JEWISH

—◦◦◦—

Does It Make a Difference?

JEWISH

DOES IT MAKE A
Difference?

Elvira & Mihai Nadin

JD | JONATHAN DAVID PUBLISHERS, INC.
Middle Village, New York 11379

Jonathan David Publishers, Inc.
68-22 Eliot Avenue
Middle Village, NY 11379
www.jdbooks.com

2 4 6 8 10 9 7 5 3 1

Library of Congress Cataloging-in-Publication Data

Nadin, Elvira
    Jewish : does it make a difference? / Elvira & Mihai Nadin.
       p.   cm.
    Includes index
    ISBN 0-8246-0420-2
    1. Jews—Identity. 2. Jews—Interviews. 3. Public opinion—Jews. 4. Judaism—
    20th century. 5. Judaism—Essence, genius, nature. I. Nadin, Mihai. II. Title
    DS143 .N33 2000
    305.892'4—dc21   99-088188
                                                                       CIP

Book Design and Composition by John Reinhardt Book Design

Printed in the United States of America

Dedicated to the memory of
Raphael Yitzchak Ephraim
ben Arye Leib Shlomo

Contents

————ⱺⱾⱺ————

Acknowledgments

———— ⌒ ————

Our first expression of gratitude goes to all the individuals whose answers appear in this book. They took time and effort when publication was more hope than promise. Several, unfortunately, passed away before they could see their answers in print. In such cases, their answers remain a testament. We would like especially to acknowledge the contribution of Mr. Edward Asner, the first to respond to our letter of inquiry. When answers were slow in coming, his encouraging words echoed in the back of our heads. We must also gratefully acknowledge Rabbi Ephraim Buchwald of the National Jewish Outreach Group in New York City for facilitating contacts and lending his moral support when other groups expressed reservations about endorsing a book that encompassed so many varied opinions about the Jewish experience.

To each respondent who provided leads to yet others, we hereby express our additional thanks. The friends and acquaintances who put us in contact with potential respondents are too numerous to list, but the following persons deserve special appreciation:

In the United States—Leibl Estrin, Edgar M. Phillips, Rabbi Abraham Ginzberg, Blossom Kirschenbaum, Arlene and Peter Rosenblum, Rabbi Yehoshua Laufer, Richard Zakia, Tamara Shamson, Yankel Pinson, Abe Twersky, Baruch Gorkin, Meir Rhodes, Hilde Kron, Barbara Nessim, Pino Trogu, Hans Janachek, Aaron Marcus, Hammet Nurosi

In Germany—Dr. Ulrike Schrader, Michael Okroy, Rabbi Menahem Stroks, Andreas Ziegler

In France—Robert Futtersack (our uncle), Michel Futtersack (our cousin)

In the Czech Republic—Richard Wiest

In Romania—Ileana Popovici

In Israel—Cornel Safirman

Thanks go to the following persons for help in translating our letter of inquiry: Leonid Goldberg, for translation into Russian; Michel Futtersack, for translation into French; Helga Maser, Sarah Halbach, and Matthias Ferch for translation into German; Robert Futtersack, for translation into Hungarian.

To our daughter Elisabeth, we owe our gratitude for gathering addresses, typing and sending out letters, reading and rereading the manuscript, and making suggestions for improvement.

This book is dedicated to the memory of Raphael Yitzchak ben Arye Leib Shlomo. Despite a lifelong struggle against cystic fibrosis, he maintained a positive attitude based on the difference that Judaism made in his life.

Introduction

—⟡—

YET ANOTHER BOOK ON JEWISH IDENTITY? After the hundreds of attempts through essays, novels, and short stories to explain—to Jews themselves as well as to others—what a Jew is, what more can be said? We asked ourselves this question before undertaking a task that, like Henny Penny's desire to make bread, met with very little cooperation.

The question posed in the title of the book—Does it make a difference?—was a point of departure from previous attempts to define Jewish identity—or, more precisely, how Jews identify themselves in the context of today's world. It evokes a question asked by many immigrants and minorities as they sought and seek to exercise their rights in work, housing, and self-fulfillment in the United States. Prejudices of the Old World were supposed to have remained there. The United States was the land of new beginnings, of new hope. That this question (Does it make a difference?) was asked in response to others ("Are you . . .?" "What kind of name is that?") shows that hope was met with prejudice even in the "land of the free." Each nationality—Italian, Irish, Polish, Russian, as well as Jewish—can fill in the appropriate "tag." The idea of the United States as a melting pot was more aspiration (of the Jewish Israel Zangwill) than reality. In *Only in America*, Harry Golden, that original chronicler of (Jewish) immigrants' progress, records all these experiences as they touched him and his time. It was only after World War II—actually, only after the McCarthy era—that Jews finally became accepted as being like everyone else—that is, not different—in the American mainstream. The American-born coauthor of this book remembers hearing with astonishment in 1970 how a lawyer who had shortened his name to "Rose" was still required, in the 1950s, to enter the office of the New York City law firm that employed him through the back door, climbing the stairs instead of taking the elevator. During interviews with respondents, we were surprised to learn of the official *numerus clausus* admission policy in universities throughout the United States even thirty years ago; fraternities and clubs totally excluded Jews.

It took generations and a new mindset before the question of *difference* took a different turn. After a time of blending, of becoming like everyone else, the consequences of this development became apparent to many Jews. Harry Golden put it in a comic light, complaining about the loss of spontaneity, tasteless food, and meager portions served at modern Jewish weddings (to which we shall refer in the Afterword). But Jewish organizations, foundations, and ad hoc movements (such as committees established in the shadow of some tragic event in Jewish history) started losing their base of support. Liberal Judaism became alarmed at the rate of intermarriage and the consequent abandonment of the Jewish spouse's connection to his or her people. As crass as this comment may seem, these groups also saw their financial base of support waning. The challenge of total absorption into the American "stew" had to be met. Several attempts have been made through celebrity testimonials and public awareness events dedicated to various Jewish causes—support for Israel, protest against Soviet treatment of Jews, memorials to the victims of the Holocaust—all intended to remind Jews to remain Jewish. Religiously oriented Jews also reached out. The work of the Lubavitch movement in getting Jews to perform traditional Jewish rituals (lighting Shabbat candles and the menorah for Chanukah, observing the holidays, attending synagogue) is probably the best known because it is so public and pervasive: "*mitzvah* mobiles" on the streets of major cities, ads in leading newspapers, giant Chanukah *menorot* on public property, appearances of the Rebbe on cable television. There is also the work of organizations like the National Jewish Outreach Group, based in New York City, and Aish HaTorah in Israel and the United States, which aim to persuade Jews to be more conscious of (Orthodox) Judaism, its beliefs and practices. The (Reform) American Jewish Committee tries to convince visitors to its website that it's great to be Jewish.

The Jews that these groups attempt to attract are made aware of what they can attain on the spiritual, cultural, and humanistic levels by returning to Judaism. By getting their fellow Jews actively involved in Jewish practices, these organizations remind their constituency that "faith without deeds is dead." This citation from the Christian Bible might offend some readers, but we find it appropriate here because it defines a first difference of Judaism, one that serves as the basis for our question. Judaism is an algorithm of deeds and beliefs that lead to positive action, whether it is washing one's hands before eating, keeping kosher, contributing to all types of charities, or fighting intolerance and injustice. This emphasis on actions stands in stark contrast to other major religions. Christianity, for example, emphasizes salvation through faith; Islam dispenses with many of its ritual requirements for Muslims living in non-Islamic lands; Hinduism preaches passivity in response to human misery. Judaism is a program for everyday practice. Jews constituted their identity through living their beliefs, their laws. Indeed, in Judaism virtues are encoded as law, not as mere desiderata. "You shall be righteous as I am righteous" does not leave much room for compromise.

Milan Kundera described this aspect in his book *Immortality*. Christians have one law, "Love your neighbor," and are left on their own to figure out how to carry out this commandment. The Jews have many laws telling them how to live this love. From the perspective of twentieth-century humanism and ethics, people living in democratic societies take for granted the laws originating in the Torah over four thousand years ago and refined by Jewish thinkers from that time through the Dark Ages of Europe. Ethics and laws assumed as rights in our century have been ignored for most of human history, if they were ever known. Seen from the perspective of its period, Jewish law is revolutionary. It took thousands of years for the "enlightened" world to catch up. Mutilation ("cruel and unusual punishment," as it is called in the U.S. Constitution) is forbidden in the Torah because it disables a person from making a living. Yet mutilation (in various grisly forms) was the law in Europe throughout the Enlightenment and is still accepted in the Islamic world. The rule of law, administered through judges, stands in sharp contrast to "the divine right of kings." This right, never granted in the Torah or subsequent writings, prevailed in Christian Europe and lingers on in regimes—totalitarian and democratic—governed by a dictator or president. In effect, the non-Jewish world became more Jewish during the very period the Jews sought to "be like other people"—the desire expressed in the First Book of Samuel (8:5) when the Hebrews demanded that a king rule over them.

It is known that down through their history, Jews have integrated into Judaism the beliefs and practices of the peoples among whom they lived: angelology and names of months from the Persians; gematria, logical argumentation, and the love of the word from the Greeks; braided bread, hamantaschen, dreidels, and a *lingua franca* from the Germans; folk superstitions and various articles of attire from eastern Europe. Sometimes it is hard to know what is intrinsically Jewish and what began as foreign. While an expression like "Christian atheist" or "Muslim atheist" is an oxymoron, a Jew can be an atheist or a Buddhist in a Jewish way, as long as the Jewish part means a way of life based on certain values transmitted over millennia. Reconstructionist, Reform, and Liberal Judaism are examples of borrowing foreign ideas (especially from the German enlightenment) and applying them to Judaism.

In the context in which non-Jewish and Jewish values coincide, does it make sense for Jews and Jewish organizations to insist upon Judaism as a distinct way of life worth nurturing and continuing? Is there still something different about being Jewish? Have humanism, enlightenment, and reason caught up with Judaism to the extent of abolishing significant differences between Jews and non-Jews on the ethical level? This is one aspect of our inquiry.

The other aspect on which we based our inquiry is related to difference from another perspective. While Jewish law and practices kept Jews at a distance from non-Jews, anti-Semitism kept non-Jews away from Jews. In most cases in the Diaspora, Jews were not only regarded and treated as different, they were hardly allowed to be themselves due to edicts that restricted their commercial and professional activities. These restrictions led to an inwardness and solidarity that gave rise to many of the characteristics considered Jewish: strong cohesion; organizations devoted to help and charity; creativity forced to the utmost in order to make a living in a restrictive environment, as well as to escape persecution; identification with oppressed groups; a sensitivity toward injustice and the demand for justice for all. The triumph of reason over prejudice, laws that extended equal rights and access to all peoples, late twentieth-century ecumenism that lifted the stigma of Jews as Christkillers—all these slowly did away with the mental and physical barriers that had kept Jews outside the mainstream. People began to notice that Jews were not so different after all.

The trend toward assimilation—Jews assimilating the practices of other peoples—took another turn: non-Jews started to assimilate not only Jewish-based values and ethics, but the Jews themselves. As we know, official anti-Semitism rose once more under two ostensibly opposing political systems, but with the same deadly effect: Hitler's national-socialist regime and Soviet-style international communism. Both fed off the economic misery of their people, and both encouraged the not yet dead hatred of the "foreign" minority among them. With the downfall of these two regimes, one can say that anti-Semitism in its officially encouraged manifestation has disappeared, at least from the Western world. But what genocide failed to accomplish is being carried out through virtual suicide. The current rate of assimilation in the United States and Europe exceeds that once reached in pre-Hitler Germany (over thirty percent). This has led some branches of Judaism to ease the rules of "membership," accepting as Jews the children of Jewish fathers and non-Jewish mothers. Traditionalists argue that such laxity will erode Jewish vitality. Judaism, in their view, is still trying to recover from the loss of over six million Jews due to the Holocaust. Many more were killed in pogroms or abandoned their Jewishness by intermarriage and assimilation. Some observers argue that despite these losses, Judaism, with all its splendid contradictions and extreme expressions of energy, is in better shape than it has ever been.

The fall of the Soviet regime led to a new displacement. Hundreds of thousands of Jews, some with tenuous claims to Jewishness and more Russian, Armenian, Uzbek, Serbian, Polish, or Romanian than Jewish in their outlook, have left their former homelands in droves, more in search of a safe economic haven than a religious one. Many were happy to be accepted into Germany, for example, with its promise of a golden social parachute, despite the Germans' low tolerance for difference. For the majority, being Jewish meant more than an ethnic designation on their identity papers. And they continue to keep in the background whatever Jewishness still remains in them. Large numbers have wound up in Israel, probably the world's second largest melting pot, living relatively free of discrimination because they are, by some definition, Jews. In Israel, Jews from the former Soviet Union have become a substantial political force, motivated to action partly by the difficulties faced by the many among them whose Jewish status is problematic.

The modern state of Israel has turned fifty, younger than many of the new nations re-established after the fall of the Soviet Union. It was envisioned as a homeland where all Jews seeking freedom could live and express themselves without fear of the anti-Semitism that might at any time erupt in the Diaspora countries in which they were always a minority group. In having their own land again, Jews have once more become "like other nations." The land of Judah became Israel; the returning Diaspora Jew became an Israeli. The persecuted minority at last became the majority in their own democratic nation.

With the establishment of Israel and the end of official anti-Semitism, the Jews of the Diaspora found themselves facing a new reality: the glaring injustices that had held them together and separate for centuries had for the most part vanished. The outside forces that attacked Jews wherever they lived and forced them into solidarity were gone. And after the downfall of the Soviet Union in 1991, many Jewish groups that had used Soviet persecution of Jews as a rallying cry for fundraising and political action were at a loss. What was left to keep Jews, especially the more liberal sects, on the Jewish track? What should keep

Jews together, let alone distinct among other groups sharing the same ethics and world view? Several articles have been written in the United States on this theme. This questioning has led to testimonials in leading newspapers (supported mainly by liberal Jewish organizations) and on the Internet. *Why Be Jewish?*, the Internet site of the American Jewish Committee, sounds almost like "Why I accepted Christ as my personal savior." Set up years after the work on this book started, it has one thing in common with our attempt: it stresses the individual's view of Jewishness and his or her relation to the religious, ethical system called Judaism.

At the time we started sending out our letters of inquiry, Jewishness was a characteristic defined mainly by scholars and writers on Jewish identity. All the answers to "What is a Jew?" written by scholars and self-declared experts tended to establish an idealized generality to which the individual had to shape himself or herself. Indeed, the standard these writers set was so general that many worthy non-Jews fit the definition. Our interrogation follows a different path: it is based on letting individual Jews question and define themselves. In other words, we do not pursue a deductive task, but rather allow those who are identified as Jews to express what they perceive to be characteristic of this denomination. Is there something different? Different acts? Different perspectives? Most important, how do these affect what they do so that each act becomes the act of a Jew, not of any other ethical individual?

Our questions posed several challenges. One was to get the respondent to think in terms of what he or she believes and does. Most Jews tended to respond in the third person. Many answers started with "The Jew" or "To be Jewish" instead of with "I." We wanted our respondents to talk about themselves, for themselves, not for every other Jew. When they did, we could only assume that what each respondent referred to in the collective case actually addressed his or her own condition. That such an exploration of Judaism is something best left to scholars and is incapable of being carried out by an individual Jew was summed up in the response of one well-known individual who epitomizes what is known as "the professional Jew," that is, one who makes a living from past suffering or present dilemma, or who takes tradition out of context, exploiting all these as a commodity: "Scholars are the ones who ask this question. I have no time."

Mark Twain realized that there was something different about the Jews when he wrote:

> If the statistics are right, the Jews constitute but one quarter of one percent of the human race. It suggests a nebulous dim puff of star dust

lost in the blaze of the Milky Way. Properly, the Jew ought hardly to be heard of; but he is heard of, has always been heard of. He is prominent on the planet as any other people, and his importance is extravagantly out of proportion to the smallness of his bulk. His contributions to the world's list of great names in literature, science, art, music, finance, medicine and abstruse learning are also out of proportion to the weakness of his numbers . . . What is the nature of his immortality?

His question served as the starting point for our book. We decided to ask those Jews who had made a name for themselves through their accomplishments as writers, scientists, businesspersons, inventors, and so on if they could trace their success to something that Judaism had instilled in them. Their unresponsiveness caused us a lot of frustration. Indeed, we were told that many Jews leave their Judaism behind once they have attained a certain acclaim. It was the realization that Judaism was supported by millions of everyday Jews silently living the values that they had absorbed through living in Jewish homes that set us on the right path leading to this book.

We sent about two thousand letters, first throughout the United States, then throughout the world as personal business took us to Europe. We were able to interview individuals living in several countries—Germany, France, Belgium, the Czech Republic, Israel—as well as those visiting Germany (where we now work and live). Travels to Spain and Italy introduced us to the non-Ashkenazic worlds of the Sephards (and the beauty of Ladino) and Roman Jews, who take pride in belonging to the oldest continuous Jewish community in Europe. The small fraction of answers in relation to requests was a disappointment that led to various speculations on our part. Perhaps Judaism was dying out, after all. We had been confident that most people would be forthcoming about their Jewishness. After all, don't Jews love to discuss their condition? In truth, we discovered that many people found it hard to express themselves on paper, whereas those who gave us telephone interviews were glad to talk about the values they find unique to Judaism. Other respondents insisted that we honestly transmit their negative feelings about being Jews, or their indifference. One thing we insisted upon in our letters of inquiry was that respondents be frank. We did not want to paint a falsely rosy picture of the contemporary relationship between Jews and Judaism.

No reader should think that letting others provide answers for us was an easy way to write a book. Many times we told ourselves that we could have written this book in less than half the time it took to elicit answers. A major frustration was the number of recognizable names who chose not to respond. In Los Angeles as well as in New York, it is a cliché that many Jews leave their Jewishness behind as they seek success. However, when Vladimir Ashkenazy rang us from his home in Switzerland one Sunday morning, we were ecstatic! Finally, a famous Jew who is so excited that he invests in an international call! Well, if we ever thought that being Jewish makes a difference, Mr. Ashkenazy did indeed confirm this hypothesis. His hasty, but very considerate, response to our letter was to set the record straight: Despite his Jewish name, he is definitely not Jewish. After he explained his antecedents to us, he added how highly he thought of our endeavor and said we could use his name to encourage his Jewish colleagues to respond. Some did, without our mentioning his name; others did not, even when we trumpeted Mr. Ashkenazy's endorsement. In a few cases, we sent letters of inquiry to individuals commonly considered to be Jewish. Some of them answered politely, if not so urgently, that they were not Jews. Others, aware of their personal history, felt like acknowledging a connection to Judaism and reflected upon how this could have made a difference in their lives. We included their answers because they are a testimony to the depth of their roots and to their willingness to allow this to be publicly known. As for all the famous names that did not respond, we concluded only that their time was extremely limited.

Persistence paid off. We received enough answers from a variety of individuals from around the world. We are grateful to each one of them. (Some of them, such as Alfred Eisenstaedt, Paul Rand, Paul Erdös, Yehudi Menuhin—each a leader in his respective field—are no longer alive.) As varied as each response is, we did see correlations, if not patterns. Some answers express plainly what other respondents could not put into words but certainly exemplify in their actions. Our first idea was to present the answers in alphabetical order and let the reader form his own conclusions as to what difference, if any, being Jewish makes in the lives of the respondents. But in this age of time-saving technology, there is little enough time to read, and precious little time for reflection. Hence, we decided to classify the replies into subject categories to provide additional guidance to the content. This solution is far from perfect. Most answers fit into several categories. We realize—and we certainly hope—that readers will draw their own conclusions. The ideal solution would be to make this book available in an interactive format that would allow readers to arrange their conclusions in categories of their own choosing.

After the time-consuming and costly effort of sending out over two thousand letters to all parts of the world, only to receive the direct mailer's standard return rate of one percent; after sacrificing needed vacation time in order to interview Jews in person wherever our travels took us; after dialing hundreds of telephone numbers accessed through area codes few people use, was the experience worth it all? After all the books and articles on Jews, can this inquiry add anything unknown or unexpected to the existing literature? We think that our approach of asking individuals to define themselves, rather than asking how they fit another's definition, reflects the networked, decentralized, and heterogenous world that we are living in more and more.

Jews were probably the first people to "go global" before the term became the cliché that it is today. Jewish communities around the world started forming their own nuclei, networking with others as the need arose. One can perceive the destruction of the center, Jerusalem, as the paradigm of an international age without a determinate center two thousand years before digital technology made this practically possible. This is probably the main reason Jews of all denominations take to and are so overwhelmingly present on the Internet. We expect that readers—Jewish and non-Jewish, casual and scholarly—will keep this perspective in mind as they read and discover, forming their conclusions and applying them to further questions. There are no final answers, only links in the infinite process of interpretation. Judaism is a fuzzy paradigm, in the mathematical sense of fuzzy logic, that proves so useful today in philosophy and technology. To come to any sharp definition of Judaism is a task as overwhelming as it is useless. The "authentic" Judaism of today would be unrecognizable to the Moses of the Torah as well as to Moses ben Maimon or to Moses Mendelssohn. In one sense, all Judaism is "reform," since it is part of a continuum of historical events that have led to myriad reinterpretations to fit circumstances not accounted for in the Torah, the "constitution" of all people who call themselves Jewish. Some Jews constitute themselves as religious; others do so in ways that escape definition.

Our inquiry introduced us to many people around the world who do or have done amazing things. Asking them if being Jewish had any bearing on what they do either elicited an immediate response or made them think. If this book can do the same for the readers, then it has served its purpose.

The Questioning Process

———— ⌁ ————

The work on the book *Jewish: Does It Make a Difference?* extended over six years, during which time the questioning process underwent slight variations. This explains why some answers do not follow the standard format of responding to the questions given in the letter of inquiry reproduced below. We solicited answers in several ways:

- Letters to persons whose addresses were obtained from various sources, such as friends, organizations, individuals interested in our book, lists, registries, Internet groups, and (in the case of reprinted material) publishers of books and magazines with content pertinent to the subject.

- Cold telephone calls, through which we contacted the individual directly or made an appointment for a telephone interview. Sometimes the respondents had already received the questionnaire, sometimes the questions were put to them for the first time via telephone.

- *Ad hoc* dialogues with individuals we chanced to meet in various Jewish settings or at social occasions. Because of the informal nature of these encounters, for some respondents no profession was ascertained and hence is not provided in the text.

It was not easy to restrict interviewees to our question format. They said what they wanted to say, and in many cases their comments yielded gems that our questions could not have elicited; we then gleaned those portions that were in keeping with the scope of our inquiry. In other cases, interviewees had such interesting things to say that we just let them go on talking and subsequently reproduced the information germane to the book. Following *ad hoc* interviews, in which no recording materials were used, the interviewer rewrote the conversation from memory as soon as possible, and when possible also submitted it to the person interviewed.

Letter of Inquiry

The world in which Jews live has changed radically in the last fifty years. Official anti-Semitism has practically disappeared. The Soviet Union collapsed. Jews have their own land in the modern state of Israel. More important, many of the values that originated in the Torah and which Jews have preserved and developed throughout millennia have been integrated in secular, non-Jewish society. In view of all this, does being Jewish matter? Better said, is there anything about Judaism that preserves or promotes a distinct outlook on life, or a distinct way of life, that is worth keeping us from becoming like other nations? With this in mind, we ask that your answer be guided by the following questions:

- Does it make a difference to you that you are Jewish? Why? How? Or: Why not?

- In your opinion, are there any values that remain distinctly Jewish? Which ones?

- How do these values guide you in your outlook and in your daily life?

- Could you give an example of an incident in which you relied on Jewish values to help you reach a decision?

CHAPTER ONE

―◦◦◦―

A Reflection of
the Human Condition

Today Jews in almost all countries enjoy religious, social, and economic freedom to an unprecedented extent. They move without restriction in the non-Jewish world. Still, every now and then Jews confront attitudes that remind them that they are different from the majority around them on both spiritual and material levels. As some of them integrate their Jewish formative structure in their thinking, they realize what it means to remain committed to values and ideals not accepted by the majority. While this may keep Jews outside the mainstream of thought, their perspective is one that the surrounding society should not ignore. As society looks into the mirror of the Jewish experience, it sees a different picture of itself.

Aharon Appelfeld

NOVELIST; PROFESSOR, HOLOCAUST STUDIES
BEN-GURION UNIVERSITY
Be'er Sheva, Israel

The Jewish soul is not capable of carrying out vengeance. In my book *The Railroad,* the son whose parents were killed in a concentration camp pursues the murderer for years, traveling the railway. At the same time, he struggles with himself over whether he is capable of carrying out revenge, or even justified in seeking it. It is not in the Jewish soul to seek vengeance, but justice.

―◌◌―

Edward Asner

ACTOR; PRODUCER
Los Angeles, California

Being Jewish has always carried that blessedness of being the minority, of encountering prejudice, of encountering bias and being held apart from the crowd—yet not too far apart. But as time went on with all the "Woe is me," the poor me, that the situation tended to create, I was still able to benefit by being automatically kept from acceptance as part of the herd.

And now since World War II, since the Holocaust, with the disappearance of the six million, the creation of Israel, with the commitment and the realization by the majority, at least in America, of the sins of the past, Judaism is no longer an affliction. It's become much more casual, it no longer provides that wonderful arena for that love-hate relationship that so many of us existed under.

I feel I've known two worlds of Jewishness. The special place of stigma; youth and the beginning steps of my creativity; into the present, reflecting something of an Everyman position.

If you are to call me an artist, then I would have to lay a great deal of that to my Jewishness. When I was a kid, all the special notoriety achieved by youth in science and art was won by first-generation Jewish kids; now, awards and honors are being taken on every side by Asian kids.

It is a great religion, a great people, but if we cease to function as the outsider, as a prodder, a reminder to the world that we *can* be and *are* different, I wonder how long we can survive.

Theodore Bikel

ACTOR; FOLK SINGER
Wilton, Connecticut

Jewish descent alone is not the determinant of my self-definition as a Jew. The acknowledgment of the "familial bond" tying together all Jews rests on active commitments made by modern and aware people. In other words, it assumes active consent. My regret is that so many of my fellow Jews treat themselves to a phoenix-like existence, thinking that one can exist without acknowledging yesterday. This casts doubt on the ability to deal with today and calls into question the entitlement to a tomorrow.

The difference that being Jewish makes in this regard is that it lends a heightened awareness of the human condition and the knowledge that where we stand, someone has stood before.

[*From* Theo, *HarperCollins, 1994. Reprinted with the permission of the author.*]

Peter Bloch

EDITOR, *PENTHOUSE* MAGAZINE
New York, New York

I was raised as a secular Jew, learning Bible stories in Hebrew school when I was little, but knowing that my parents had little, if any, use for the religious trappings of Judaism. At the same time, however, I know that by submerging me in their intense love of reading and learning, by teaching me how to question things and argue about their meaning, by refusing to blindly accept anything "on faith" (except the sanctity of FDR and the trade union movement!), my parents gave me a permanent Jewish identity.

While the evils of organized religion (Judaism included) have scourged mankind from its earliest days right up to the present, Judaism, unlike most other religions, also encourages a quest for knowledge that often undermines that very organization. Despite themselves, Jews from Eve onward have asked "Why?" when their immediate prospects might have suggested quiet obedience as the more prudent course. It is no wonder that the way in which we view the universe, and ourselves, has been a reflection of questions asked by Moses, Jesus, Marx, Freud, Einstein, and so many other Jews who could not simply "let things be."

What I do as editor of *Penthouse* is obviously far from that exalted level. But I'm proud that the articles that we publish have encouraged millions of people to question some of the fundamentals of their daily reality. Rather than simply extolling the consumer society, our point of view is one of skepticism and disbelief. During the twenty years I've been with *Penthouse,* I've published hundreds of articles on such subjects as the government's abandonment of our Vietnam veterans, how the medical establishment ignores new scientific advances, the greed and hypocrisy of political zealots cloaked in religious garments. So when I assign a reporter to write up the truth about American prisoners in Vietnam, I, too, am following in the tradition of not "letting things be."

I have three daughters who have given me more than my share of pride and happiness, especially when I see that they, too, love to read, to study, and to question their world. No religious ceremony, not even a *bat mitzvah* at the Wailing Wall, could remind me more of their heritage, or make me swell more with pride, than the fact that they always, constantly, carry a book with them. Then I know that the proudest Jewish tradition, which I learned from my parents, is now theirs.

—✦—

Sophie Brüss
SOCIOECONOMICS STUDENT
Cologne, Germany

Being Jewish is a challenge to the mentality of the masses, a reminder that one should not give in to the pressure of the majority. I am the product of the marriage of French and German, traditional enemies. But to my parents, as Jews, these modifiers refer only to citizenship. Being Jewish gives me a chance to teach. Many acquaintances who know about the Holocaust want to know what it feels like to be Jewish, what is different, and especially, why we make ourselves different. My answer is that if we were not different, if we did not have a sense of difference, we would not be here.

Our religion is like a small house that we retreat to not to hide, not to withdraw from the world, but to pause in order to gather strength.

Joshua Fishman

SOCIOLINGUIST
Palo Alto, California

A Jewish citizen of the world and a citizen of the Jewish world is how I consider myself. Among my other identifiers—American, sociolinguist, husband, father, grandfather—being Jewish is my most basic identity and has influenced all that I am and do. My Jewishness is expressed linguistically, culturally, and religiously; it is evident in my diet, my informal reading, my organizational memberships, my charitable contributions, my voluntary activities, my choice of residential neighborhood, my political preferences, etc., etc. My multiple identities constantly interact with each other and I am the result as well as the regulator of those interactions. As a result of all these, I am not quite at home with any one group in Jewish life, but that is the price one pays for being a complex human being of any kind.

At times, there are conflicts between my Jewishness and one or another of my identities, conflicts that are conducive to growth, to personally relevant solutions. I may accept rabbinical or other Jewish authority in one area but not in another, but that is no different than not fully or finally accepting any political or theoretical formulations whatsoever. Judaism, more than any other culture, has always respected minority opinions as well as majority opinions, and it seems to me quite in accord with a Jewish (as well as with a general scientific) outlook to be less than fully in accord with a dominant view pertaining to any subject. However, to be Jewish is more than just to be disagreeable; it is to be eccentric on a solid Jewish foundation.

Having done my best (with the decided help and even leadership of my good wife) to guarantee and enrich the Jewishness of my three sons, I am now working away at guaranteeing and enriching the Jewishness of my four grandchildren. I want them to have the same deeply historical perspective, the same indomitable optimism, the same sense of making a difference in the world, the same identification with the underdog, the same certainty of their own basic identity, the same thorough familiarity with the culture of their forebears, the same willingness to experiment with the new coupled with a readiness to try the old carefully before tampering with it or discarding it, and, finally, the same freedom to make up their own minds regarding in what ways and to what extent to be Jewish, which I have found so rewarding.

Esther Flath
SOCIAL PSYCHOLOGIST; MARKET RESEARCHER
Paris, France

I would not be what I am—a social psychologist—if I were not Jewish. When people ask me what I am, I tell that I am Jewish, that Yiddish, not German, is my mother tongue. My parents are Holocaust survivors who met and married after World War II. Because my mother got pregnant, they stayed in Germany, where my brother and I were raised. So my education at home gave me the impression that I was different from the other children in Münster, the city where I was raised. We Jewish children did not have to attend obligatory Christian religious education classes. Neither did we participate in the Christian holidays that play a major social role in Germany. The one hundred fifty Jews left in Münster formed a refuge, a small family. We remained home during our holidays. And when we returned to classes, the German children looked at us to see if we had changed in some way.

My parents were Orthodox and religion gave me a framework for my view of the world. They taught me to believe what is in my mind, not in material things. In the 1970s and 1980s, I got caught up in the leftist movements because their demand for social justice sounded like what I had learned through Judaism. And this is when I decided to study social psychology. At the age of fifteen, I made two major decisions. I knew I did not want to remain in Germany because all that my parents had told me made me realize that I could not feel German. So I had to choose between Israel and some other country in which to live. I decided on France by chance and stayed there to study, because that is where the major research in social psychology was going on. I am a French citizen, but only the adjective denoting the country where I live has changed. I still feel the outsider, the one who looks in from the outside of mainstream society. This also played a role in my becoming a social psychologist. In France, most of the people in this field are Jews. We are the observers. As Jews, we try to understand how people act the way they do, especially under stressful situations that lead to such things as persecution.

I also decided to be a Jew, but not a religious Jew. This means that I have a history and a culture, both of which I want my children to inherit through me. I want them to feel comfortable as Jews. Of course I know that they will not receive from me what I received from my parents. They will not learn Hebrew from me. I am a Diaspora Jew who left Israel because I am universal, as well as idealistic.

I am not sure one can say there are values that are exclusively Jewish.

All good people share similar values about justice and family. Jewish education transmits values in a way that seems to fit into one's outlook on life. Whereas other religions do a kind of mental gymnastics to get a humanistic view, Judaism does not. Religion is more important than humanity for Christians, for example. They bring people to religion, but not to reason or to life. Judaism encourages a freedom of expression and questioning, not passive learning. This questioning leads to personal autonomy and independence, to thinking for yourself, not letting another entity think for you.

—◦◦◦—

Arthur Gelb
EUGENE O'NEILL BIOGRAPHER; FORMER MANAGING EDITOR OF
THE NEW YORK TIMES
New York, New York

Since childhood, I have always been conscious of my Jewishness. It has been rooted in my very bones, a mystical fabric of feelings bequeathed by embracing parents, who came to America from a Carpathian village. I never met my grandparents, but I was regaled with stories of their Jewish warmth, quest for learning, humor and courage. Because of this heritage, I always associated Jewishness with a yearning for liberty and a lust for knowledge.

For me, Tolstoy was wisest in his attempt to explain what is a Jew: "The Jew is the source and well from which all other nations have drawn their religions and beliefs. . . . The Jew is the discoverer of freedom. . . . The Jew is a symbol of civic and religious tolerance. . . . The Jew is a symbol of eternity."

Yevgheny Khaldei
PHOTOGRAPHER
Moscow, Russia

People look at my photographs and admire my ability to catch on film moments that belong to history. Now that there is more past than future left for me, I was wondering what I would have done without a camera. The answer is that I probably would have told the story of all that I experienced. The Red Flag over the Reichstag in Berlin is probably as well known as Eisenstaedt's photo of Victory Day in New York. The photograph of the Hungarian Jews liberated from the ghetto is less known, but not less important to me. These people were like me, but caught in a situation where they could only wait for someone to free them before they were carried off. My heart beat so strongly when I saw them that I was scared. They were alive, and their survival meant a lot to me. This solidarity in the survival of our nation impresses and intrigues me.

Many Jews live in Moscow. Some are living in misery after a hard life of work and hope for a better society. Others prosper, often to the detriment of their heritage. But as different as our lives are, we belong to something deep in our hearts that we cannot always explain. I hope that my photographs captured this feeling.

William Klein
PHOTOGRAPHER
Paris, France

An American in Paris—this was a Jewish story, too, wasn't it? Only this time around, it was my life. Rue de Medicis is not exactly the corner of 108th Street and Amsterdam Avenue, or the Upper West Side, where I was born. There I could relate to the kids of other Jewish immigrants and pick up Yiddish jokes. Nothing like that here. Still, I am as Jewish here in Paris as I was in New York because being Jewish is a matter of attitude. Just like in America, there are two kinds of photography here: Jewish and non-Jewish. Jewish photography is urban, emotional, funky, marked by fear—the photography of Diane Arbus, Robert Frank, Weegee, the fashion photography of Penn and Avedon. This photography is part of my past, too: my work for *Vogue*, my work with Liebermann, the comical quality of my images. Non-Jewish photography is the great American outdoors, the photography of Adams, Weston, Evans.

My Jewishness pertains to my attitude and is the reason for the conflicts I became involved in and for my exile in France. Vietnam was not a Jewish theme in itself. Its moral implications were, however. And my photos of Muhammad Ali, Little Richard, Eldridge Cleaver, and so many themes that polarize people are also Jewish through their moral implications.

An outsider in America, an outsider in France—some people might read into this a reflection of my being Jewish in a world not willing to accept us as different even when we don't want to be.

Solomon Marcus
MATHEMATICIAN
Bucharest, Romania

My Jewishness was established through two avenues: my family, that is, my parents, who spoke sometimes Yiddish, sometimes Romanian, and who observed Jewish traditions; and the discrimination emanating from the local sociopolitical environment, during the rise of fascism in Romania. The Judaism transmitted through my family never marked me. I was obliged to mechanically repeat words that were never explained to me, and to follow a ritual whose symbolism was foreign to me. On the other hand, the negative aspects marked me deeply. The first shock was when a schoolmate beat me up for murdering Jesus. Other episodes followed that left deep wounds in my adolescent soul. I will never forget how a professor of Romanian literature humiliated me before the class because I could remember only eighteen lines of a thirty-two-line poem. During the German occupation, we had to wear the yellow star, and we Jewish students were excluded from the schools. I took refuge in Romanian, French, and—strange as it seems—German literature. I was always dominated by a tendency towards universalism, towards what brings people together, not what separates them. That is probably why I chose mathematics as a profession, a field that has given me the greatest spiritual satisfaction, even during the tragedy that followed fascism: totalitarian communism.

But even during this period of internationalism, I could not escape the negative part of my Jewishness, the collective guilt that people have put on Jews down through history. In the army, when I had to fill out the military form, I declared my nationality to be Romanian. The form came back, altered. It stated my nationality as Jewish. Since then, I don't say I am a Romanian national except when I am outside of Romania. So, even though Romanian culture has marked me profoundly, I am a Jew in my country.

My dilemma can be illustrated through the following hypothetical situation: Let's imagine a collection of a thousand marbles, nine hundred sixty of them white and forty of them blue. If something happens to one of the whites, we will be tempted to blame the blue. On the other hand, the behavior of a blue marble will not be correlated to the other color. Now let's imagine people instead of marbles. The whites will tend to see any blue as a representative of all blues, who, in turn, run the risk of becoming obsessed with this state of affairs. The whites will attribute any anomaly that occurs to them, and for which blame must be sought, to all types of obscure aggressive intentions among blues who maintain a solidarity imagined by the whites. At such a moment, the whites form at least two categories, depending on the degree to which they cast blame on the blues. But the blues also face a dilemma: after they were victims of their own color, they run the risk of extending this scenario to the situations in which color is irrelevant. Suspicion is fed from both sides.

To try to elucidate in which way a Jew is different is as difficult as it is interesting. But it should not be turned into an obsession. You cannot go around in life asking how you are different. It is as troublesome as it is unproductive.

The question I am responding to threw me into a dilemma due to the two sides of my Jewishness, one side for the others, one side for me. Was I untrue to my Jewish culture? Is Jewishness a thing in itself or is it based on context? Some scientists say that every five years, the atoms of which the human body is made are completely replaced. If this is true, then our biological identity is not material, but structural, relational. Could it be possible that our spiritual identity follows the same pattern? I am still working on an explanation.

Leon Poliakoff

HISTORIAN AND AUTHOR, KNOWN FOR HIS EIGHT-VOLUME
MAGNUM OPUS, *THE HISTORY OF ANTI-SEMITISM*
Massy, France

I am what I am, which means I am different because I am an individual. My parents were enlightened, assimilated Jews, as much as they could be at the turn of the century. My "conversion" to Judaism was on a rational basis. Christianity is the most stupid philosophy. As one rabbi asked—I forgot his name, but it's in my book on the history of anti-Semitism: How can anyone believe that God would attempt to save the world by nothing better than having a son born through the womb of a young virgin, having him go through a thousand tortures, only to have no effect in the end? During my research, I learned what so-called enlightened scientists of the sixteenth and seventeenth centuries were expounding and trying to prove: the effects of impossible cross-breeding and that Negroes are the result of breeding between apes and men. So when I read that Moses said that every animal must breed after its own kind, that you cannot cross-breed two different kinds, I realized that the Jewish religion was based on rationality.

Obviously there are some differences between Jews and non-Jews. For example, there are many Jews in France who are in journalism. One recalls that in the Middle Ages, Jews knew what was going on all over the world. They knew that, at any moment, they could be subject to persecution, so they kept up to date on what was going on all over the world.

Jews are pains in the neck. In order to resist assimilation after such heavy persecution through the centuries, they had to be. Today, they are less of a pain in the neck than Christians, not so fierce, so ferocious. They do not go around killing people who do not agree with them.

I would choose a Jewish doctor over a Christian one, because of what I believe the inner qualities of Jews are. Look, among all the scientists and mathematicians, and Nobel Prize winners, the greatest proportion are Jews. There must be some explanation for that that transcends education and upbringing.

Roger Rosenblatt
DIRECTOR, DELACORTE CENTER FOR MAGAZINE JOURNALISM,
COLUMBIA UNIVERSITY; JOURNALIST; PLAYWRIGHT; ESSAYIST
New York, New York

Being a Jew allows me the power of powerlessness. That Jews are small in number; that we have been persecuted for centuries, everywhere; that we have always been on the run—these facts bestow a kind of pride, because they prove we have endured. But for a Jewish writer, the power of powerlessness is more specific. Being "out of things," we are born on a different—often lonely—perch, and we look at the world from that perch, from which the world, in turn, also looks different. So, being Jewish gives me two blessings: It makes me part of a group; and it permits, indeed encourages, me to live apart from any group. It gives me others and it gives me myself.

—cᴧɔ—

Jacob Seela
Turku, Finland

There are three aspects to the Jewish difference in my life. First is the religious aspect. It is difficult for me to judge how religious I am. The outward forms of religion demand that I go to the synagogue every Shabbat and keep all the holidays. My inner feeling is a sense of trust in the Lord. But I do not keep kosher, and I work on Shabbat. I feel sorry that I do not obey these important Jewish laws, but I do not consider them a "must." Many would judge my religion by these criteria. The religious aspect also requires that I make a distinction between myself and my non-Jewish friends.

Then there is the difference on the ethical level. Finnish Jews have been striving for acceptance in Finland since they first arrived in the middle of the nineteenth century as retired soldiers of the Russian army. Finland was the last European country to give Jews full rights as citizens (in 1918), and the older Jews are still cautious. So each of us tries to live at an ethical level that will keep the non-Jews from saying, "That filthy Jew!"

Last, but not least, is the difference that Zionism makes. Every day and every moment, I think about what is good for Israel, how to explain to non-Jewish friends why the Israeli government made such and such a decision, and why the army has moved in or out. My friends face no such problems.

Jewish values define the Jew. I am not referring to holiness, because according to the Torah, we are a holy people and true Jewish values can only be found in serving the Lord. I am speaking about very subjective values, since I cannot objectively discuss Jewish values that I myself accept or reject. I think that the values which are contrary to those of the contemporary world are Jewish values. To swim against the tide. To feel the importance of criticizing what today is wrong and bad, but at the same time to be constructive. And when you feel it is necessary, to protest against the status quo. To be in opposition. But to develop new ideas, to be creative. Particularly Jewish is the ability to organize (for instance, social work), to withstand suffering, to educate your children and yourself. And, of course, never to put your hand on a human life (or the life of animals, as with hunting). To me, especially important is to be critical, to be social, to accept the commandment, "Thou shalt not kill." To know by educating yourself. And to always remember that you are Jewish.

—◌◦◌—

Arnold Wesker
WRITER
Hereford, England

In 1982, when invited to deliver a paper to a Rockefeller Foundation conference on "the survival and transformation of Jewish cultural and religious values in literature written since the Second World War," I indulged my taste for intellectual speculation and at the same time grappled with the nature of Judaism. At least a nature of Judaism which would explain me to myself, perhaps identify a quality in my work which made it sit uncomfortably in the English tradition. I quoted from Isaiah 1:11–18:

> To what purpose is the multitude of your sacrifices unto me? saith the Lord. I am full of the burnt offerings of rams, and the fat of fed beasts; and I delight not in the blood of bullocks, or of lambs or of he-goats. . . .
> Your hands are full of blood. Wash you, make you clean; put away the evil doings from before mine eyes; cease to do evil; learn to do well; seek judgment, relieve the oppressed, judge the fatherless, plead for the widow. Come now, let us reason together. . . .

In Isaiah could be found one of the roots of Jewishness: "let us reason together." It is a Jewish trait to believe in the power of reason and it is both our strength and downfall. From Isaiah to my mother: "Come, sit down, have some tea, be calm, talk to me, discuss, say it, be reasonable. . . ."

Then I turned to Genesis: "So God created man in his own image, in the image of God created he him: male and female created he them."

What a strange concept: "in his own image." What could it mean? That God was of supreme importance for creating humankind or—and here begins a Jewish heresy to which "we hold life cheaply" is anathema—that humankind was more important because it was created in God's image? From this simple but glorious declaration in Genesis, I concluded, stemmed the two roots of Judaism. Conflicting roots. Between those who revered God more than people because he created them, and those who revered people more than God because they were created in his image.

I believe the bias of the majority of Jews is towards the rational. Of course, in some of us there is the one and a touch of the other, but . . . most Jews—and I speak of writers and intellectuals because I myself am one—are the inheritors of the first: that reverence for, and greater preoccupation with, man and his ways rather than with God and the rituals surrounding the glorification of his name. And that inheritance includes the tradition of prophecy, the spirit of justice and tolerance, and the Jewish energy for action; and by prophecy I do not mean futurology, the visionary forecasts of doom-laden or beautiful times to come, which is messianic prophecy and something quite different. I mean prophecy as criticism, chastisement, warning. How this spirit was handed down, what paths it took even unto the agnostic son and daughter is something for which I cannot account. I know only that it traveled through the ages, that it touched many of us, that we drew strength from it, that we warmed more to dicta like those of Moses Mendelssohn's—that Judaism only judges action and not religious opinions—and that it made us feel we could justly lay claim to the identity: Jew.

Elie Wiesel

NOBEL PEACE PRIZE LAUREATE; ANDREW W. MELLON
PROFESSOR IN THE HUMANITIES, BOSTON UNIVERSITY
Boston, Massachusetts

I still believe that to be Jewish today means what it meant yesterday and a thousand years ago: to seek fulfillment both as a Jew and as a human being because Judaism and humanity must go together. To be Jewish today is to recognize that every person is created in the image of God and that our purpose in living is to be a reminder of God.

To be Jewish is, above all, to safeguard memory and open its gates to the celebration of life as well as to the suffering, to the song of ecstasy as well as to the tears of distress that are our legacy as Jews. It is to rejoice in the renaissance of Jewish sovereignty in Israel and the reawakening of Jewish life in the former Soviet Union. It is to identify with the plight of Jews living under oppressive regimes and with the challenges facing our communities in free societies. A Jew cannot remain indifferent to human suffering, whether in former Yugoslavia, in Somalia, or in our own cities and towns. The mission of the Jewish people has never been to make the world more Jewish, but to make it more human.

[*From* Why Be Jewish? *Reprinted with the permission of the American Jewish Committee.*]

CHAPTER TWO

---ⴰⵏⵓ---

"If I Am but for Myself...?"

Hillel asked, "If I am but for myself, what am I?" Jews are encouraged by their religion to seek individual well-being, materially as well as spiritually. But the Torah instructs that they must also be concerned with the spiritual and material well-being of their neighbors and of fellow Jews close to home, in Israel, and around the world. The responses placed in this chapter reflect this awareness and dedication.

Shoshanna Ahrens
REBBETZIN
Cologne, Germany

Ahavat Israel. Love of one's fellow Jew. Here in Cologne, women come to me to ask about the *mitzvot* pertaining to women, especially the ritual of the *mikveh*. Of course, I am happy to help them. I never question their motives, no matter how much I question myself inwardly. Consideration for the sensitivity of others is another value that has a particular Jewish flavor to it, and it is something I must keep in mind. So I never question a person's motives. Who knows what one *mitzvah* will lead to?

Franz Auerbach
EDUCATOR
Johannesburg, South Africa

I am a person with multiple identities—male, Jewish, educator, white, a citizen of South Africa, but born in Germany, of which I still remember scenes from my childhood. But it is probably my Jewishness that plays the most important part in my life because it gives me the guides by which I live in any of my other identities. And this is the Talmud's summary formulation of Jewish morality: "What is hateful to you, do not do to your fellow men." I have to admit that I do not have a total commitment to all the religious precepts of traditional Judaism or to the six hundred thirteen traditional *mitzvot*. But I cannot accept that this makes me less of a Jew.

The tenth commandment, "Thou shalt not covet," speaks to me especially in the context of the acquisitive consumer society. How can besting one's neighbour through competitive practices be regarded as success? I think that modern society has to tame the desire to possess, the desire for self-gratification. This is suggested in Hillel's famous dictum. "If I am not for myself, who is for me? If I am but for myself, what am I?" That is a fair balance between egoism and philanthropy, and yet commits one to a life of action instead of to a life of waiting for the opportune moment, which may never come.

Maurice Avigdon

PHARMACIST
Lyon, France

We of the Sephardic tradition are more emotional and outgoing than the Jews of eastern Europe. Here, as a visitor to the Old New Synagogue in Prague, I do not feel a stranger. We Jews have enough in common so that we feel at home among each other no matter where we find ourselves. Although I do not understand the native language of the Czech Republic, I understand the body language of my fellow-Jews.

Being Jewish makes a difference in that I carry out my duties with a sense of responsibility to help others, Jewish or not. Probably Jews were always interested in medicine and pharmacy because we care for others.

Joel Berger

RABBI
Schwerin, Germany

An important dimension of our Jewish identity comes from the commandment of respecting the memory of the deceased. Our rules are more restrictive than those of many other nations. It makes a difference for a Jew, a simple Jew or a rabbi, who lives in Germany that the graves, when graves exist, be held in respect, that cemeteries should be preserved, and that the memory of the millions who perished during the Nazi regime be acknowledged. I live in a town where, after the so-called *Wende,* i.e., the "turn," many East Germans rushed to capture their piece of prosperity and well-being. Nothing bad about this. We Jews are encouraged to look after our well-being, a good deed that expresses social responsibility. What is bad, and what prompts me to insist on this particular experience, is that things dear or even holy to us as Jews were ignored. In the years of the East German communist government, this happened often. But as the East and West were reunited, we were assured that in the new Germany, the sad experience of subjecting Jews to offense and discrimination would not be repeated. Here I am fighting for our cemetery, for the peace of those for whom we pray. Part of the cemetery was sold, the remnants of the deceased carted off to another place, only because those in power wanted to build their new mansions in a quiet area for which little money, if any, was requested of them.

The lesson: It makes a difference to be a Jew because in respecting those who have departed, you are sure that those following you will pay respect to you. It might be only a very small issue, less critical than our rules of sharing, of helping the needy and the sick. But it has a lot to do with our continuity as a people. This is why, from here in Schwerin, a community you might never have heard of, I can relate only to a concern that definitely makes a huge difference in my life as a Jew.

∾

Frania Bestornik
RETIRED TEACHER
Vilnius, Lithuania

To many Jews, Lithuania means Orthodox tradition. For me, it is the place where I grew up and the place from which I was taken to the concentration camp. Today I am asked if I want to live in Vilnius or if I want help in order to emigrate because I suffered so much. If I go, like so many do, our traditions will disappear from this place. The graves of the wise Jewish people of our community will disappear. And nobody will remember that we had our schools and synagogues, our Jewish theater, our music. If I stay in Vilnius, I will be exposed to the new face of anti-Semitism, the people who say that we Jews brought all the misery upon them. I wish I knew the right answer.

My heart says, "Stay. Help the ones who are not ready to come out from hiding under a different identity. Sing with them and speak Yiddish. Celebrate the holidays with them and talk about the extermination camps."

I, for one, believe that the difference it makes to me to be Jewish is that I end up taking the more difficult road. Probably because only what takes effort makes us realize who we are and to be happy with what we are.

Please come visit us in Riga and Vilnius!

Daniel Boari

SOCIAL WORKER
Rome, Italy

Judaism makes a difference in that I learned to be a good person, though not necessarily a "good Jew." The first aspect is important to the rest of the world. Being a good person means I am kind, polite, obey the laws of the land. The second aspect is being a good Jew, helping one's fellow Jew, and relying on the Torah as a guide to one's thinking and acting. Some Jewish practices make absolutely no difference to the rest of the world. In some cases, being a good Jew makes non-Jews hostile. Sabbath is one example, as are the other holy days.

On the other hand, my study of Judaism is a study in freedom. Judaism teaches us to be free of the constraints that the world places on the human soul; it gives the Jew something higher to contemplate. Belief in God, even under very difficult circumstances, makes one free.

Helen Brustman

COMMUNAL AFFAIRS DIRECTOR, JEWISH COMMUNITY COUNCIL OF VICTORIA
Melbourne, Australia

My parents (of blessed memory) were Holocaust survivors who brought me up with strong traditional Jewish values. I practice my Jewishness by attending an Orthodox synagogue every Shabbat and observing all the Jewish festivals.

I am strongly involved in working with and for the Jewish community of Melbourne. And I believe in the state of Israel as the homeland for Jews. My values are the ones based on the Torah: the six hundred thirteen *mitzvot*.

Rosalie Cohen

"GRANDE DAME" OF THE NEW ORLEANS JEWISH COMMUNITY
New Orleans, Louisiana

Jewish is what I am. It started with my birth. My family was devoted to each member, and to the family itself. My parents gave me a Jewish and secular education. In New Orleans, they brought the Hebrew poet Ephraim Lissitzky to educate us daughters. Although New Orleans is one of the oldest Jewish communities in the United States, it is isolated from the main centers of Judaism in the North. We are only twelve thousand Jews here. So I feel it is my responsibility to contribute to the community.

One way I do this is by supporting the learning and knowledge of Hebrew. It is one thing to read a translation of the Torah and quite another to enter in its spirit through the spirit of the language it was written in.

It is not only the language that makes Jews different. Our survival is due to the values we inherited and the responsibility we felt to carry them out and to transmit them. This is where our consciousness of being a chosen people comes from. We are, after all, to be a light, an example, to the other nations. It is not only the commandments that define us, but our commitment to the six hundred thirteen *mitzvot*. All six hundred thirteen lead to a person's becoming a decent, honest, compassionate human being. Of course, many nations now obey some of the same laws. But it is the commitment to God's law and the spirit in which we live the traditions that make us different.

We carry out the law in the belief that these are acts of righteousness, that these acts bring us closer to God. Especially meaningful are the *mitzvot* of *tzedakah*—of helping and giving—and *emet*—truthfulness, honesty in our dealings and our lives. Both of these combine in our sense of responsibility to society.

Josef Domberg

HONORARY PRESIDENT OF THE B'NAI BRITH OF EUROPE
Munich, Germany

One cannot choose how or what one is born as. I am a Jew because I was born as one, and this has marked my life in several ways. First of all, I was raised in a religious home and received a Jewish education. I will never forget the day of my *bar mitzvah* because that is the day my town in Poland was bombed. Being Jewish led to the need for me to emigrate, to leave the land of my birth. That is another difference that being Jewish made in my life. On a more positive note, being Jewish meant that I was born to a wonderful history and destiny. Therefore, I try to live up to the demands of being a Jew and to live proudly as a Jew in the Diaspora.

Being Jewish makes a difference in how I deal with people in my professional activity. I work here in Germany with Germans, with German politicians and members of the government, with German bankers, and with such professionals from other countries. I do not hide my Jewishness. Although I am not Orthodox, I do hold to our traditions. My offices are closed on the Jewish holidays. I try to be a bridge between the traditional Jewish world, which I try to represent, and the nonreligious, or at least non-Jewish, world.

Another difference that being Jewish makes to me is that I participate in Jewish-oriented activities, for Jewish causes and charities. This I do for my soul and spirit. They take a lot of my time and money, but as our tradition says, "Man does not live by bread alone."

I believe that our tradition encompasses the most beautiful ethical and moral principles. These are transmitted through the home life, from parents to children, down through the generations. We have the Ten Commandments, which we Jews gave to the world, to other religions of the Western world. Giving charity, *doing* charity is probably one tradition that remains specifically Jewish. There is a peculiar character to the Jewish way of charity. It has a very high priority. Helping others not only with money, but with your time and with all your resources. Giving of yourself as a human being because there is a religion that you carry in your heart.

Tzedakah—the Jewish way of charity—is the value that I would say guides me in particular. Helping not only other Jews, but all people in need. Fighting discrimination and racism. As our law says, you shall not have one law for the home-born and another law for the stranger. We are all children of God.

Kirk Douglas

ACTOR
Hollywood, California

I don't care about Israeli politics or various sects in Judaism. I don't care if someone goes around with *payis* down to his ankles, or whether he votes for Likud or Labor. I am a Jew and all Jews are my brothers. Better said, I try to be a Jew by studying the Torah and donating my money so others can study it in order to become better people.

M. C. Galaun

CHAIRMAN, LUSAKA HEBREW CONGREGATION
Lusaka, Zambia

I have a feeling of pride in being Jewish, but am also aware of the responsibility this entails. I am proud of achievements of other Jews, but feel shame when other Jews discredit our people. To me, as a Jew it is important not to discriminate on the basis of race, religion, origin, or social class, and to oppose discrimination in any form. That is, we have to apply the commandment to treat others as we want to be treated and make no difference between others and ourselves as Jews. In addition, I believe it is an important Jewish value to deal honestly, humanely, and generously with others.

Peter Gyori

DIRECTOR, BEIT PRAHA
Prague, Czech Republic

Being Jewish makes a difference in everything. My work in directing Beit Praha comes from being Jewish and having a sense of helping my fellow Jews, among others. But there is a difference in helping Jews as a Jew, and helping others. As part of my training in community service, I had to serve in South Central Los Angeles. You cannot help feeling that you are looking from the outside in. But you feel an attachment to other Jews when you are Jewish. Just like when I go to Israel. It is not just a place that I visit, like when I go to Italy. I always keep in mind what Hillel said: "Do not separate from the community."

Being Jewish means that I ask myself questions in light of the fact that I am Jewish. "What is my Jewish future?" "How do I pray as a Jew?" "Should I even consider intermarriage?" One thing I learned and took to heart as I studied Judaism is, there is no such thing as a stupid question. As you become more Jewish, you feel a certain separation from others in the world, you acquire a certain way of looking at things. You become more conscious not only of differences, but of your role as a Jew and as a human being among thousands, some Jewish, many not. You become sensitive to others who are different and who suffer injustice and inequality only because they are different.

Being Jewish means that I can rely on values that hold us together: the traditions celebrated with family, the Shabbat, learning. These values do not belong just to the Orthodox. I direct a group that appeals to Jews who do not want to be Orthodox, but who want to maintain what is valuable to them as Jews. Ah, this reminds me of another value that I really have to rely on: creativity. Jews come up with all kinds of ideas. Sometimes in my work, I really have to be creative in order to bring together all the Jews of various degrees of belief, from Orthodox to those who rarely think of going to a synagogue.

———⌒ல⌒———

Mireille Hadas-Lebel
PROFESSOR OF HISTORY, SORBONNE
Paris, France

The fact that I am Jewish imposes upon me an accrued assortment of responsibility, because I have the impression that my behavior is not for my sake alone. Moreover, if the behavior is a matter of possible blame, the judgment or reaction that it entails could have consequences for the entire community.

I don't know if there are any Jewish values that remain uniquely Jewish. The values mentioned in the Bible have been spread throughout civilized countries. The values that formed Jewish life in the Diaspora are respect for study and faithfulness to an ancestral tradition, which other ethnic groups can also have.

The vacuity of a life without intellectual study or research of any kind frightens me. And I am full of admiration for the generations that faced persecution down through the centuries and remained faithful to Judaism. This fidelity, often heroic, forbids me to break a very long chain.

—◦◦◦—

Erica Ioil
ADMINISTRATOR FOR THE WELFARE OF THE ELDERLY,
MUNICIPALITY OF JERUSALEM
Jerusalem/Gilo, Israel

Growing up in a city in Transylvania where Romanians, Germans, and Hungarians lived, *I* did not feel different because I was Jewish. Other people made me aware that I was somehow different, which means not equal to them, the Christians. With my blond hair and blue eyes, I do not look Jewish. But in the German grade school I attended, the kids beat me up because I was Jewish. When I grew up and went to the university, colleagues would ask me why I always stated that I was Jewish when I could easily pass for a non-Jew. But I did not want to be anything other than what I was. Maybe being Jewish was beaten into me by Christians. Religion was not. My parents were communists, but my aunt, who raised me, was Orthodox. I grew up in many different worlds.

As a Jew, I am different because I am part of this people. And I want to see the Jews as a people continue. I want my children to marry Jews and to continue our culture. We did not survive thousands of years of persecution to disappear through assimilation. This attitude is not particularly Jewish. Other nationalities and groups fight absorption and reassert their customs.

Just as Jews laid the foundation for Christianity and Islam, Jews gave the world its human values, so these values are no longer exclusively Jewish. I think that religion has a role in moral education, so long as religion is not taken to fanatical extremes. The most moral people I know have some religious feeling. I intend to study religion myself, but from a historical perspective, to see how our Jewish morality developed.

I work with old people. We Jews still respect the elderly and care for them, as we do for the poor and the sick. The state takes care of old people in Israel. This care for the elderly and the unfortunate goes back to our foundation as a nation. The government of Israel is in many ways based on the Torah, not in the sense that fanatics give it, but in our social laws. Israel is full of different types of Jews from almost every country in the world. We are each marked by the land we come from. The only thing we have in common is the heritage that derives from the Torah.

Baruch Korff
RABBI; SCHOLAR (DECEASED 1996)
Providence, Rhode Island

Being Jewish means, above all, helping other Jews. This is what guided me during World War II, when I worked for the Emergency Committee to Save the Jewish People of Europe, and also worked to provide funds and passports so Jews could be saved from certain death.

It also means loyalty. It was the grateful Jews of the Touro Synagogue of Newport who lent money to George Washington so that he could equip his army. Many of these Jews never got their money back. But they were loyal to the country that gave them the chance to live as human beings. During the time of the Watergate episode, I felt I owed loyalty to the presidency, to the ideals on which this country is based. This is why I founded the National Citizens Committee for Fairness to the Presidency.

Heinz Krymalovsky
REALTOR; MEMBER OF THE GERMAN NATIONAL JEWISH COUNCIL
Cologne, Germany

Being Jewish plays a big role in my life. I was born Jewish, my parents were Jewish, I was raised Jewish. During my youth, I was a member of several Jewish organizations. My children were raised Jewish. For me, being Jewish is not a burden and I see no reason to assimilate, even here in Germany. There is no question of shame. Some of my employees are German, and they see the *mezuzot* on the doorposts.

I am not religious, in the accepted understanding of the word. I do not observe the strictest religious rules. But I respect the people who do. That is why I support them by supporting the synagogue here in Cologne. I support it as an Orthodox synagogue because there are still Jews who want to be Orthodox in this city. Tradition is important for the future of Judaism here in Germany, as opposed to the liberal Judaism, a "lite" Judaism. The service should be conducted in Hebrew, not German. Our children should learn Hebrew. That is the language of the Torah. After all, they have to learn English, French, even Latin in the public schools. So they should at least be given the choice of learning their own language. And isn't Hebrew an international language? Jews live all over the world!

Lia van Leer
FOUNDER AND DIRECTOR, ISRAEL FILM ARCHIVES
Jerusalem

I was born Jewish and I would not want to be anything but Jewish. My family left Belz for Israel, and here I do not feel that I am a second-class citizen. Here I feel part of an international nation. But I do not see my being Jewish as a religious question. Jews are known for their humanism, their humanity. This comes from being a persecuted minority. All Jews believe in fighting for the rights of the individual. However, in Israel we are less humanistic than we would like to be. One cannot be a "nice occupier." One cannot preach human rights for one group, but only offer some rights to others, to non-Jews. On the other hand, "If I am not for myself, who am I? If I am not for others, what am I?"

My work reflects my life, my beliefs. I founded this institute. It brings together people from all over the world in order to share in the experience of film. Israeli films are not better or different by virtue of being Israeli or being produced by Jews. Our best films explore the human condition. Israeli films are very critical. Take, for example, the racism rampant here on the part of Jews from eastern Europe. Our films take a harshly critical perspective of this attitude, of our own racism.

Samuel Lieber

PHYSICIAN
Antwerp, Belgium

Life is sacred for us Jews. This, I think, is why so many illustrious physicians have been of Jewish origin. Even when prohibited from certain trades, Jews proved to be dedicated to the health of their brothers and sisters, as well as of non-Jews. In becoming good doctors, they carried out a humanistic ideal. They are good listeners, observe well, and care for others. Even in the world of high-tech medicine, these are characteristics that cannot be replaced by anything else.

For me, it makes a difference that I am Jewish because I am happy to be able to practice the respect for life and its maintenance in that unique way that comes from having a Jewish perspective on life as being holy.

Jan Murray

COMEDIAN; GAME-SHOW HOST DURING THE EARLY YEARS OF TELEVISION; ACTOR
Beverly Hills, California

When I was a child growing up, being Jewish had no special meaning for me. It was what I was. I didn't have to study. I didn't have to have special training. I didn't have to pass a test. It was the way I was born—an American Jew.

When I went to synagogue on the High Holidays and fasted on Yom Kippur; when Passover came, and my mother changed the house from *chametz* to *pesachdik;* when my father presided over the two Sedarim for all the relatives in our tiny apartment; when I went to Hebrew school to learn to read Hebrew so I could *daven;* when I was bar mitzvahed—never once did I feel different or special, because most of my friends were doing the same things. A few of the Christian friends I had prayed differently, in a church instead of a synagogue. And they had many different traditions, of course. But what did it matter to us children? As Americans, we shared so many things together—schools, athletics, social life, etc., etc.

It wasn't until my late teens and early twenties that I began to realize that my Jewishness indeed made me different. Slowly but surely, I was learning the mind-boggling fact that there were people on this earth who hated and despised me. Some even wished I were dead. Imagine, people who never even knew me! People who didn't know if I was dumb or smart, interesting or dull, cruel or kind, good or evil. And yet they hated and despised me only because I was a Jew!

Because of that, I feel a kinship, a brotherhood, and I have a concern for every Jew everywhere. Because of that, there is no way I could ever be anti-Black, anti-gay, anti-Christian, anti-European, -Asian, -African, or -Latin American.

However, any individual, any group, any organization that I perceive as evil can arouse violent hatred in me. So it's evident to me that for better or worse, most of who and what I am has been influenced by my Jewishness.

✧

Elvira Noa
MUSIC TEACHER; PRESIDENT OF THE JEWISH COMMUNITY
Bremen, Germany

Being Jewish gives me a standard to live by. I tried to find this in other religions, but could not. For me, it is important to pray. I found I could do this in Judaism. My mother is Catholic and my father is Jewish, but she did not believe in her religion and raised me as Jewish. As a child, I had to take religion classes in Germany, as the school system requires, so I studied Catholicism. But I can pray directly to God in Judaism. The development of religion from the inside is important in Judaism and provides inner strength.

At home, we celebrated the major Christian holidays, Christmas and Easter, as national holidays, without spiritual content. We also celebrated the Jewish holidays. My mother, the Catholic, insisted on this, as well as my father.

The humanistic values remain strong in Judaism, even though non-Jews have accepted them. Strong also are justice and knowledge and love of one's fellow human beings. But to me, the most important values are kindness, mercy, and charity. I am part of a state committee for integrating foreigners here in Bremen. I hope that I practice these values in this capacity.

Edgar M. Phillips, Jr.

INVESTMENT ADVISER
Beverly Hills, California

Without a doubt, the word that comes to mind is charity. My parents taught me to help the other man and woman, and through the years I have been involved to a great extent. In fact, many a time I have told my wife that if we win a lottery, the big winner of the day would be charities. In addition, the people we have met who are likewise charitable have enriched our lives.

Kindness to others in general, visiting those who are ill, teaching others how to live by setting a good example, are other values that I find to be especially Jewish and which I live by. Last, but certainly not least, is having a son (a Lubavitcher rabbi raised in a Reform family!) and a daughter and a wonderful wife who, in the spirit of our Jewish heritage, make our family a great team, helping others wherever and whenever possible.

—⬥—

Lilo Plon Federsdorf*

PRESIDENT OF THE JEWISH COMMUNITY
Alicante, Spain

Being Jewish is not a matter of race, since there are Jews among all races. It is not a matter of tradition, since I did not have a Jewish upbringing (my mother married a non-Jew). It is not a question of religion, because, although I believe in God, I do so in an unconventional way. That is, I observe all the traditions and holidays, but not as the Orthodox do. I have given lectures in schools about Judaism and Israel. And I can say that for me, as a Jew, Israel and Zionism are the most important. At age eighteen, I joined the Zionist Youth Organization, and that meant more to me than having a religious wedding and giving my children a religious upbringing.

Of all the Jewish values, I believe a love of peace is the most important. The word *shalom* is the most beautiful word of all the languages in the world, even though there is so little of it in everyday life. And then there is tolerance for all religions and viewpoints.

[*Daughter of the director of the film* Lang ist der Weg, *a full-length feature about German Jews preparing to leave Germany for after World War II for the future Israel.*]

Any Rapaport

HEAD OF FONDATION POUR LE JUDAISME FRANÇAIS
(FRENCH JEWISH FOUNDATION)
Paris, France

My parents were nonobservant, leftist. There was never any particular manifestation of Jewishness in our home. Nevertheless, I remain Jewish. I married a Jew who was somewhat more observant than I, which is not saying much. But we made our home more observant than the one I grew up in. My husband and I divorced, but I keep up some of the customs we observed together. I work here at the Foundation, so I am involved in Jewish life every day. The humanistic aspect of Judaism is what I feel closest to, the idea that we should care for others. I learned this much even during my childhood.

Edmund de Rothschild

FINANCIER
London, England

As a member of the fifth generation of Rothschilds to live in the United Kingdom, I feel strongly about preserving the Jewish quality of the family. I married Jewish and my children recognise their heritage. This heritage has been the major influence in my supporting Jewish charities and non-Jewish entities, which means double work.

Also, I support Israel, in a nonpolitical way, though, especially working towards solving the problem of water for Israel, the Gaza Strip, and the West Bank. I am proud of the fact that when Sir Winston Churchill authorised the formation of the Jewish Infantry Brigade Group, I commanded Battery 200 Field Regiment Royal Artillery, comprised of Jewish refugees, sabras, and a handful of British officers. In this way I was able to serve my people and my country.

Sheldon Schaffer

BUSINESS AND ECONOMIC ANALYST
Birmingham, Alabama

My Jewishness is a twentieth-century phenomenon. I am a secular, rationalistic, humanistic, nonreligious, largely unaffiliated Jew rooted in Diaspora life. My Jewishness is the most important nonphysical characteristic of my being. It provides me the foundation for much of what I am or do. Being Jewish makes a difference because I want it to make a difference. Being Jewish impels me to put into practice what I perceive to be an ethically satisfying Jewishness with worldwide applicability for achieving peace, tranquility, and a certain amount of harmony in my everyday life and in the life of all the people around me and in the world. I look on the Jewish difference as a support system that provides me with helpful, exploratory guidelines as I throw myself into a constructive and sometimes confrontational, active, but changing life. Even as I do, I wonder whether there are other people who might be using their own different guiding support system in the same way and for much the same reasons. But because of the widespread and pervasive presence of evil, evil created by humans around the world, I am less than confident that there are really truly effective alternative operative systems out there. We Jews do violate the very laws we established. But don't we do so with a special sense of guilt and bewilderment and a special felt need for constraint, which often result in somewhat more restrained negative behaviors than are acted out by other societal groups? Don't we Jews display a more humane and compassionate attitude in the constraints we would impose on those who deviate? Not only do we place an especially high value on even a single life, but don't we often take the extra step in seeking redeeming value in those who deviate.

For me, the treasurable part of the traditional Jewish system is the enunciation of ethical precepts, as in the *Ethics of the Fathers*, which emphasize the desirability and attainability of peaceful, harmonious, tolerant, cooperative human behaviors. I perceive these as human constructs that require no God-ordained involvement. They require only a self-imposed obligation, in covenant with other people who think similarly, and who are bound together through a variety of tribal or ethnic or even congregational reinforcing agents. This is why, after our children were grown, my wife and I affiliated with secular-humanistic Judaism and the Society for Humanistic Judaism.

My view of Judaism challenges Jews to be completely positive and forthright about their Judaism and to disallow the constraining and negative effects of anti-Semitism on Jewish life. My operational definition demands that I and every other Jew openly and vigorously oppose bigotry against any and all groups, but especially our own.

Maurizio di Segni
FORMER BUSINESSMAN
Rome, Italy

Jews came to Rome over two thousand years ago. Our community is probably the oldest in Europe. My ancestors came here as agents of the Jews living in the Holy Land, that is, for the Jews who needed support to study Torah. I am not saying this in order to retell our history, but as an introduction to the variety of people that fall under the qualifier "Jewish." As a Roman Jew, I am different from Jews in other parts of Italy and in Europe, who were expelled from the Holy Land. My history is part of Jewish history, but only in a dimension you will not find in Poland, Morocco, France, England, or America. So I feel not only that being Jewish makes a difference in a Roman Catholic city and country, but that being a Roman Jew makes me different from other Jews. Except for one thing all Jews have in common: solidarity in time of trouble.

We have seven synagogues in Rome representing different attitudes, different ways of praying, different ways of burying the dead. They arose when three thousand Jews from all around Rome were squeezed into this small ghetto, the first ever: seven streets long on the edge of the Tiber that overflowed its banks every spring. Non-Jews saw them as a homogeneous mass of undesirables. Yet there is probably more diversity among this small amount of people that constitute the Jews of the world than in one huge unified church or nation.

Hans Stecher

BUSINESSMAN
Port of Spain, Trinidad

If I had not been born Jewish, I would have become Jewish. Why would I want to be part of a people who have been slandered, defamed, despised, and persecuted for over two thousand years? I am proud to be part of a people who, despite all these severe trials, have held true to their religion, ethics, and values. Proud to be part of a people who gave the world its first ethical and moral code—the Ten Commandments—and whose Torah became the foundation of Christianity, which conquered the world, and of Islam, which conquered almost all of the rest.

But it is not enough to be proud of one's history. My history compels me to not break with the past through inaction. When my wife and I arrived here as refugees from Nazi Vienna, we joined other Jews in forming a synagogue and providing services to the Jewish community, practically all refugees. To be Jewish means not to forget that you are Jewish and therefore to have a responsibility to each other, even those Jews no longer physcally present. To this day, as our community in Trinidad dwindles, I take care of the graves of Jews in the Jewish area of the Mucurapo Cemetery.

Irving I. Stone

CHAIRMAN AND CEO, AMERICAN GREETINGS
Pittsburgh, Pennsylvania

I have always felt the key to Jewish continuity to be providing young Jews with a good Torah education. The Jewish people have always been at the forefront of educational literacy. We were the first nation, some two thousand years ago, to institute universal education. In medieval Europe, there were only three groups that were literate: the nobility, the clergy, and the Jews. Tragically, today many Jews' zeal for education has been limited to secular studies and the magnificent, deep wisdom of our tradition goes unlearned.

I have dedicated much of my time and resources over the years towards trying to provide many of my fellow Jews with an opportunity to learn about their heritage. My fifty-odd year association with the

Hebrew Academy (for many years, the largest day school in America), my support of various outreach organizations, and my sponsorship of various books and publications have all been towards this goal. I have always felt that when your fellow traveler is thirsty and you can provide him with water, you have an obligation to share. G-d has been good to me in so many ways, first and foremost in making me a Jew. If many more of our people were given the opportunity to learn about their tradition, I'm sure they would feel the same way.

Katalja Talyigas
SOCIAL WORKER
Budapest, Hungary

Only a few years ago, questions like these would have meant nothing to me. My first goal was to become a leading sociologist. I knew I was Jewish, but this was unimportant to me for my everyday life. Today I work as a Jewish social worker in a Jewish social support foundation, and I do my best to help people who need my skills from the particular perspective of our people. What is this perspective?

In 1993, I took part in a three-week program under the auspices of the Buncher Leadership Program in Israel. Strengthening Jewish communities in the Diaspora is the major goal of this program. To strengthen means to make something viable. Our viability is based on our unique perspective of the human being and a human society passed down through a long tradition of ethics and values. To take care of older people sounds like something all people hold as a value. But our history has made this concern for the elderly, the sick, and the needy part of the Jewish ethos. We are particularly sensitive to these conditions and needs. I resigned my comfortable position as a sociologist and became a social worker. It is my obligation to help, and to fulfill this obligation means to live like a Jew, with a special consideration of people who need help.

Suzan Tarablus

JOURNALIST
Istanbul, Turkey

A few months ago, the president of Turkey made his first and historic visit to Israel. I was one of the journalists accompanying him. I witnessed a ceremony in which I heard the national anthems of both Turkey and Israel sung one after the other in Jerusalem. No one else could feel what I felt at the time, since I was the only Turkish Jew among them.

Practicing Judaism is not difficult in Turkey, but it still makes one feel as "the other" in a land where ninety-nine percent of the population is Muslim. Of about sixty-three million people in Turkey, twenty-seven thousand are Jewish. To maintain a Jewish identity takes a lot of personal effort.

One of the values that helps is unity, especially the unity of the family, which even in Turkey is unique to Jews. The concept of *tzedakah*—helping people who are in need—the concept of human rights, and so many other concepts derive from the Torah, which I believe is a gift to humanity. Although I am not at all religious, nearly all the concepts and values of Judaism are part of my belief and daily life. The importance of togetherness, helpfulness, and considering "the other" as my equal shows up in my outlook towards life in general.

Nowadays, it is not enough to be a Jew oneself, and I believe that it is most important to bring up Jewish children in full awareness of their Judaism.

Boruch Wahrhaftig

Los Angeles, California

Jews are unique in that their souls, whose source is God, are directly connected to the Creator. This leads to a strong connection among individual Jews, almost like a family relationship, and stimulates a feeling of community responsibility and service to fellow Jews.

Mike Wallace

TELEVISION JOURNALIST
New York, New York

Being Jewish—for me—is a matter of some pride, for I believe I'm
an inheritor of a remarkable ethnic gene pool. I'm not especially Jewish in a religious sense—despite the fact that I invariably say the Shema
before going to sleep each night. Rather, I am Jewish through my
parents, through lessons learned in the Reform Sunday School I attended in Boston a long time ago, through identification with the remarkable history that goes back several millennia.

I try to live by the Golden Rule, and that, I believe, has its heritage
in Jewish history.

Maciej Welyczko

PRESIDENT, JEWISH STUDENT ASSOCIATION
Wroclaw, Poland

My mother is a Polish Catholic. My father is Jewish, but an atheist.
I am also an atheist and attend services, with my father, at the synagogue. In Wroclaw, the synagogue is Orthodox, but I get along very
well with the people there. The only practicing Jews in Wroclaw are
very old, but they are my friends. Because the Jewish community in
Wroclaw is small—only three hundred people—it is very open to others. It is also a dying community.

In Judaism, knowledge is very important, and this is something that
I consider to be great. In Catholicism, in Poland, the most important
thing is faith. I am very skeptical of faith alone since I am a scientific
type. My major is history and Judaism is my area of specialization. My
master's thesis is on the history of Jewish communities in western Poland.

The Association of Jewish Students in Poland is doing many things
to make sure that we Jews survive and thrive. One of the most pressing
problems is the very old Jews. We help them to keep up a Jewish way of
life until the inevitable happens. For those on the other side of the age
continuum, we have started the Jewish Boy Scouts, along the line of
pre-Israeli groups of young people. The Lauder Foundation came to
Poland and tried to reestablish Jewish religious life by convincing young

people to be either Conservative or Orthodox. For me, the future of Jewish life in Poland is important, no matter what type—religious or liberal. What is important is that this future be Jewish of some type.

It is important to save Jewish culture in Poland. That is why the association of Jewish Students also has cultural programs to educate both Jews and Poles. The association also protests manifestations of anti-Semitism that arise from time to time, and tries to effect change in a low-key, legal way by appealing to the authorities. In the case of this priest who is stirring up people against the Jews, the friend of Lech Wałesa, he is now under investigation due to our protests. [The events took place in 1994–1995.] The association is made up of young Jews, liberal or not religious. Despite the title, it is not a religious organization. Our only criterion for membership is, do you feel Jewish?

Sylvie Wittman
EDUCATIONAL TOUR ORGANIZER; RESTORER OF JUDAICA;
CHAIRPERSON, CHEVRA BETH SIMCHA
Prague, Czech Republic

My mother was not considered *halachically* Jewish, so I had to go through conversion to become what I always was: Jewish. I am not the only one who went through this difficulty, and to understand it, you have to understand something of the post-World War II experience of Jews in what is now the Czech Republic. Religious Jews emigrated. The men who returned from camps to Prague married non-Jewish women and did their best to avoid the consequences of Judaism. Then, due to communism, Jews had to remain invisible again. Children were not raised Jewish either out of a fear of anti-Semitism or out of disgust of associating with collaborators who went to the synagogues to report on other Jews. The small Jewish community was closely watched. The communists permitted only Orthodox Judaism, and most of the men were paid to attend services so as to show the noncommunist world that there was religious freedom under communism. Dictatorships need loyal minorities. And Orthodoxy makes no trouble for its supporters, only for other Jews. Children were hidden from Judaism. Now that they are adults and the land is free, they face the *halachic* question of who is a Jew. That's why many of the leaders of the Orthodox congregation converted to Judaism from the state of nonreligion they used to be in. The majority of Jews in this country have not been Orthodox for one hundred twenty years.

I am a duly elected chairperson of a *chevra,* not a synagogue. It is called "alternative" because in a country that woke up from authoritarianism, what is not mainstream is alternative. The mainstream is not the majority here, but it is the most powerful because it receives financial support from organizations in the United States and from the tourists. I am not mainstream, which means I do not belong to the Orthodox group. The chief rabbi of Prague, a good friend of mine, is not my representative, nor my priest before God, only my friend.

I started the *chevra* because I do not believe in centralization. There is nothing in Judaism that says we have to be organized under a central authority. The tragedy of central Europe is that its development was arrested by a hierarchy. Judaism was headed towards Reform in this part of the world. We get help from the European Board of the World Union for Progressive Judaism. A young woman from our *chevra* is studying at the Leo Baeck College and will be our rabbi. Our *chevra* is made up of students. On the holidays, about ninety-two people attend services; on *kabbalat Shabbat,* about thirty. We do not delve into the backgrounds of our congregants. It is important to be inclusive. The people who do not want to be Jewish will eventually leave; they will not try to make Judaism into something it is not.

So, as you can see, Judaism is very important to me. Jewish values are very different from mainstream Czech values and the cultures based on Christianity. Christianity is based on manipulation and unchanging dogma. The people are not encouraged to be well educated in their religion. Neither does Christianity know anything about its own foundation, which is a little Judaism and some paganism, as can be seen in their idol worship. It is institutionalized hypocrisy. This is not to say that Jews are not hypocrites, but there is no institutionalized space in Judaism for hypocrisy. There is no one human being who is held to represent absolute truth. There is no dogma of submission. Faith is based on fulfilling the *mitzvot.* Doing is more important than believing. The ground rules are more important than the author.

It is very important for me that I am Jewish because I believe that it is important to be human.

CHAPTER THREE

"An Exemplary Constructive Power,
Practical and Generous"

I n spite of its unequaled traumas, Jewish destiny proves itself to be an exemplary constructive power, practical and generous," wrote one
of the respondents. The answers placed in this cat-
egory tend to regard Judaism or Jewishness above
all as a force that leads to creativity. To them, it
represents a motive for positive action, often expressed in innovation, humanization, or popular-
ization.

R. O. Blechman

ILLUSTRATOR; ANIMATED-FILM MAKER; AUTHOR
New York, New York

The melting pot was boiling at high heat when my parents were youngsters. Second-generation Jews from eastern Europe, they tended to mix smoothly into the American stew. Born Samuel, my father became "Chuck." His brothers, Nathan and Abraham, became "Nat" and "Ack." With their snappy monikers, tweed knickers, and hair parted down the middle and slicked down with Vitalis, they fitted nicely into the American scene of the Roaring Twenties.

But in time there was a complication. My brother and I were born. I suppose that my parents feared that we would lose our Jewishness entirely, so as youngsters we were trundled off to Hebrew school. Classes started at four o'clock, so for five days a week, we had to run home from public school, gulp down our chocolate milk, and rush to the East Midwood Jewish Center, where we would struggle with the funny-looking characters of the Hebrew language. Hebrew school meant little, if any, time for playing stickball or riding our Schwinn bikes, and this struck me as cruel and unusual punishment. "For what?" I had to wonder.

Further punishment came along when my European-born grandmother moved into our home after my grandfather's death. She kept a kosher house. Banished were the glory of bacon-lettuce-and-tomato triple-deckers (my favorite sandwich), and milk with any kind of meat, except when they were sneaked at a drugstore lunch counter. We even had to exchange the glitter of Christmas for the sobriety of Chanukah, although we managed to create an uncomfortable hybrid celebration. Christmas gifts were exchanged along with Chanukah gelt. No Christmas tree, however, although paper Santa Clauses sometimes found their way near the *menorah*.

I had blond hair as a child, and friends of my parents sometimes remarked admiringly to them, "He looks just like a *shaygitz* [Christian boy]." My parents beamed with pride. So clearly, it was considered good to be a Christian. But if this was the case, I wondered, what was I? Or to pose more precisely the question that this young boy asked, his blond eyebrows raised high: "What should I want to be?"

The question was answered when I was eight years old. Kristallnacht shattered any illusions I might have had that being a Jew was a good thing. Clearly, it was not, or why were those awful things happening to Jews? Of course, it was difficult to conceive of a non-Jewish world, since everybody I knew was Jewish, except our maid, Grace (née Gretchen), a farm girl from Germany.

So there I was, a *shaygitz* Jew, a strange and lone ingredient floating unassimilated in the melting pot.

With the passing of my blond hair to brown, and my brown hair to white, I came to accept my Jewishness, if not with open arms, at least not with folded ones. Perhaps I hedged things by marrying a Christian.

I have come to realize that Jewish elements have entered my work. In an animated retelling of the Nativity story for a PBS Christmas special, there is a scene where Herod's troops are about to enter Bethlehem. The townspeople take down their signs welcoming Jesus and toss them into a bonfire. A friend remarked that my staging of the scene reminded him of the Nazi book-burnings.

Maybe so. But more to the point, I observe that my narratives are heavily loaded with the language and rhythms of Yiddish.

I sometimes wonder if even my idiosyncratic style of drawing—the nervous line, the visual counterpart to Woody Allen's anxious patter— isn't a reflection of my Jewish background. Perhaps, in a profound way, my style of thinking may reflect my Jewish heritage. In a pure sense, creativity is a matter of expressing oneself uniquely, of leaving the herd in order to take the lonely, less trodden path. I think that being born "different," or perceiving oneself as being "different," may promote the individuating process that is at the heart of true creativity.

Rudy Boschwitz
U.S. SENATOR FROM MINNESOTA, 1978–1991
St. Paul, Minnesota

Being Jewish is a state of mind—and it is always there. It drives me to excel. It drives me to help our people, because I know how much earlier generations—and mine—have suffered just because we are Jews. It's a warm and wonderful feeling that fills my heart with pride.

Joseph Burg
EDITOR OF *DIE TCHERNOWITZER BLÄTTER*
Czernovitz, Ukraine

As a Jew, I continue to write and live in a city that used be known throughout Europe for its Yiddish culture. Here in Czernovitz, at a conference in 1908, Yiddish was consecrated as a literary language. Here were born and lived Rose Ausländer, Paul Celan, and Aharon Appelfeld. Here creativity in writing and theater thrived among Jews, not just in Yiddish, but also in Romanian, Russian, and German. I do not take credit for all these achievements, but they serve as an inspiration for my own work as writer and editor. The Holocaust, World War II, and communism turned this multicultural European capital back into a provincial town in the area known in Romanian as Bucovina.

As a survivor of all these cataclysms, I want to keep these accomplishments from fading into oblivion. Whenever I can get the necessary money—with help from Jews around the world—I publish the newspaper in Yiddish to ensure the continuity of our heritage and creativity. How long this will last, I do not know. People are leaving for places where they can make a living, where they can have a future with other Jews.

George Burns
COMEDIAN; ACTOR (DECEASED 1996)
Beverly Hills, California

Do you want to hear the best joke? "I am Jewish." Each time I said these words, people would start laughing. Even Gracie would. I could hear the wheels turning in their brains "What's new, Georgie?" as they laughed. I would look at them as a *nebechel*, as though I did not know why they laughed, and wait for an explanation. To be Jewish means to be born contaminated with humor. Those who hate us cannot stand that even when the going gets tough, we take it in good spirit.

Leonardo Coen

JOURNALIST
Rome, Italy

Jewish journalists are under double scrutiny: by the readers, as all journalists are, and as Jews. As a Jewish journalist in Italy, I am more an exception than a Jewish journalist in France or England or the United States. Even when I do not want to acknowledge the pressure of the situation, it comes out in my reporting. But don't get me wrong; I do not take this in a negative sense. Being Jewish makes me sensitive to themes that other journalists conveniently ignore: injustice, discrimination, as well as exceptional accomplishments. As a Jew, I am dedicated to making things better, not to sensationalize them. This does not automatically make me a good writer or a good reporter, but it gives me a sense of direction. The Jewish culture of the word, and especially the tradition of splitting hairs, of engaging in discussions about fine points that do not seem very exciting at first, also affect my writing. When I hear that some of my opinions excite the public, I feel that belonging to a tradition dedicated to open debate and critical attitude has helped me a lot. In the superb line of great Jewish journalists who have made a difference in Italy, I am but a testimony that their contribution was not an accident.

Lou Dorfsman

GRAPHIC DESIGNER (CREATOR OF THE CBS "EYE")
New York, New York

I grew up in a neighborhood that I would say was a mixture between Polish and Jewish. My first idea that Jewish was different came when the Polish kids in the neighborhood would pick on the Jewish kids. And then my father told me stories about the Russians and the Poles and the things he and his family and friends went through as children.

When I entered the advertising world, a little before World War II, it was a very WASPy business. So I decided to work in exhibition design, World's Fair exhibitions in 1938, 1939, 1940. It was a field open enough so that there were no restrictions in terms of ethnic background. When I joined the army, they found out, through primitive computers, that my background was in exhibition design, and they put me in charge of this giant, giant traveling exhibition for the army. Since I was considered some kind of talent or artist, my Jewishness did not enter into things. They needed me.

After World War II, the WASPy business of advertising agencies opened up. One of the partners of Birnbach, Doyle and Behn was Jewish. So they were known as a Jewish agency, so unusual it was. A Jewish agency that began to attract big accounts. Its biggest account was Volkswagen, of all things. Here's this Nazi car and a "Jewish" agency that did an incredibly magnificent job of launching that car in the United States and making it a success. The quality of Birnbach was so high that they set a new standard. The competition tried to harm them by hiring their own Jews and other non-WASP types.

I began working at CBS after the war. And I have to admit that I was not what you'd call an open Jew. The world was still not ready for that. I acted like a real American, which is what a lot of Jews did. I'm probably more Jewish now than I ever was, only because I think of where I was as a younger person. I'm a little more outspoken about it. On the other hand, I don't regularly go to temple. I sort of don't believe in organized religion. But I moved to Great Neck because it's a Jewish neighborhood, and I wanted my kids to grow up here. They went to a Yiddish school. They learned to speak and read Yiddish. I feel good that they will carry on.

If there is anything in Judaism that I would like to leave to my children and grandchildren, I would say: All of it! There's a deep-seated sense of intellect in Jewish culture. A nonviolence in Jewishness. Hard to tell in Israel, but the violence is coming to them and they're responding. And there's still that thing about knowledge and education. Those basic tenets that I feel strongly about. As I glance around, as I've done for fifty years, I see Jews excelling in so many areas and I think to myself occasionally that it's kind of miraculous that a little people, a tiny people, in a country like this, stands out in so many areas of activity—show business, cultural activities, music, art, my business. It can't be because they're Jews, but there they are. And when I see Jews doing the wrong thing, it bothers the hell out of me.

I was on one of the early teams to design the Holocaust Museum. I wanted to do the job for nothing. By some standards, I am not very Jewish. But I wanted to work on the Holocaust Museum for nothing. For my *kishka* I wanted to do this job. No matter what, it would be worth it to me just to do it.

Josif Elgurt

PAINTER
Odessa, Ukraine

From my apartment window, I can see the harbor. I can paint what I see, just as I paint clowns, cats, and fantastic images. But I cannot paint what I experienced—the murder of my parents in the Ukraine, mass graves, scenes from concentration camps. My Jewishness is expressed in the depth of my memories, not in feeling sorry for myself. There is a strong feeling of destiny to my Jewishness.

Giora Feidman

WORLD-RENOWNED KLEZMER INTERPRETER; FORMER CLARINETIST
IN THE ISRAELI PHILHARMONIC ORCHESTRA
New York and Israel

Jews are born singers and dancers. The holy glue of a people is their music. It is a language. We are born with the instrument of song. *Klezmer* is composed of two syllables: *kli* and *zemer*. The letters *k*, *l*, and *i* refer to Kohen (the high priest from the tribe of Levi who served in the Temple), Levi (the tribe that took care of the Temple), and Israel (all the other Jews from the eleven remaining tribes). That means all of the Jews. *Zemer* is the instrument of song. If we rearrange the letters, we get *remez*, which means "a hint of something," or *zerem*, which means "pressure" [*sic*]. We use only a hint, a small part of the knowledge of God.

"*Ani ma'amin* [I believe]" refers to a belief that is the result of knowledge. This is what differentiates Judaism from other religions, in which faith is an escape. Judaism is approached through prayer, and when Jews pray, they sing and dance. God does not need our words. Words serve only to educate our own brains through a language so we can approach God. *Niggun* (the Hebrew word for melody) is not a melody but the energy that results from interpretation. This energy is manifest in any art. The human message that music brings out through the Jewish conception is unique, but it applies to all humans. It refers to knowledge given to the Jews through Moses and when it comes, we do not need more "religion."

Jews must start to learn why all that happened to them has happened. One reason is that Jews don't fulfill their role in the human family. They do not live the values of Judaism written into the Torah. I do not mean all the interpretations around the Torah, but the Torah itself. The only thing that makes Jews different is the Torah. And this is why I am Jewish. We have to use our energy to live and teach Torah. Jews are the best professors, but we are not teaching the right things. We serve society the wrong way if we are only the best doctors or lawyers or professors. I cannot emphasize this enough. We must live the Torah.

It's no secret that the Jewish world is in a crisis, and that this reverberates on another level. Again, this is because Jews do not know the values of Judaism and thus do not understand their responsibility to be a light to the Gentiles, a light to all the other members of the human family. That's why Jews have become a nation more than a religion. This national feeling has held us together for more than two thousand years and it brought us back home. But that is not enough. It is even dangerous because we go to our home, Israel, without knowing why we really left our nation in the first place. This came about as the result of strife among brothers. Jews returned to Israel, but Judaism did not.

If the motive behind Judaism is only a reaction to some event or events—the Holocaust, the bombing of a synagogue in Argentina, the assassination of Rabin—then Judaism will disappear as soon as Jews are no longer attacked. Judaism must be preached, not just studied, so that we ourselves learn the values of Judaism and be what the Torah said we should be, a light to the universe.

Laszlo Fekete
CANTOR; OPERA SINGER
Budapest, Hungary

Here is one difference that being Jewish makes. On Shabbat, when I am dressed in a dark suit or a caftan and a hat, the men who exchange money on the black market approach me by saying "Shalom." During the week, when I am in everyday dress, that is, not dressed as a Jew, they approach me by asking, "Change money?"

My family was traditional. My mother lit candles and my father and I went to the synagogue on holidays. I learned enough about Judaism to get me through my *bar mitzvah*. As a child, I believed in God.

School under the communist regime caused me to have doubts about His existence, but I still had a desire on the rational level to learn about Judaism and God. I stopped believing in God after a while, but I could not live without one. I acted under God's control despite my rationality.

When I was in my twenties, a Baptist colleague who understood my doubts asked me "Why do you want to know who we have to believe?" This question woke me up and my soul felt relieved after this incident. My commitment to Judaism grew. It manifested itself through music.

I was a bathroom soloist who got his first chance to perform when the star soloist was too sick to perform on stage one night. Everyone in the audience woke up as I sang! And everyone told me that my future lay in singing. So I explored Jewish music in my free time, while I was employed as a baritone *buffo* in the Hungarian Chamber Ensemble. But I wanted to be a cantor. And this was something I had to be good enough to do, to prepare myself for. Not the other way around, which would be to practice being a cantor while serving as one. This meant for me to immerse myself in the Jewish way of life, our laws and traditions. The difference that being Jewish makes is that it is something to which I aspire, and do not take for granted.

Being Jewish is not a yes-or-no matter, it is a continuum, a continuous development of feeling and practice. I was twenty years old when I first saw my mother praying in the morning and found out that she prayed every day. "Do you believe in God?" I asked her. She answered that God's existence was never something she questioned. And here is another big difference that Judaism has for me: Whether there is a God or not, we are to practice the *mitzvot* in our lives.

Gyorgy Friedlander
LITERARY CRITIC
St. Petersburg, Russia

I wish I could answer the question for what it is worth. My lineage goes back to Bergson, and thus to a Jewish way of thinking that affected the Western world in many ways. Jews are provocative thinkers, rebellious; they tackle hard intellectual questions, and they have a good sense of humor. They are the service providers of the many places in which they settled: as merchants, singers, poets, performers, teachers,

carpenters, shoemakers, barbers, bankers, and critics of art and literature.

Living in Russia, I probably became more Russian than I am Jewish.
Or so I thought. I was called the most influential authority on
Dostoyevsky. But then my dedication to Russian literature was de-
nounced as tainted because I am Jewish. It seems that the more we try
to be like the others, the more we face the danger of being reminded
that we are not.

As I answer your question, I realize that my Jewishness is manifest
through my interest and ability to interpret. Jews are accused of being
parasites because they appropriate the themes and ideas of other peoples
in their own music, art, literature, philosophy, and humor. Is this because Jews, knowingly or not, see something in the work of others that
they can take further or improve upon?

Basia Frydman
ACTRESS
Stockholm, Sweden

When I came to Sweden in 1948, I was a Polish-Jewish princess. As
early as I can remember, I tried my best to eradicate all traces of my
immigrant background. If I succeeded, at the very least by trading in
my Polish accent for a homespun Swedish one, the metamorphosis was
not entirely complete. There is still that *other,* my Jewishness.

Once, in the first grade, I came home from school and threw myself
into my mother's arms weeping. In those days, like most of my peers,
I collected paper bookmarks, and through a trade, I had just acquired
a beautiful baby Jesus in glitter. "Mommy, " I cried, cradling the cov-
eted bookmark in my hands, "How could those horrible Jews murder
such a sweet little baby"?

My mother answered, "Basie, we are those 'terrible Jews' and we
did not kill Jesus."

All at once, the pieces fell into place. Wasn't it I who, as a three-year-
old, with passion and ardor, stood on a stool before an audience of
appreciating Jews at the community center and recited Yiddish verse,
which my father had taught me over dinner while my mother fed us
gehackte leber [chopped liver] and a dose of *gehackte tzuras* [troubles]?
Of course we were Jewish. But having well understood the fact, I was

still not satisfied. If we were Jewish, couldn't my parents at least try their best to be Swedish Jews? From what I observed around me, this was a state far less compromising to be in. According to me, Swedish Jews had style and class, almost like real Swedes. In their homes, guests were invited. They dined in sumptuous surroundings. In our Jewish home, people just dropped in and were so many that friends referred to our house as "the café." It was these great contrasts that made the Swedish Jew, for me, so worth emulating. While growing up, I believed that Swedish Jews spoke in sober tones and never raised their voices. This was not the case in our immigrant Jewish home. Here we sang and yelled and sweated, moving bodies and hands wildly to the songs we sang. One night, our neighbors even called the police. They thought we were beating each other to death.

There were more comparisons. Swedish Jews did not pinch their children on the cheek in front of everyone. Swedish Jews were not overly emotional, getting hysterical over the slightest little thing. Swedish Jews did not wish their children the successes of Shirley Temple or Elizabeth Taylor, twisting their girls' hair into tiny corkscrews to achieve at least a semblance of greatness. Swedish Jews did not squirrel food for possible hard times ahead or fight the hopeless battle of a never-emptying plate, which was filled by a loving mother every time one turned her head in conversation at the dinner table.

On the other hand, those desirably refined Swedish Jewish children did not, like us, get everything they pointed to. We children got oil paints and canvases to turn us into Picassos. We had a piano, paid for in installments, to be able to play like Schubert by the time we were six. However, whatever the comparison, there was no getting around the fact that we were all Jews.

I remember how we celebrated all the Jewish holidays and how Mamma cried when she lit the candles on Shabbat eve, even if we otherwise never prayed at home. Having gone to *yeshivah* as a child, my father knew all the prayers. But he was an atheist, and Jewish education became the children's responsibility. We were sent to religious schools. I understand now that my father, for most of his life, just couldn't get along with God, even if in his old age he came nearer than ever before.

I have become neither a Picasso, a concert pianist, Shirley Temple, nor Elizabeth Taylor. And as for my religious-cultural identity, whether I am Swedish, Jewish-Swedish, Swedish-Jewish, who can say? I am a mother because I have children. Am I a Jewish mother? My children— are they Swedes first, or Jews? Mine is a mixed marriage. I realize now that my Jewishness, bequeathed to me at birth, and which I have loved, hated, and loved again, has always stayed with me, no matter what I did to try to rub it out, soften it, exaggerate it. Still, that which I've always taken for granted and seen as obvious is, in fact, not at all such a given. My Jewishness can die, or it can live on. And Jewishness as I know it? Will it always remain fixed and immutable, or will it grow in new directions? Or disappear?

Culture. Traditions. Religion. Religions. Philosophy. Diaspora. Israel. Yiddish. Chaos. Chaos that weakens. Chaos that strengthens.

I would like my Jewish culture, my Jewish religion, my Jewishness to live on.

For years, my husband nagged me (thank God for his Finnish obstinacy) about how very much a Jewish theater was needed on the dramatic scene. Finally, we took the initiative to begin a professional Jewish Theater in Stockholm. In 1991, with the help of the director Pierre Fränckel, financier Robert Weil, and many others, we turned our dream into reality. Although we have no permanent stage, we have performed for the Royal Dramatic Theater, television, radio, and film, besides holding cabaret and literary evenings. We also visit many schools in Sweden, perform small plays about anti-Semitism and racism, and conduct discussions between the students and actors. On my own, I have made a CD of Yiddish songs, entitled *Basia oif Yiddish-Farbotene Lider*, and am working on a new one with the help and inspiration of Salmon Schulman, a Swedish pediatrician, author, and the country's foremost translator of Yiddish literature and poetry into Swedish. He has opened many new doors for me to my beloved Yiddish cultural heritage.

[*Translated from the Swedish by Nancy Miller.*]

Frank Gehry
ARCHITECT
Santa Monica, California

In my work—and I work in many different countries—I seem to be very adaptable; I bring my language to France, and to Germany, and to Spain, and Korea, and adapt to the local cultures easily. People who work with me think that this is a very Jewish thing, and I suppose it is. We Jews are always on the run, so we learn to adapt, right? I think it's a value to be able to do it, because that means that you're adaptable to a changing world. You don't get bogged down in the past; you go forward, you're willing to accept change as inevitable and work with it. That's very valuable. And I think that's very Jewish.

Until my *bar mitzvah,* I was raised by a father who was not religious, but my grandparents were. My grandfather was the cantor at his little shul, and my grandmother was very religious. I was part of their culture. My grandfather used to sit with me and read Talmud, and I went to Hebrew school and studied Talmud. I think this stimulates the questioning spirit. The young man asking the old rabbi to tell him what was most important while he stood on one foot. You have to search your soul for the essence of life.

You don't presume perfection; you don't presume that you're right; you don't take things for granted. You work for them and prove yourself time and time again. I think questioning, constant questioning, leads to a creative response. There are a number of great artists and scientists and musicians who have been innovative as well as creative. How about Richard Feinman, Barnett Newman, Lillian Hellman, Alfred Eisenstaedt, Steve Jobs, Andy Grove? The bad thing—for me, anyway, is that the Jewish tradition, because of the "no graven images," makes being an architect, an artist, not so important in the Jewish equation. You're much better accepted if you play the violin. If you go to Israel now, there's very little architecture. The Arabs have it better, architecturally. Architecture is the golden calf. It may well be because we never put down roots, because we're always on the move, architecture never took hold. But that's Jewish, too, publicly admitting that you don't know everything.

Jews are adaptable: They move into a society and are realists; they don't take the place and try to change it; they use what's there and take it forward. They take and create within a given milieu. They extend the culture that they find themselves in. I'm willing to be a realist, to accept the time I live in, to work within the time and context, and to try to extend it, and use it and work with it in a creative way, which is what Jews have always done.

My family changed its name from Goldberg to Gehry, something I agreed to a long time ago. But my wife, who is Latin American, wants to change it back to Goldberg, and she's Catholic. Hitler proved to us that you can't escape, you can't assimilate into a culture and be other than what you are. Once you are born a Jew, you are stamped for life and you might as well accept it. To try to hide or to try to pretend you're not is useless. The first thing I told the people in Sicily the other day, when I met with them about designing a Catholic facility, was that I am a Jew. They said that they knew that, and that was not an issue for them, that I was talented and they just wanted me. I have always identified myself before someone identifies me.

When I was a boy, the kids in my neighborhood beat me because I was Jewish. I was not allowed into the architectural fraternity at the University of California because I was a Jew. I don't go to the synagogue, I don't practice, but I still identify myself as a Jew and always will.

⌘

Allen Ginsberg
POET (DECEASED 1997)
New York, New York

I'm Jewish because love my family Matzoh ball soup
I'm Jewish because my fathers mothers uncles grandmoth-
    ers said "Jewish," all the way back to Vitebsk &
    Kaminetz-Podolska via Lvov.
Jewish because reading Dostoyevsky at 13 I write poems at
    restaurant tables Lower East Side, perfect delicatessen
    intellectual.
Jewish because violent Zionists make my blood boil,
    Progressive indignation.
Jewish because Buddhist, my anger's transparent hot air, I
    shrug my shoulders.
Jewish because monotheistic Jews Catholics Moslems're
    intolerant—
Blake sd. "6000 years of sleep" since antique Nobodaddy
    Adonai's mind trap—OY! such Meshuggeneh absolutes—
Senior Citizen Jewish paid my dues got half-fare card
    buses subways, discount movies—
Can't imagine how these young people make a life, make a
    living.
How can they stand it, going out in the world with only
    $10 and a hydrogen bomb?

[*"Yiddishe Kopf," October 1991. Reprinted with permission of the author.*]

Yevgeny Komisarenko
STUDENT
Cologne, Germany

After twenty-one years in Russia, in Ukraine, and four years in Germany, I went to Israel but returned to Germany. After comparing the way of life in each country, I found Germany to be better for my career. I started attending college. It was here in Germany that I discovered my religion and tradition. My family was never religious, and I was never interested in a Jewish way of life because I never saw anything in it to make me love it enough to embrace it.

But when I discovered the world of religion here in Germany, I was afraid of this overwhelming feeling. I learned to love it enough to become a *bar mitzvah* and to be circumcised. I started to learn about Judaism, about ethics and tolerance. I find in Judaism a source of positive energy and a determination to achieve.

There is also tolerance, although I will never say that I have learned tolerance to the degree that I can abide those people who oppressed me because I am a Jew. Here I learned that anti-Semitism is not confined to Eastern Europe. We Jews are outsiders and prefer to remain that way. We are inwardly proud of being in the minority—half arrogant, half perverse, an explosive combination. It is a source of the force underlying our existence. It is a motive for action.

Jaron Lanier
INVENTOR OF, AND RESEARCHER IN, VIRTUAL REALITY;
PROFESSOR OF COMPUTER SCIENCE, COLUMBIA UNIVERSITY
New York, New York

Most people are surprised to learn that I'm Jewish. Lanier is a French pen name that my father took and which I inherited. Although both my parents are Jewish, I personally have come to believe that Jewishness is a certain intimate identification. Having both parents Jewish does not necessarily make someone Jewish. Nor does not having Jewish parents make someone not Jewish. I've always felt very intensely Jewish. I have come to believe that the heart of Judaism is much more an intimate, personal phenomenon than a ritualized one. So I've decided that I am Jewish, and a practicing Jew, even if I am pretty sporadic about attending services. On the other hand, it's important to realize that Jewish practice does vary considerably through history among people who consider themselves devout.

Judaism has always struck me as a "chamber music religion," one that is practiced in the intimate space of the family. Now I might have a special feeling for that side of it because Judaism has a special connection to my mother, who died while I was a child, and who was a concentration camp survivor. So I think of it most intensely as a bond with her. But it's also an entirely unique experience. The bond between people who are Jewish tends to be very personal. We have to remember that, except in very rare cases, Judaism has never been a religion of a majority. I think of Judaism as like a string of pearls, in which the pearls are families that are all intensely connected through their emotions. That makes Judaism a more emotional, more intimate, and therefore a more sweet and sad and neurotic kind of an occurrence than other things it might be compared to.

The other thing that always struck me about Judaism is that in comparison to the notion of God in the other major religions, in Judaism, God himself—or herself—is quite abstract, on the one hand. The Jewish God will say "I am what I am." On the other hand, the Jewish God has emotions, is very personal. I think of the Jewish God as another member of our family. Once again, this leads to a much more emotional and intimate sense of spirituality.

You can say that I have a Jewish approach to virtual reality. I see it as a way of bridging our interpersonal gap. Virtual reality will become a personal, emotional experience. Here you could see virtual reality as a way of looking into someone's heart or looking at stock market behavior. A non-Jewish way of thinking about virtual reality would be perceiving the virtual world as merely conveying data or as displaying abstractions of some sort.

What is interesting with virtual reality is that it bridges; it is the first thing in the physical world that is objectively present among people, and that is subject to infinite possibilities. What I would hope is that virtual reality will eventually wend its way to being a new bridge between people, a new way of sharing imagination, a new form of communication. That's what I would call it first of all: communication with the notion that if you have a world in which you can make anything at all exist, you may not need symbols or intermediaries such as words or diagrams or that sort of thing. We could actually make the world directly as we might imagine it.

What does this have to do with Jewishness? First of all, Judaism, I think, created a sort of new intensity about what a text was. I can't think of any other ancient tradition in which text is quite so revered as in Judaism. In Judaism, text took on a life of its own; in a sense, it became a primary reality. In a way, the work I'm doing with virtual reality, as I understand it, is seen as almost the antithesis of Jewish tradition in the sense that I sort of propose that not only might words not be primary, they might not even be necessary. But then, I think in a deeper sense, perhaps the reason why Judaism focused so much on texts as primary reality is part of what I perceive as being an abiding concern of Judaism from the earliest of times, which is a reconciliation of the most intimate, most emotional, most personal experiences with the most epistemological, most cosmic, most ultimate question. I mean, if words connect people, then from the Jewish perspective words are no mere abstraction. They take on a personality, a fire, a reality of their own. And I think that that sense of primacy of interpersonal contact and of the sort of refusal to let the most abstract cosmic things escape emotion or escape interpersonal neuroses is something common throughout Jewish history.

Joshua Lederberg
PRESIDENT, ROCKEFELLER UNIVERSITY;
NOBEL LAUREATE IN MEDICINE
New York, New York

My father was an Orthodox rabbi, born and educated in Israel, and thus had more prestige, higher intellectual aspirations for his children, and less income than most of his neighbors. Like many other first-generation Jewish youths in New York City at that time, I was recruited into an efficient and calculated system of Americanization, fostered by the rich opportunities and incentives of the educational system.

My earliest recollections aver an unswerving interest in science as the means by which humankind could strive for understanding of its origin, setting, and purpose, and for power to forestall its natural fate of hunger, disease, and death. The Jewish reading in *Genesis* of the expulsion from Eden makes no presumptions of the benignity of Nature: "By the sweat of thy brow. . . ." This may have been the most acceptable deviation from the Orthodox religious calling of my family tradition. These images were reinforced by the roles of Albert Einstein and Chaim Weizmann as heroes whose secular achievements my parents and I could together understand and appreciate, regardless of the intergenerational conflicts evoked by my callow agnosticism.

I could not then see how the monotheistic world view and the central teachings of the Old Testament, and their ethical imperatives for contemporary life, related to the tribal rituals shaped in the Diaspora. But the utopian-scientific ethic offered an acceptable resolution. My own career could advance our shared ideals in a modern, American idiom. Science would be a path to knowledge of the cosmic order. It would also be a means of alleviating human suffering. The Jewish tradition is remarkably tolerant of skepticism: I have in mind Maimonides' teachings of the unknowability of God. The agnostic mindset thereby permitted, together with my reaction to my father's Orthodoxy, carried over into my reflex response to other sources of authoritative knowledge.

Erwin Leiser

FILMMAKER; WRITER
Zurich, Switzerland

Like many German-Jewish families before World War II, mine was assimilated into German society. If being Jewish did not make a difference before the age of ten, it certainly did afterwards. Hitler came to power and all we Jews in Germany learned what the difference was. In my case, too, being Jewish meant there were certain things I could not do: I could not be a full member of German society: I was an outsider at school. But through a friend, the grandson of a rabbi, I learned that Judaism was a positive force. Despite the isolation and persecution in Germany, I still found this positive force to be stronger than the troubles coming from outside myself. Judaism contains an invisible force that not even the Nazis could touch. We sing to an invisible God, and these songs reach Him. Only by killing all the Jews can you rid the world of this song. Hitler tried, and he failed.

In 1939, at the age of fifteen, I left Germany for Sweden, knowing nothing about my future. A group of us Jewish boys was placed in a home where we had only each other. We became a family, and we learned very early the importance of life, of survival. I do not think about death, which I know will come, but about living, about making the most of my life on earth. I see myself as part of a long chain that goes back thousands of years to Abraham. In retrospect, I can thank Hitler that he considered me different. Had he considered me a German, I would have been taken to the army and probably killed. Many were killed in Auschwitz and the other camps. People ask how God could have allowed this. God made a world and left it to humans to govern. Auschwitz was a human invention, not a divine one.

The fact that I survived the Holocaust places me under the obligation to be a witness to the events of that time. I want to be of use to others, to society, through my experience, skills, and knowledge, so that human beings and the world can be better. I do this through my films. I am a witness, not a commentator or judge, but a witness who informs others. As a writer and filmmaker, I am fortunate to be doing what I enjoy. Again, this goes back to the positive force in Judaism that obliges us to live life to the fullest, to glorify life. Not many people take this perspective to heart. They glorify suffering over living life positively. Such people hide from reality in suffering. Jews do not have a philosophy that allows them to escape from reality. A Jew must deal with reality in order to survive.

Clara Leví de Benaím
TELEVISION JOURNALIST
Barcelona, Spain

First the obvious: the history and culture of the Jewish people impress upon one the great difference between Jews and Catholics. But I feel a difference in a personal way, and this needs some explanation. Wherever Jews lived, they held true to monotheism. But whatever did not violate this faith, they absorbed and then carried from land to land as they were expelled from where they lived. Jews embodied skills and attitudes that led Franco to invite them back into Spain after four hundred fifty years of expulsion. Today, Jews in Spain continue this function of cross-pollination. I look back on five hundred years of a history of wandering and absorbing the best that other cultures had to offer and am motivated to continue along this line of cross-fertilization so that life for everyone will be better.

Jakov Lind
WRITER
London, England

I was born in Vienna, raised in Holland, lived and worked in Germany—with false papers—made it to Palestine, and now live in London. Some might envy this life of the wanderer and find it adventurous. For me, it was, and still is, a big joke. I survived by not giving in to fear. My books are an expression of this Jewish sense of humor and *chutzpah*.

Rabbi Jonathan Magonet
STERNBERG CENTRE FOR JUDAISM, LEO BAECK COLLEGE
London, England

My Jewishness was a given, something I always had. I grew up in England with a very distinct sense of being part of a minority within a larger, supposedly pluralistic, society. So the sense of being different was clearly there. It was part of the culture, and you either had to fight it or go along with it. The options were to get out and hide, become a successful psychiatrist, which I would have been, or to somehow take seriously the intuition that there was some value in this otherness. And I suppose I made that choice. It's a question of a rule: We choose a religion at some stage in life.

The Judaism that I have come to know—Liberal Judaism—I find very acceptable. There are aspects of Judaism that I don't like and would fight against. The other options, Islam or Christianity, were not very attractive. The figure of Jesus was so remote and peculiar that it didn't make any sense. Islam is an attractive alternative, but even that lacks things that Judaism has, particularly a sense of humor, which probably derives from being outcasts for such a long time. I find Judaism to be a very sensible and life-promoting religion.

There's another strange game. I think that by being a minority—because of the history, the Third Reich and all that happened, the Holocaust, and now Israel—that you are in a very privileged position. There is a district rabbi in England who is always on a platform with the Catholics and Protestants because, as he says, they represent millions of people, but he represents six million dead. You have a voice that can be heard precisely because of the absurdity of what Judaism appears in the eyes of the rest of the world. That is, we're a voice people will listen to precisely because of that past. As a Jew, you can have an impact, which is unexpected—certainly in Europe. In America, you're part of a wider, more pluralistic society. But in Europe you are still a minority, a minority that makes people nervous, and therefore they listen.

We seem to overlook the fact—because in a sense we've been hijacked—that the Bible is ours. Christians have taken it over. But our way of reading it is quite unique, very special. The whole tradition of commentary is a very useful way of giving you a perspective on contemporary values. You see them through the eyes of different peers in Jewish history. So you have a certain ability to be moved and caught up by the voice of revelation and at the same time to have a certain detachment in order to recognize where this all takes you in that it raises problems. So there is a self-critical, evaluative mode within Judaism, an intellectual mode, which I think is so important. Curiously enough, we tend—because we are so ignorant of our tradition—to treat Judaism as a mystery religion. You know, the mysterious rabbi who knows all those things that we don't know or care about. This mystery stuff is closer to what some of what the old Catholic orthodoxy was about.

We should rather celebrate the rationality, the intellect, the questing that is so much at the heart of Judaism, that takes nothing for granted, that allows nothing to be unchallenged—at its best. At its worst, this characteristic is a bloody pain in the *tochas*. But at its best, it does lead to the opening up of ideas. Nothing is ever resolved; things vary with the circumstances because I am many things. I am a man, but I live among women. That's a new tension that one is made aware of. I am a white person in a society where Blacks may be persecuted. That puts me in another circumstance. I'm a mixture of all of these things, as well as of the Jewish element. And I would rather recognize the pluralism within me that matches the pluralism without me and learn to live with it. Perhaps the very self-consciousness of this condition is something different about Jewishness, along with the willingness to live with it and be comfortable with it, as opposed to denying or running away from it. It may also be part of the Jewish quest for truth, the acknowledgment of reality, which is a very strong Jewish characteristic.

The tragedy is that we split our intellectual curiosity and questing from our commitment to tradition. So the Jews who made the great new moves of the last century and a half did so outside the borders of Judaism, in the wide world. We have not learned how to integrate them back into tradition. Freud would have been a rabbi a couple of generations earlier and would have gotten to the top. So there is a risk of stagnation because the best minds have gone somewhere else and have not been admitted to the charmed circle of those who know enough to be able to work within the tradition.

Norman Manea

PROFESSOR OF LANGUAGE AND LITERATURE, BARD COLLEGE;
WRITER; RECIPIENT OF MACARTHUR "GENIUS" GRANT
New York, New York

In a world that is more and more incoherent and centrifugal, identity seems to many to be an instantaneous magic answer to the individual's growing sacred and profane uncertainties. Unfortunately, uncertainties do not miraculously disappear through belonging and collective association. Even more so in the case of an ancient and scattered people, continuously victimized, without the calm of an untroubled place in the world to call their own. It's hard to forget Kafka's words: "What have I in common with Jews? I hardly have something in common with myself and should stay quietly in a corner, content that I can breathe."

All in all, Jewish destiny is nothing but exacerbation, through suffering, of the destiny of humankind, a passing exile on an earthly adventure, a sarcastic initiation in the drama of being a person among people. The mirror that the Jew holds to the world is not at all pleasing, but the history of the persecuted who, in all his stopping places, stamps his unusual creativity on the culture of people he comes across remains one of the most impressive of human acts. In spite of its unequaled traumas, Jewish destiny proves itself to be an exemplary constructive power, practical and generous. Something that does not simplify, but complicates, its definition.

Freud rightly asked what remains Jewish when one is no longer religious or nationalistic, when one does not know the language of the Bible; that is, what remains Jewish in a Jew who has lost everything that defines him as such? Much, maybe even the essential, the ultra-assimilated Austrian Jew answered, but without defining the essence. The millennia-long Jewish Diaspora made it difficult to define a Jewish identity, not just because a Jew is also Russian, Austrian, Argentinian, American, or even Israeli. Jewish transcendence remains contradictory,

JEWISH: DOES IT MAKE A DIFFERENCE?

paradoxical, unclassifiable, but resistant to disasters, just as easily demonizable in the hostile world in which it always reveals itself.

Of course, identity is, before anything else, filial. My memory frequently calls forth the image of my mother, herself the essence of the Jewish ghetto, animated by great expectations and fear: feverish, altruistic, acute, and spiritualized in an extraordinary fervor of ideas and feelings, of bitter humor, brave and traumatic, vulnerable and vital, of incomparable human intensity, amplified to paroxysm, between the most torrid passion and the most cutting glacial lucidity. A rich and strange inheritance, with unforeseeable potentiality.

History hastens, however, much too frequently for the Jew, a dark explanation. When you discover your Jewishness at five years of age, in a concentration camp, you are instantly connected to an ancient collective tragedy that annihilates your options. The Holocaust was my brutal initiation to existence at a much too early age. Later, communist totalitarianism meant not just prohibition and annihilation of tradition, but also a complicated and complete education in being marginal and suspect. Finally, exile returned me, at the threshold of middle age, to the condition of alien and nomad, to which I thought I had found a solution by immersing myself in the language and culture in which I was born.

The Jew is nonetheless not defined through the adversity of others, as Sartre believed, nor is it sufficient to be born of Jewish parents, like the rabbi Jehoshua of Nazareth. What history makes and what each of us makes out of this "misfortune," as Heine put it, in the end defines us. The writer justifies himself through his work, alive to the extent that it is unique and his alone. Art is the most individual of professions, but belonging, implicitly or explicitly, to a community enters too capriciously in the oft fluid equation of creation in order to foresee its effects. A book stands alone before judgment, no ethnic emblem can save it, just as the writer's uniqueness cannot be pacified through a simple communal lineup.

Without any intention of affiliation or militancy, I have still felt, ever since my literary beginnings, and especially in years following, how biography inevitably marked the themes, tension, and tonality of my writing. Experience that went by the names Holocaust, communist anti-Semitism, exile, was augmented through the extreme experience of literature. A binary and complementary positioning in the far reaches of the growing risk and growing intensity of existence. If the poet was always considered a type of Jew, the Jewish writer, early accustomed to the jokes destiny plays, could, on account of his *belonging,* lay claim to the privilege of a double calling.

Leonard Nimoy

TELEVISION AND FILM ACTOR
Beverly Hills, California

Although I learned early on, at street level, about anti-Semitism, my family made me feel loved and secure. Judaism and Yiddishkeit were very much alive in our home of immigrants from eastern Europe. With this sense of security, I felt I could be anything I wanted to be. And I wanted to be an actor. As a boy, I learned that the ability to separate the fingers into two groups of two was the sign of the Kohen. Through that Vulcan salute, I connected with every Jew watching *Star Trek*. Why did I think of that hand gesture? Like practically every actor, I look for something personal to bring to my performance. Maybe it was the convergence of my spiritual and artistic lives.

[*From* Why Be Jewish? *Reprinted with the permission of the American Jewish Committee.*]

Richard Raskin

AUTHOR; ASSOCIATE PROFESSOR, DEPARTMENT OF INFORMATION
AND MEDIA SCIENCE, AARHUS UNIVERSITY
American living in Denmark

In *Hannah and Her Sisters* (1986), the character played by Woody Allen asks his parents why there is so much evil in the world and why there were Nazis. His father replies, "How the hell do I know why there were Nazis? I don't know how a can opener works!" Funny as it is, this exchange has a deeper meaning and expresses what I think is one basic Jewish attitude toward dealing with larger issues: a sense that it is important to keep our feet on the ground and not to overestimate our ability to explain everything. Related tendencies include (1) a sense that reality is not only multifaceted, but essentially incongruous and riddled with inner contradictions; (2) a delight in comparing alternate perceptions of some issue, seen as potentially (though not necessarily) balancing and complementary; and (3) a basic mistrust of intellectual or ideological constructs which pretend to settle fundamental questions of meaning once and for all.

Another and very different Jewish tendency is the attitude in face of life-threatening situations: namely, a refusal to accept the loss of life as an inevitable outcome, a refusal to write off as impossible the inventing of some way out. This tendency is both expressed and mildly made fun of in the following joke, which dates from the cold war period:

> An American strategic bomber is flying over the North Pole and accidentally drops a hydrogen bomb. It explodes and the polar ice cap begins to melt. Scientists calculate that in forty-eight hours, water will cover the entire world. In the face of this catastrophe, the world's religious leaders are asked to address their people. The pope tells the Catholics of the world to take the last sacrament. The Protestant organizations send out the message that all Protestants should prepare to meet their Maker. The chief rabbi of Jerusalem tells his people, "So, we've got forty-eight hours to learn how to live under water!"

This life-affirming joke, which proposes a problem-solving stance rather than resignation, even in the face of seemingly hopeless odds, beautifully illustrates that central aspect of Jewishness that Israel Knox so aptly described as "tragic optimism."

Iosif Sava
MUSIC DIRECTOR FOR ROMANIAN RADIO AND TELEVISION
Bucharest, Romania

At the age of eighteen, I would never have known that I was Jewish if I had not lived in a home in which a *bar mitzvah* was a real celebration, in which Jewish music was often played, and in which Pesach and Rosh Hashanah were observed. Religion was not emphasized, but life carried on in the leitmotif of ancestral traditions.

The postwar years were supposed to bring us the awaited utopia, but a visit to Russia after Stalin's death lifted the blinders from my mind's eye. I was obliged to live parallel lives: one as the husband of a woman from an enlightened Jewish family, the other as a historian of Romanian music, promoting Romanian culture through my books and the radio and television programs I produced. My attachment to Judaism grew within me, even though I could not acknowledge it publicly.

In 1989, I began to breathe again. I felt that I could finally express myself freely. After one year, the forces of reaction descended once again. The extreme rightists began to attack me despite my professional life spent in promoting Romanian culture. Pointing to my Jewish background, they interpreted my work to suit their agenda, even challenging my right to express myself on political questions.

My reaction was normal. I became prouder of my Judaism and began to strengthen my ties to the Jewish community. I began work on a series of books, published by the house Hasefer, entitled *Fiddlers on the Roof*, in which I emphasize the contributions to music that Jews from small cities in the Eastern countries have made in the past two centuries. For as long as stupidity and fascism rule the political scene, spreading anti-Semitism despite the evidence of history, my books will try to cast light on at least one aspect of human life: its music. On this path of resistance, my Jewishness gives me spiritual balance and tranquility.

Glenn Spearman
SAXOPHONIST; COMPOSER
New York, New York

My Jewish mother and my African-American father define my identity. Although I did not live like a Jew when I discovered the music of the Falashas, I realized that I am probably more Jewish than I was aware of. I believe that I expressed my Jewishness in my music, *Blues for Falasha,* which I hope will become part of my legacy. This music is my way of thanking them for allowing me to better understand who I am.

Imre Stern
CANTOR
Brussels, Belgium

Judaism gives me a sense of life, a source of vitality. My family was dedicated to being Jewish. I was born in a small town in Hungary called Janoshalva. My father was a very busy man, but he always found time to teach me our traditions, to teach me Hebrew and the Chumash, and to implant the spirit of our laws: love of God and of our fellow humans. He made the sacrifice to send me to another town to be educated in Judaism. His last words to me before he was taken to a concentration camp were, "Never forget that you are Jewish."

Could I do less for my own children than he did for me? They were also brought up with *kashrut*, *mishpachah*, and *mitzvot*. These are what give flavor to life.

Michael Vana
Prague, Czech Republic

Being Jewish means having hope, hope that things will be better for oneself, for one's family, for the community. More people attended religious services here under the communists. But I have the hope that young Jews will find out that there is more to our new freedom than long weekends and buying what until a few years ago was out of reach. If we don't meet to pray, we will meet in our hope.

Henri Wald
PHILOSOPHER; LOGICIAN
Bucharest, Romania

It is only natural that a people that has had more time than space, more history than geography, more future than present be messianic—that is, to believe in a better world, to believe that humans can be educated in order to bring about better relations between them, to be critical about the present, to destroy any idol that obstructs the path to progress, and to hold human creativity in high esteem. Last, but not least, Jews cultivate the word, the only means that makes us able to speak about the future, more so even than images.

To me, Jews have been a civilizing influence in the nations they have lived in. To be Jewish means to make a positive difference.

Eliezer Wayman
DIAMOND MERCHANT
Antwerp, Belgium

"Diamonds are forever" is the slogan of my trade. "Jews and Jewishness are forever" is my own deep conviction. From Russia to Belgium, I went through many stages to rediscover what I actually am. The diamond business is hard work. So is being a Jew. Diamonds are polished with diamonds. Jews become better Jews in connection to Jewish life. Diamonds make the world more beautiful. So do Jews, if they live like Jews should. It took me a long time to find this out, but I am grateful that I eventually did.

I may never become rich. That all Jews are rich is another fallacy invented by people who want us to give up being what we are. But in being Jewish, I have a richness that translates into my continual attempt to be a better human being.

Joseph Weintraub
PRESIDENT, THINKING SOFTWARE, INC.; THREE-TIME
WINNER OF THE LOEBNER PRIZE FOR ARTIFICIAL INTELLIGENCE
Woodside, New York

It seems that Jews, as a group, have been blessed with an extra helping of intelligence. We also seem to have a tendency to work hard and achieve to our maximum potential. Freud, Marx, Einstein, Jung, and Wilhelm Reich are only a few examples. The important advances in my field—computer science and artificial intelligence—have also been made by Jewish scientists, such as Marvin Minsky and Joseph Weizenbaum. As Jews, we should concentrate less on religion and more on achievement.

CHAPTER FOUR

————— ⌀ —————

"...My Home Is Jewish..."

The Jews are a people of time, not space. In all their wanderings, the only "real" estate that Jews took with them was their relation to an idea, to a way of life. In one sense, a Jew can physically travel to any Jewish community around the world and feel at home. In another sense, Jews have learned that they own a space that is not limited by physical boundaries. In some cases, it is the only home they can return to. There are a character and a legacy, in religious as well as secular Judaism, that transcend time and space and that make Jews what they are wherever they are.

Heinz Abosch

WRITER
Magdeburg, Germany

In 1933, I abandoned Germany. In 1944, the Gestapo arrested me in Lyon. In France, that is, in Strasbourg and Paris, where I lived after 1933, I found my place not in the Jewish community, but among Trotskyites. I fought in the underground and was tortured by Klaus Barbie's troops. I jumped from the train taking me, and so many others, to certain death, and I am unable to get rid of this feeling of guilt for having survived. In my mind, there was only one obsession left: a democratic world was the only alternative. No room for Jewishness in my thoughts.

My parents came to Magdeburg from Galicia, from a typical *shtetl*. I remember the place from a visit with my sister to my grandparents, before I became *bar mitzvah* age. Now, I am at the end of my life's journey, back in Germany, but still not at home. Yes, homeless, despite an address. The book I am working on is subtitled "From the Life of a Homeless Man." I suppose that the Jewishness I ran away from is the home I have been searching for so desperately all my life.

Marcos Aguinis

NOVELIST; ESSAYIST; MINISTER OF CULTURE (1983–1987)
Buenos Aires, Argentina

As the son of European immigrants to Argentina, and as a writer, I have a deep appreciation of the fact that the Torah is our home. Throughout the Diaspora, Jews have regarded our written word as the one entity to which we owe allegiance. Whether conservative or liberal, mystic or agnostic, scientist or artist, we carry this love for the word.

[*From* Why Be Jewish? *Reprinted with the permission of the American Jewish Committee.*]

Rifat N. Bali

BUSINESSMAN
Istanbul, Turkey

To be Jewish in Turkey, a country in which ninety-nine percent of the population is Muslim, means that you are constantly reminded that you are a "foreigner," or you will be used as a propaganda tool for promoting the tolerance image of the Turkish Republic. These are the two positions of being Jewish in Turkey, and that is what makes my life different from other people's lives. Being a Turkish Jew means differentiation, if not discrimination. You will always be reminded in one way or another that you are a Jew, and most of the time not in a positive way. You are addressed as "Mösyö [Monsieur]" instead of "Sir," for example, or you are told that Jews are liked and welcome in the Ottoman land of tolerance.

Being a nonobservant Jew, I think that the only value that guides my life today is the fact that my father and mother fought to remain Jewish by marrying each other. If we want to continue their legacy, we must pass on a Jewish consciousness to Jewish children. But in passing the torch of Judaism to the next generation, I feel that I have failed.

Jerzy Bawol

ACCORDION PLAYER IN THE KROKE KLEZMER BAND
Kasimierz/Krakow, Poland

There is an inner harmony that I feel with our music. It is me. I want it to be me. It makes me want to discover my roots, to discover that I belong to something greater than a small community in Krakow. There are cases of Jewish Poles who immigrated to Germany because they felt they could not live as Jews in Poland. But in Germany they are also afraid. One such person told me how nervous he is about being a Jew in Germany and hides the fact that he is Jewish. He felt that he could live more like a Jew in Poland, with less fear. He was happy to hear that after the Berlin Wall fell down, there were still Jews in Poland, that Jews could continue living as Jews. There was an awakening, and we realized we could live as Jews.

I realized what being Jewish meant when I learned something about my roots. This happened to me around age twenty. I can say that God was with me. Everything that I am was so deep in me that it just came out on its own. I started to get interested in Jewish culture, especially in Jewish music and the Jewish soul. My fellow musicians in Kroke and I started to talk this language of the soul and about this language of the soul. We didn't have to ask ourselves why we came together and learned to love klezmer music.

—◦◦◦—

José Bendayan Emerguí
OWNER OF AN EXPORT/IMPORT BUSINESS
Seville, Spain

Being Jewish makes no difference in my daily life, or so it seems. Although I am active in the small Jewish community of Seville, I am a Jew who observes no Jewish laws or traditions, no Shabbat. Moreover, I am married to a gentile woman. Still, my family history, as it was retold to each generation, goes back to the first Jews who settled in what was to become Spain. My direct ancestors refused to convert and remained Jews despite the hardships this imposed upon them. Other ancestors converted and received the privilege of being called *marranos*, pigs, and even treated like them by the very intolerant Catholic society. Those who could not take the humiliation left and reconnected to a Judaism that had evolved differently from the one they knew. Other distant relations practice Catholicism to this day. But they tell me that they feel they have lost something that was originally theirs. This short history is a summary of how Jews live among and work with non-Jews in Spain, not wanting to be different, but still considered different even when they try hard to be like the majority. It is not a comfortable life. The past is with us even when we try to run away from it.

I was born and raised in Morocco, in a community of five thousand Jews. Looking back, I remember it as my paradise on earth. It was easy to be Jewish, and a pleasure. Morocco gained independence and the Moroccans, once treated as second-class citizens by the French and Spanish imperialists, started treating Jews as second-class citizens. My family did not want to reexperience the history of our Spanish ancestors. So at age twenty-nine, I wound up in Andalusia. After centuries of resistance to keep Judaism alive, that part of the family history came to an end with me.

However, my Jewish history is alive. I feel at home among the members of the small Jewish community here. They stirred me to set the community on a solid financial footing to serve as a basis for community aid. For this aim, I summoned up the courage to approach the Catholics and ask them for aid. And they gave! Not out of guilt, but because they are impressed with the contributions Jews make, through their values of work and family, to the places they live and work in.

I am Jewish enough to have experienced the pain of being treated as despised by the majority and the laws of the ruling parties. This is why I deplore any situation in which individuals are treated as second-class citizens in lands where the majority has won independence: Morocco, Algeria, the Balkans, even Israel. Although I am not a typical Jew, I feel part of the community here and I support those values that I recognize as characteristic of Judaism: equal justice, tolerance, pursuit of knowledge, and family unity.

Jacob Blum
Melbourne, Australia

If you asked me this question down in Australia, I would have said that my family taught me to live like a Jew, keeping the commandments and traditions. And I do. Being here, in the oldest synagogue in Europe [Old New Synagogue, Prague], I feel that being Jewish makes a difference in how I relate to history. My parents told me a lot about anti-Semitism and pogroms, and here I can relate to that history and to the people here who went through that. I sense my fellow-Jew and they sense me. I cannot explain what this is and how it works. This sense of belonging makes a difference.

Radu Cosasu
WRITER
Bucharest, Romania

Schwer zeyn a yid [It's hard to be a Jew]. I have heard this saying since the day of my birth. Being Jewish in Romania means that I could never instinctively identify with the general population. I am not Romanian, but I feel neither Jewish nor foreign. I never felt like an outsider in Romania because I am Jewish, but because I am an intellectual dissident.

Nevertheless, I could identify with the Jews of my reading: Isaac Babel, Saul Bellow's *Herzog*, and the Romanian Jew, Mihai Sebastian. They are my family. Just as the heroes of my novels—six volumes entitled *Survival*—are all myself: the boy who had his *bar mitzvah* in 1943 and who in 1947 was carried away by the messianic hope of the international proletarian movement; the Jew who, with all his family emigrated to Israel, was never a Zionist; the Jew who believed the necessary lies of communism, but also the Jew who once spoke the truth in public—Down with censorship!—assuring for himself a decade of unemployment and ostracism from public life.

I am the Jew of Henry Roth—the New Yorker who wrote his last novel at the age of ninety—about whom he said, "He was a Jew because he had to be. He saw no virtue in being one, prisoner of an identity he could never escape." But there is a difference. I never felt a prisoner of Judaism and never even thought of escaping from it. I am a synthesis, a man from Bucharest who will never deny that he is Jewish or Romanian, no matter how impoverished either label might sound. I have the same feeling of irony for my aunt in Tel Aviv, who kisses the *mezuzot* on the doorposts of every El Al agency, as for the anti-Semites in Bucharest—who outnumber the Jews—when they are too inimical to my synthesis. They are both right that, after Auschwitz, being Jewish, anti-Semite or anti-anti-Semite is no longer a Jewish problem.

Herschel Davis

FORMER PROFESSOR OF HISTORY
Melbourne, Australia

For over five decades since the end of World War II, I have often been asked what it means to be Jewish by non-Jewish academicians. I have always responded that I am a member of the worldwide Jewish community who happens to have been born in Australia and that I am not an Australian Jew, but a member of the Jewish faith with Australian citizenship. My father was born in a shtetl in a part of eastern Europe belonging to Poland or Russia, depending on which country had won the most recent battle. After a pogrom in his hometown, during which he was jailed, his stepbrother in London managed, through some miracle, to have him shipped to England in steerage. My father could have remained in England, living in London's East End ghetto. Again as a steerage passenger, he emigrated to Australia in 1912, where he worked as a master tailor for the rest of his life.

It is probably due to this background of the wandering Jew that I have formed my strong opinion against national boundaries and all that such a policy entails. And this is why I identify myself as a Jew first of all, who just happened to be born in a certain place, Melbourne. And this is probably the greatest difference that being Jewish makes in my life.

We have a wonderful, vibrant Jewish life here, due to the Jews who came here and maintained their Jewishness. I am active in the local *shul* and a member of the *Chevra Kadisha* and many other Jewish organizations here. Currently, I am writing the history of one of the oldest *shul*s in this area, the St. Kilda Shul. I could not imagine being anything other than Jewish. Judaism defines my life, my actions, and my goals.

⎯⎯⎯ ❧ ⎯⎯⎯

Paul Erdös
MATHEMATICIAN OF LEGENDARY FAME (DECEASED 1996)
Budapest, Hungary

My entire life was marked by being a Jew, even though I was never an active Jew. More to the point: I wanted to study mathematics in Germany. Too bad! Hitler made that impossible. That started my career as a mathematical preacher and wanderer. Even a wandering Jew cannot avoid borders. When America closed its doors to me, it made a difference that I was Jewish because Israel accepted me.

The Jewish gang from Budapest—von Neumann and Teller are the most famous from among others not less gifted—prompted many people to write all kinds of stories. Some are even true. For instance, we were all aware of the famous revolving-door joke. How do you recognize a Hungarian in a crowd making its way through a revolving door? The Hungarian always comes out first. But the Hungarians protested: We are civilized. The pushy Jews come out first. Jews fought for survival and came out first in many fields. But for all the fame we got, the lives of those who were killed because they were Jews are more important and cannot be replaced. There is a lot to wonder about the mathematical equation of Jewish survival.

People know that I have said that all mathematics is kept in a book written by God. We humans must discover the mathematics that the book contains.

Yet how Jewish I am is something others know better than I do. If I think of my mother, then I am very Jewish. She understood that I do not want to carry a national identity with me. As a Jew from Hungary who never settled in a house and never owned more than his mind, I remained connected to Budapest because we all need an address and friends. Borders and passports are limiting. Thinking is limitless. I did not want Israeli citizenship not because I feel more Hungarian than Jewish, as some said, but because I feel a citizen of the world. Maybe this is what being Jewish means.

These are the disparate thoughts of an old mathematician who never thought he would talk about his Jewishness. Mathematically this was always irrelevant to me.

Daniel Gerson

BASS PLAYER IN AND MANAGER OF THE KROKE KLEZMER BAND
Kasimierz /Krakow, Poland

It's very hard to explain in a few words what it means to be Jewish. It's a matter of thousands of years of existence. Of course, it means something to me personally to be a Jew. First of all, it is my religion, my culture, my experience. It is my self. But in Poland, in the historical background of the last fifty to sixty years, what could we do with our culture?

I was born in Poland in 1958 and lived there until I was eighteen years old. Then my family moved to Western Europe. In 1979, I went to Israel and lived there for ten years. After that, I went to Canada, went to the army, and finally, two and a half years ago, I returned to Poland, where I started to do something for Jewish culture. It was in Poland that I realized and recognized how Jewish I am. This is connected to Kasimierz, the only Jewish city in the world. I found my Jewishness against the background of a dying Jewish community. Then, I and a few other people realized that if we don't save some of what was Jewish in Kasimierz in some way, the only Jewish city would disappear as such.

Music was the way we discovered to save the city. It is a way to be most easily understood by everybody. Music is a form of transmitting a culture and a feeling without resorting to language, words, or any other indirect means. Later, we organized a Jewish restaurant, which is a second aspect of Jewish life that is very easy to understand—to taste, see, and touch without much philosophy, dogmatism, or deep Torah learning.

The older generation in Poland has various opinions about Jews: some positive, some neutral, some negative regarding Jews and the role of Jews in history. The reaction of the young people in Poland is the most important, especially in politics. Young people were fed with lies about history and everything, even about us Jews. They learned in school to be against Jews, or at least to be skeptical regarding Jews. The same people who are unsure or indifferent to the role of Jews, when they hear our music, they start to think, to question, and to open up. For our group, this is a most beautiful moment: when you start to realize how other people's feelings change when something we convey through our music echoes in their feelings. It has never happened yet that someone has a negative reaction to our music. Never. The style of Jewish music has something to do with this. It is not an aggressive or tendentious type of music. It is one of the few types of music in the world that is totally international. It has no religious or language problems. It is actually the expression of feelings, human feelings.

Margaret Heppner
Auckland, New Zealand

What difference does being Jewish make in my life? Quite a lot. First of all, as a Jew, I always feel aware of being an outsider in a country in which only five thousand out of three and one-half million people are Jews. Moreover, that country is Christian, Anglo-Saxon, and fiercely British. For some reason, this translates into being anti-Israel. In this sense, I often feel like a lone voice in the wilderness, loving a country that everyone else seems to hate.

As a traditional, but nonreligious, Jew, I attend *shul* regularly. I do not keep kosher, but will not mix meat and dairy and eat vegetarian when I eat away from home. As a Jew, I feel I have to treat others as I would like to be treated, in being a *mensch* and dealing fairly and justly with fellow human beings.

Hermann Kesten

WRITER
Basel, Switzerland

Should I say that I don't know whether being Jewish made a difference in my life? Those who have heard of me (because almost no one who knew me is still alive) would think that I am again being difficult. Of course, being Jewish made a difference. I was born in Nuremberg and was celebrated in Weimar (the Kleist Prize, in 1928). I wrote about Spain, lived in Amsterdam—that is, I survived there under rather good conditions, which allowed me to help others in need. I became an American citizen, returned to Germany, got involved in all kinds of intellectual conflicts, lost my wife in Rome, and am about to follow her from this sad place in Riehe, near Basel in Switzerland, where I spend my last years.

I reread these last sentences, trying to figure out what they say. Now I have to smile and conclude: Here it is! The difference. Being all over—Germany, Spain, Holland, America, Italy, Switzerland—but nowhere at home. That's what the anti-Semites have said about the Jews, and keep repeating it, to show that we are not able to be faithful citizens. I see it otherwise. Being all over, but because of my choice, while rooted in the eternity of my Jewish destiny. Observant Jew? Not exactly. Fighting Jew? Always. And a man of the book. Of books. Not only mine, but of those wonderful books written by others without the reading of which my life would not make too much sense.

Thomas Kukurba

MUSICIAN (VIOLA, VIOLIN) AND VOCALIST IN KROKE KLEZMER BAND
Kasimierz/Krakow, Poland

One day, my uncle took me aside and said: "What you're doing makes me very happy. Did you know that your grandparents were observant Jews? Because of everything that happened during the war and later under the communists, we never wanted to tell you anything about this."

In 1989, when the communist government broke down, Jewish culture started a kind of a renaissance. It started to grow and express itself through the people. Books, music, and other material started to appear. Only after the band had been playing for a while did each member of Kroke ask our families the why, what, and where about the music. Even when our families didn't exactly want to answer, they started to open up. A bit of vodka, maybe too much, helped.

In America, there is a history of klezmer that goes back one hundred years. People there can live normally, play, dance, wear a *yarmulke*. Here in Kasimierz, I feel all the past, the Holocaust and everything that has happened since. I live in this atmosphere. Even worse, the community is dying. I see death and hopelessness every day. Last year, the Jewish community had one hundred eighty people. Today it has one hundred sixty-six. Every month, the list of community members shrinks. Young Jews live with this prospect. There are nine synagogues in Kasimierz. The spirit of Judaism hangs heavy in them. But that's all there is—ghosts. To get a *minyan,* we have to call old men who come, sometimes in spite of the aches they feel. Now, we are coming back to life, and we want to keep it that way.

But we do not want to live only in the past. That's why we play our music only in Kasimierz. Each week, about two hundred people hear us. About fifty buy our tapes and take them home. We don't know where to, because our audience is made up of Poles and tourists who come from all over. So our sound is going around the world. I would not call our music our cry for help, but it is a voice against all the circumstances and plans of nations to destroy us. We exist. And we may be only a few, but we are powerful. This music is our voice of power. It's our hope. Nothing is lost forever.

Thomas Lato
BASS PLAYER IN KROKE KLEZMER BAND
Kasimierz/Krakow, Poland

Through the music the band plays, I undergo a kind of inner connection with Judaism. And I want to pursue this direction. There are a lot of older people who want to forget that they are Jewish because of all the hardship they went through. But I do not know any of this. I want to look ahead, to keep the Jewish spirit alive. The music of eastern European Jewry is my instrument for this goal. The music transmits a strength of spirit that goes beyond boundaries and time.

Maureen Lipman
ACTRESS; WRITER
London, England

Being Jewish makes a difference to me and to the perception others have of me. Sometimes this works for me, sometimes against. It gives me a membership, a faith, a universal sister/brotherhood, a sense of belonging, an historical perspective, an understanding of humour and the rhythm of language, a handle on the seasons, and a love of family and traditional values. It means I feel at home in New York and at one in Jerusalem. It informs my opinions, my cooking, my politics, my taste and my choice of a partner. Yes, of course being Jewish makes a difference. It makes me feel special!

Sometimes it certainly also makes me prejudiced or biased, oversensitive, paranoid, anxious, angry or furtively ashamed because, like a child, I want to be like everyone else. Sometimes I'm convinced that "they" only see me as a "Jewish" actress, as a "Jewish" writer, which lessens my Englishness. Sometimes I'm aware of a glass floor and ceiling which stereotypes me and loses me any classical work. Often I feel that the only directors who see me in a rounded way, capable of playing princesses and nuns, are Jewish directors who are without prejudice themselves. Sometimes I believe a Jewish actor in England can get so far and no further because of unseen barriers and can only be really appreciated if they are more successful overseas. Sometimes I think this makes me sharp-tongued and cynical, sometimes merely shortsighted. Sometimes I'm suspicious of the amount my Jewishness is discussed in company—how it always arises when other people's religions don't—and that under the pretext of curiosity and interest lurk envy and ingratiation. Sometimes I think I encourage this myself, subliminally, to bask in my "difference." Would I want it any other way? Sometimes yes, sometimes no.

I don't think there are any specific Jewish values; they are all to do with survival in the Diaspora: family affection, demonstrative shows of affection—not dissimilar to Italian displays of same—pride, often stiff-necked, in rising above the average—as in most immigrant populations not specifically Jewish; hard work and application of good sense, likewise.

Mordechai Mark

UNEMPLOYED RUSSIAN IMMIGRANT
Bremen, Germany

Am I a Russian living in Germany, or am I a Jew living in Germany? Is this your question? I am a Jew, although I did not live like one in the Soviet Union, nor in the Russia that came after it. I am here, in the synagogue, because of something I must do as a Jew. Almost a year ago, my father died. He was religious but never tried to make me become like him. Now I am here to say *Kaddish* over him. To respect the memory of those we lost is part of being a Jew. We all say *Kaddish* and in saying it, we feel that every other Jew is saying it with us, taking part in our grief. So each one of us is part of a bigger family.

I speak Russian and feel lost in this country that caused us Jews so much pain. The fact that there is a Jewish community here gives me courage to start a new life when others are making plans for retirement.

If my father could see me praying here, he would say, "Mordechai, I always told you. Don't run away from yourself. Your Jewish soul will eventually catch up with you."

Imo Moszkowicz

FILM DIRECTOR
Ottobrun, Germany

Your question bothered me so much that at first I hardly knew how to answer it, mainly because I had to learn that it is not so healthy to be a Jew or to cultivate one's Judaism.

Practically the whole world hates us. Why? Because we were "chosen"? The misinterpretation of this label from the Old Testament has caused lots of suffering. So, being Jewish means first of all to share in a common fate with other Jews. All the wonderful traditions that we inherited through our religion have become indistinguishable; all the ideals have become a shabby normalcy in which I can perceive only the tiniest glimmer of something special. But perhaps it is this normalcy that can set us at peace with the world, even with God.

I recognize that the special feeling of being Jewish also distinguishes our inadequate human striving towards something good. The daily strife of the new old land of Israel is proof of this point. Am I being too critical? Then so I am, and gladly. Because I am Jewish. Examination of our existence, the probing of our communality, the inquiry into the most lapidary utterances—these are specific to Jews and to myself, even though I sometimes wish this were not so.

Yet I often ask myself, why are there so many Jewish film directors? Preoccupation with the word, which goes back to the receiving of the Ten Commandments, is at the bottom of a talent that is at the depths of the Jewish soul. Just as is the quest for something else, something that ennobles life, even if it means escaping to a world of fantasy. The way of Chasidism was led by this feeling, as the poet Beer-Hofmann expressed it in "Lullaby for Miriam":

> . . . the rumbling of what is to come
> The blood of our fathers, unrest and pride.
> All are in us, who can feel alone?
> There is no inheritance here for anyone. . . .

This knowledge about ourselves is our heritage; it obliges us to rethink our Jewishness over and over again and to give ample room in our thoughts and emotions to doubt—the holiest power of humankind.

With this doubt regarding the specialness of being Jewish, I begin to live a new stage of Jewishness, which is accompanied by an extraordinary loss, by barely conceivable persecution, by the inability to put up with certain things going on around me. And certainly by the godly feeling of having found the strength, despite everything that I have been through, to not have given up entirely on my own Jewishness.

Susy Norten Maczka
DIRECTOR OF INTERNATIONAL RELATIONS, CENTRAL COMMITTEE
OF THE JEWISH COMMUNITY OF MEXICO
Mexico City, Mexico

For me, being Jewish is not a question of religion. I am a Mexican Jew, but it is my Jewishness that rules my life. My culture, education, and my family values are all based on Jewish law. Of these, I will pass on to my daughters the ones that help you to be a better human being.

In general, these values deal with honesty, kindness, and charity. We have a wonderful religion that teaches us the real meaning of *tzedakah*, the satisfaction one feels by helping those of our own kind and anybody ese in need.

Identity is a very important issue in the formation and education of youngsters. It gives meaning to their lives and helps them focus their interests and concerns in a constructive manner. I want my children to have a sense of belonging, to feel comfortable with their culture and beliefs, and to be proud of being Jewish. How sad it is to see our own young people joining cults, other religions, or nothing at all because they "can't find themselves." It is our duty to show them the way that guided the lives of our parents and grandparents. Judaism gives us the tools to improve positive relations among people, to respect one another, and to make this world a better place to live.

Zigu Ornea
DIRECTOR, ROMANIAN CULTURAL FOUNDATION
Bucharest, Romania

Being Jewish is a fact of birth, a state of mind and soul that sets the Jew apart. I know that and have lived with it my whole life, in spite of all the problems it entails for a Jewish intellectual in the Diaspora. Although raised in an environment of assimilation, I was forced to leave home, as all the Jews of our town were, and to wear a yellow star. I was not allowed to graduate. In my professional life as a historian of literature, I never forgot I was Jewish. I could not because I was always reminded.

The values, traditions, or ways of thinking associated with Jews of the European Diaspora are part of me: a constant feeling of not being at home, a spirit of justice, a critical bent, a constant state of semi-revolt, which led many Jews to join leftist movements. None of this necessarily has to do with religion.

As a Jew of a country that has gone through the Holocaust and totalitarianism, anti-Semitism and anti-Semites neither trouble nor paralyze me. To the contrary, when I come up against them, my spiritual creativity is stimulated. They do not stop me from pursuing my work in Romanian culture and literature, in which I was able to make a place for myself.

Amos Oz

WRITER; PROFESSOR OF HEBREW LANGUAGE AND LITERATURE,
BEN-GURION UNIVERSITY
Be'er Sheva, Israel

The non-Israeli Jew, who speaks a non-Jewish language and lives in a non-Jewish culture, lives a kind of part-time Jewishness. Someone like me, a secular Israeli who speaks Hebrew all the time and works within the prime—and original—Jewish language, has no more trouble sorting out his cultural identity than a French person who lives in France and speaks French, or a Dutch person in Holland, who lives inside Dutch culture. The main difference is, perhaps, that I feel close to other Jews, wherever they are, and when a Jew suffers for being a Jew, I know it means me. We are still a tribe, and if someone bites our thumb, our ear hurts, too. If a member of the tribe gets killed on the other side of the world, we feel panic, outrage, fury, and sorrow. If some Jewish trickster in Lower Ruritania is arrested, the whole tribe shudders at what the world will think. If a functionary or manager is convicted of embezzlement, I personally cringe with shame and embarrassment. I am willing to share my homeland unconditionally with every Jew who wants or needs Israel for a home. My language is essentially my culture and my home. As Hebrew is a Jewish tongue, vibrating with Jewish sensibilities, Jewish memories, Jewish conceptions, I can simply say that my home is Jewish by definition.

When Israel declared its independence, I was nine years old. I remember my father coming to my bed and lying beside me in the dark. "When I was a boy, I was beaten in school in Russia and then in Poland for being a little Jew. You may still get beaten in school, but not for being a Jew."

I am a Jew and a Zionist. In saying this, I do not base myself on religion. I have never learned to resort to verbal compromises like "the spirit of our Jewish past" or "the values of Jewish tradition" because values and tradition alike derive from religious tenets in which I cannot believe. It is impossible to sever Jewish values and tradition from their source, which is revelation, faith, and commandments. Consequently, nouns like mission, destiny, and election, when used with the adjective "Jewish," only cause me embarrassment or worse.

A Jew, in my vocabulary, is someone who regards himself as a Jew or someone who is forced to be a Jew. A Jew is someone who acknowledges his Jewishness. A Jew, in my un-*halachic* [not based on Jewish law] opinion, is someone who chooses to share the fate of other Jews, or who is condemned to do so.

[*From* Under This Blazing Light, *translated by Nicholas de Lange, Cambridge University Press, 1979. reprinted with the permission of the author.*]

Aaron Paley

EVENTS ORGANIZER
Hollywood, California

My parents sent me to a *Volkschule* that was very left-wing, socialist, non-Zionist, nonreligious, but Yiddish. So I have a very strong sense of Judaism, a very strong background in Jewish history and Jewish culture. And I speak, read, and write Yiddish. I can't say one sentence in Hebrew; I maybe know one prayer, and am not very comfortable in a synagogue because it's just not something all that familiar to me. On the other hand, I have a very highly developed sense of Jewish identity and am interested in continuing that and passing it on to my children. I'm doing what I can in the community to raise awareness of the things that to me are important to Jewish identity, like social consciousness and concern for others, and having a good sense of history, which is where the Yiddish part of it comes in: knowing where we came from and how we got here, using that as a guide to figure out where to go.

Judaism means a lot to me, even though my wife says it doesn't mean much to her. So I think that our children will find Judaism important. I would like to have them have a Jewish identity, and you don't need two parents for that. I mean they could have a Jewish identity and a Japanese identity, if I were married to a Japanese woman. There are plenty of people out there who have mixed identities. We're all running around with American and Jewish identities in the United States. And even in Israel, they're running around with Jewish and Israeli identities, and those aren't the same. I think that in mixed marriages, or where you have two different cultures, the critical thing is that both parents have a strong sense of their own culture; then that will get communicated to the children.

I'm a professional festival organizer, and now I am organizing my first Jewish festival. For this, we're really pulling from secular Jewish culture, as opposed to religious Jewish culture. We have klezmer, storytelling, films, and workshops for kids. We have Yiddish language classes, we have forums on the history of Yiddish theater, Jewish genealogy, and exhibitions on Yiddish on the Internet. The only thing that is even remotely religious is that one of the workshops for kids is *tzedakah* boxes, and we're looking at the different designs from eastern Europe and teaching those to kids.

The cultural aspect that Yiddish entails is important to me. Yiddish was the *lingua franca* of Diaspora Jews in Europe for over one thousand years. It became a culture apart from the Hebrew, and out of that culture grew many things: music, film, and stories, and literature, and proverbs, and a way of thinking, and a way of looking at the world. I think that a religious Jew would say that the reason why they continue to use Yiddish is because it provides them a way to have a Jewish way of speaking to each other that's not sacred. I think that an argument that bolsters the whole concept of Yiddish and the nonreligious language is cultural identity. It's an alternative to the constructive identity of Israel. Israel constructed a new Jewish identity in this century, which I think was one of the things that contributed, along with the Holocaust, to the demise of Yiddish. Israelis chose Hebrew as the national language and constructed a new Israeli culture. On the other hand—and I find this very encouraging—the fall of communism opened up Eastern Europe. All of a sudden, people realize that you can go there, to this place where Yiddish was a way of life, and people still speak Yiddish there. In Belarus and Lithuania, I met a lot of people, from twenty years old to eighty, who spoke Yiddish.

Roberta Peters
SOPRANO WITH THE METROPOLITAN OPERA
New York, New York

As is usual with most people, I identify with the religion into which I was born. As an active Jew, I attend synagogue and for the past twenty-five years or so I have sung at High Holiday services. My husband and two sons participate as well because we feel that it is important to preserving our Jewishness.

I have worked actively for such organizations as UJA Federation, Israel Bonds, Hebrew University of Jerusalem and Ben Gurion University. These organizations represent hope for present and future generations, particularly of Jews, but for other peoples as well.

Ann Roiphe

WRITER; NOVELIST
New York, New York

Today I have pictures in my mind of the destruction of the Temple, of the exile from Spain, of transport trains. I know the stories of Gluckel from Hameln and Rabbi Nachman of Bratislava. I have seen tomatoes growing in the Negev and can imagine the Baal Shem Tov dancing in the forest. I was proud at Entebbe, my heart skipped beats when Scuds flew over Tel Aviv. I am no longer the child who asks what this has to do with me. I believe that we Jews have a purpose, a destiny, a reason for being. I am no longer a mere particle of genetic material spinning out a single life span. I have a past, present, and future among my people.

[*From* Why Be Jewish? *Reprinted with the permission of the American Jewish Committee.*]

Wendy Schwartz

ASSISTANT TO DIRECTOR FOR PRODUCTION/BROADCASTING
RADIO FREE EUROPE/RADIO LIBERTY
American living in Prague, Czech Republic

Judaism is my family and my history. But I see religion connected to spirituality, not to family history. When I was in Bulgaria on the eve of Rosh Hashanah, I went to the synagogue. It was also the occasion for the rededication of the synagogue, and I was really happy as a Jew to be part of it. The next day, I went to a Greek Orthodox church, as a visitor.

Being Jewish gives me a concept of self that includes the fact that I am Jewish. In addition to keeping the holidays wherever I may be, I am sensitive to Jewish issues and have a vested interest when I hear something about Jews and Judaism. When the fact that I'm Jewish comes up in conversation, I am happy to respond to people's questions with a sense of sharing. Judaism is not especially a lifestyle for me. For example, if I were to get married, the man's religion would not be an overriding factor in my decision to marry him. It would be a subject that we'd have to discuss and reach an understanding about.

Ethical and moral values are cross-cultural and shared by religions.

The more I learn of other religions, the more I see that they are similar, in that they promote kindness, love, charity, and prohibitions against "sins" such as adultery, murder, and stealing. I am not deeply schooled in Judaism, but I do not think that good and evil are the domains of Jews only. My values are humanistic, without a capital *H*. I value differences. I think I am tolerant in the Jewish sense. My ideal is summed up in the sentence, "Do justice, love mercy, walk humbly," which I believe is cross-cultural.

Yefim Slobodinsky
ENGINEER
Columbus, Ohio

I arrived in the United States in 1987, after waiting eight years for an exit visa from Russia. I had the opportunity to become acquainted with some aspects of Judaism, and I'm grateful for that. In Judaism, the people who do not know anything about the laws and traditions are considered to be children born into slavery. This is the case of many, many Russian Jews. Our passports were stamped "Nationality: Jew." And we lived with unwritten but well known restrictions against Jews. So we learned how to circumvent these obstacles (and became even more despised). This mentally ingrained itself in the Russian-Jewish soul to the extent that living in a new, different country cannot change things. But the young Russian Jews here in the United States will find their way to Judaism, overcoming the same obstacles which have to be overcome by young American Jews.

In view of all this, what does being Jewish mean to me? The same as before! It is inside! I cannot be without this feeling. I'm part of all Jews. We have one common soul. Every Saturday, I go to synagogue. I cannot not go! My neighbor does not, but I do not consider him a bad Jew. He still has not come to the "right" point. Some day maybe he will, or his children, or grandchildren.

It takes time to be awakened. The main point is that practically all of us "Russians" have a Jewish soul.

Gary Smith
DIRECTOR OF THE AMERICAN ACADEMY
Berlin, Germany

Although you might call my parents assimilated, they raised me to be Jewish. Our hometown in Texas had such a small Jewish population that Jewish children had to be "imported" from nearby towns and even from Mexico so that the community could have a Jewish summer camp. In my youthful zeal, I even convinced my parents to keep a kosher home.

My mother was a refugee from Nazi Germany; my father came from another country. They had the Yiddish language in common and spoke it to each other while I was a child so that I would not understand what they were saying. This only sparked my curiosity about their history, the culture they came from, to learn why the Holocaust happened where and why it did. So I concentrated on German studies in college, something that led me away from Judaism, but also back to it.

Because of my interest in Walter Benjamin, the great German-Jewish philosopher before World War I, the DAAD (German Educational Exchange Service) awarded me a grant to study in Germany. Like many Jewish intellectuals of his time, [Benjamin] did not attend synagogue or observe the holidays. He came to Judaism through a negative association, which in the end led to a positive one. During an intellectual debate in 1911, he was asked how and why the German Jews became the bearers of German culture. The question was provocative and anti-Semitic. So he began studying Judaism to find out what led Jews toward intellectualism. He discovered something that I could describe as the imagelessness of beauty, the sublime. Most people associate beauty with some physical representation. Jews, in keeping with the biblical injunction against fashioning imagery, did not stress the physical, but the invisible characteristics that could be described as beautiful.

As I discovered how Benjamin came back to his Judaism, I grew away from mine. I stayed on in Germany to pursue this intellectual tradition. My wife, a German, an art historian by profession, had learned Hebrew. This endeared her to my parents, who had only bad memories of everything connected to the land they fled. She converted to Judaism and today we invite friends to *Kiddush* and to the Seder at our home in Germany. Rituals hold Jews together. I discovered that no matter where I go in the world, our Jewish rites are recognizable and familiar, even though not one hundred percent the same. I can *daven* in any community in any part of the world.

As a Jew and as an American, I know that I represent both cultures in dealing with Europeans. I rely on the values I learned from my Jewish upbringing. The *mitzvot* as a whole articulate a certain view of character and instill ethical norms that become a guide for daily life. I hope that this is what people see behind my academic entrepreneurship.

—∽—

Aldo Zargani
ARTIST
Rome, Italy

Pope Leo XIII declared Jews *personae non gratae* in Rome and established the ghetto. Another pope, Pius XII, asked his bishops to accept Jews into monasteries and other establishments of the Catholic Church. This saved many lives, mine included. Now, another pope, John Paul II, is trying to clear up a muddled history. But his document stops short of doing what we Jews all hoped for: Look history in the eye and admit that the Church more often than not looked the other way during acts of anti-Semitism, if it did not promote them.

But this is history. You asked me what difference it makes to me that I am Jewish. I am a product of this history, I lived part of it. Being Jewish made a difference to the extent that I did not want to be anything else. This determination caused me harm, but it left me with something precious. Where others cannot live the truth, even today, I, a Jew who survived, am happy to remain faithful to our truths.

CHAPTER FIVE

---◦◦◦---

Children of the Shoah

Many responses reminded us that the Holocaust did not end with the defeat of Hitler's Germany. For many individuals, the events of the Holocaust and anti-Semitism had or still have such a strong impact on them that these experiences serve as a major motivation for their present actions or attitudes. Anti-Semitism can be stricken from the books, but not from the hearts and minds of people looking for excuses for failure and misery. In some cases, old fears remain in the surviving Jewish populations. In other cases, Jews serve as reminders of a past that the ethnic majority would like to cover up. In eastern Europe, the anti-Semitism put into an artificial sleep by international communist ideology is reawakened at a time of economic struggle. One respondent reminded us that persecution was not limited to national socialism. Yet others feel challenged by the memory of the Holocaust to revive Jewish religion and culture in places where it once flourished and played an important role in Jewish history.

Radu Alexandru
WRITER
Bucharest, Romania

To be "guilty." But let me qualify this statement by putting it in the framework of recent eastern European history. Now that the horror that was communism is over, a question has been put before people who now have freedom of expression: "Who is to blame for everything that happened?" This question was posed with a sense of urgency that has no apparent justification. It is interesting to observe that the question did not originate with the persons who really suffered and who are still waiting for justice to be done. The question was thrown out to the public, almost as a provocation, by exactly those individuals who served the communist regime most zealously. Their reason for doing so is obvious. They had to offer something to "the Romanian people"—in whose name they spoke and continue to speak with no real authorization—an alibi for the long dark night that they went through. They need an alibi to which they can transfer their own guilt for the inexplicable misery they imposed. "The Romanian people were always anticommunist. They were betrayed by foreigners. By Hungarians, but especially by the Jews, who represented the interests of the Soviet Union. The Jews brought communism to the country and they are guilty for all the evil that came with it!"

To a people [the Romanians] that does not even know the history of the time they are living, a people who are shaking off the confusion of the concentration camp (a metaphor to which there is more truth than poetry) they have just left, any affirmation uttered with some emphasis has the chance of being accepted as truth written in capital letters. This is true especially in the light of a belief that has endured for millennia. That Jews are among the people who obtained positions of influence under the communist regime is emphasized out of proportion to the greater number of non-Jews who slavishly served the regime. Jews have always been guilty, so it is easy to blame them, only because they are Jews.

To the Jewish population in Romania, with an average age of sixty years and numbers decreasing for obvious biological reasons, the unceasing accusation of guilt causes a certain feeling of discomfort and, naturally, a defense reaction. Not only in the Jew, who after centuries of such accusations is almost immune, but in the state of justice. Democracy should start to exercise its wings. This is happening in other eastern European countries, but not in Romania, where the so-called leadership is engaging in an age-old practice: casting blame on others. As a Jew, I am again on the receiving end.

Anonymous
POLISH IMMIGRANT TO GERMANY WHOSE FAMILY WAS KILLED IN AUSCHWITZ.

To be Jewish means to be cursed and damned.

[He married a Christian woman after the Holocaust, and his children live as Christians in northwest Germany.]

∽

Siegfried Birkholz
PRINCIPAL, PESTALOZZI SCHOOL FOR CHILDREN WITH LEARNING DISABILITIES
Cologne-Wiehl, Germany

"You are as old as he would have been, if he would still be alive." Silence, then a deep sigh and trembling lips, "Your name should be Jonathan . . . yes, Jonathan."

Today, more than thirty-five years later, I hear Zwi's voice, I see the images of the eve of Rosh Hashanah 5721, before my twenty-fourth birthday. I see Zwi's shaking head and feel the strong embrace of this man who came so close to me. "Your name should be Jonathan." I remember the time in the night when questions and thoughts over-powered my desire for sleep. "Why did I come to Israel? Only to work on the Gevim kibbutz? Why did my mother tell me, as her face took on a surreptitious expression, 'You must go there!' Did I want to learn more about the unfathomable Shoah, more than what I picked up from the Jewish students at the University of Bonn as they discussed their experiences during the night? Why did Zwi have to tell me, of all people, his life story? Why did he have to tell me, the young man from the land of the murderers, the name of his slain son? Why did he make me, the *goy*, promise to say *Kaddish* for both his sons when I would visit Auschwitz? How did all this fit together?

Was I looking for something in this country that was lost, some-thing that I desperately needed? Were my reasons for coming to Israel different from those of the friends I traveled with? If that were the case, how was I to find the connection? And what would I do once I found it?

I did not find the answer in Israel, but the process was set in motion and became more intense over the years. Only much, much later was the mystery solved, near the end of my parents' lives. They finally put in words what they had kept hidden for decades: that the mothers of both parents were of Jewish ancestry. They showed me pictures of relatives murdered in Auschwitz, Theresienstadt, and other places that until that moment had only been names to me.

Curiosity drove me to learn more and to go back to the source and discover my ancestry in order to become part of that family. My progress was slow, as I overcame hindrances and faced hard decisions, as I bid farewell to the familiar and made a new beginning. I started to study the Talmud and learned that the journey is more important than the destination. Now after many years of being led by God, after meeting new friends, I am asked if being Jewish has made a difference in my life.

First, I understand what Zwi wanted to tell me when he gave me his son's name: "The Lord gives." I understand that it is God who gives. So each day, when I see the earth and the sky, I am conscious of the fact that God created it. As an essential part of myself, this name and the way back to "my Israel" turned out to be a priceless gift. I also learned that each of us is part of that creation, and I should neither judge it nor discredit it or any part of it.

Second, I am a product of this creation, along with everything else that exists: the healthy and the sick, the people who are as intelligent as I am, who are more intelligent, and the people who need help in bringing their intelligence to expression. I am not the lord of this creation to do what I want with it. "The earth is the Lord's and the fullness thereof" an elementary declaration in the Hebrew Bible and a basic principle of Jewish belief and life.

Third is a principle that I first came upon as a young man and moved me even then: the people who had gone through the horror of the Shoah believed in the One and Only. They told me that this belief was central to the faith of the Jews and that I should study it. That the God of the Torah is faithful and true motivates me every day anew in my work with the troubled young people at my school. And I would like to mention a fourth difference: The gift of the Sabbath has become a basic need, an experience that I enjoy each week. And I try to share it with the young people entrusted to me, Jewish or not Jewish.

Zwi understood much more. "Your name should be Jonathan." The Lord gives! This reality is enough of a difference for a lifetime.

Pania Brankowskaia
HOLOCAUST SURVIVOR
Vilnius, Lithuania

When I was growing up in Vilna, Jews made up 40 percent of the population. During the war, almost all were killed. I am among the few who came back.

To all who ask me if I hate the Lithuanians who took part in killing us Jews, or the Germans, I say no. But I also say that we have a right to this place; not to own it, but to continue our particular Jewish life here. In the history of Vilna, Jews made a difference that no one has a right to obliterate or forget.

Naomi Bubis
WRITER
Tel Aviv, Israel

By chance, I was born Jewish, and certainly this circumstance has had an influence on my life. I would probably not be living in Israel today were I not Jewish. But if I look back over the thirty years of my life in Germany, my being Jewish had a big influence on my existence. But never in a religious sense. The most determinant was the company or society around me. It is not written on my forehead that I am Jewish, but as soon as my name was spoken, the usual—but never direct—questions arose. It was never "Naomi: Isn't that a Jewish name?" But more often: "Naomi, what an interesting name. How did you get it?" This ever-repeated occurrence is indicative: It reveals the deeply seated tension, the enduring fear of a natural, unforced attitude towards Jews; the frequent repressed reactions—in the permanent fear of saying something "wrong"; the mark of the foreigner. In regard to the latter, I can actually say that I never felt that I was German.

So my being Jewish had a strong influence on my identity as an individual between two nations. In retrospect, I can say this in a positive sense. I find the duality to be enriching; it opened my horizon and sharpened my sensitivity to certain themes and conditions in life. A life as a Jew, that is, as a member of a minority in Germany, has an inevitable influence; it inures one to intentional or unintentional animosity.

Yes, there are still values that are Jewish. From the original religious values, an entire moral code developed through the ages. There is a value system based on long Jewish tradition. The family, respect for mother and father, and the importance given to children play a great role in this tradition. The history of our people, with all the tragic manifestations of anti-Semitism and all the murders, especially the largest industrially organized mass murder that history knows of, is, according to me, part of this people, and has led to the growth of a sensitivity in relation to human rights and towards minorities. There were and are concrete examples of this, which have been conveyed to me as values. Civil courage in daily life is one, as well as a keener perspective, the tendency to not look away, the desire to want to hear, see, and speak out wherever injustice takes place and human rights are trampled underfoot. And this goes on every day!

Shmuel Cederbaum
FORMER BUSINESSMAN; AUTHOR
Munich, Germany, and Jerusalem, Israel

Twelve children—I see them still before my eyes—killed brutally in that extermination camp which I survived by some miracle. My wife survived Auschwitz. Another miracle. This experience taught me that nothing happens without a reason. And this has guided my life.

Friends know that we Jews have a "tradition" of asking questions. In this way, we try to understand how life is given meaning, how events can be interpreted. The extermination camps caused many Jews to give up faith, others to blame Divinity. Some Jews gave up being Jewish altogether. My faith was strengthened. I may never know the answers to all the questions, or the meaning behind all the events I went through. But I will not give up trying to find out. This is part of my Jewish soul.

Hermann Flath
FORMER BUSINESSMAN
Munich, Germany

After surviving the extermination of all my family, I had to face a difficult situation: how to relate to the Germans who either took part in the killing, or who did not do anything to stop it. Being Jewish made a difference in that it led me to realize that we can come to grips with our destiny by giving our lives a sense of future, not living in the past.

After the Holocaust, I lived in Münster, and our community numbered around one hundred twenty survivors, some who returned to the place of their birth, others who were searching for a new beginning in a devastated world. Hate and intolerance dominated our discussions. Martin Buber and Leo Baeck took a different position. Arguments from the Torah, as well as arguments that developed in Jewish tradition, spoke in favor of not answering hate and destruction in kind. Instead of letting hate drive my life and actions, which would have only made me more unhappy, I have come to peace as a Jew living in a world that does not necessarily love us.

Emmerich Fuchs
DIAMOND MERCHANT
Antwerp, Belgium

My childhood is marked by the hostility I felt around me in my native Hungary. The non-Jews always reminded me that I was different from them, by which they meant inferior. This gave me a deep complex, which I have never completely lost and which made me sensitive to hostility. I deal with many non-Jews in my business, especially now in eastern Europe, and make sure I conduct myself in such a way that if they find anything to complain about working with Jews, it is not my fault.

I was raised to be observant and have lived that way all my life. It is a traditional life, tied to the values that Jews hold dear: strong family ties, duty to family, and passing on our beliefs and practices. While non-Jews may have similar values, I think that Jews cling to them more strongly because continuity is not to be taken for granted. Among the values I hold most dear and make an effort to practice are caring for the sick and helping people in need. Especially taking care of the dead. When I first had to do this, in a concentration camp, I was repulsed, until another Jew told me that this is the highest *mitzvah* of all because you know that there is no way you will be repaid or even receive a word of thanks.

Anja Gerson
ASSISTANT MANAGER OF THE KROKE KLEZMER BAND
Kasimierz/Krakow, Poland

My parents fought physically against my efforts to explore my Jewish roots. But I kept searching. Until today, my grandmother is horrified about what will happen to my children. She already warned me that if I give birth to a son, I should not to have him circumcised. "You know, things are not so bad now. But things can change. I want to die in peace, thinking that my children and grandchildren will be able to live in peace. So don't do anything that will mark you as a Jew." This is the climate in Kasimierz.

The music that I first heard the Kroke band play led me to discover something I wanted to identify with. What is important for me is family. And Judaism has a strong family element. It is part of the religion. Against all odds, I want to raise a Jewish family. What I have not yet learned about being Jewish, I will learn with my children.

The most important thing in life is the freedom to be what and who you are, and to have a strong, healthy, Jewish family. This is the basis of our almost six-thousand-year-old culture.

Ralph Giordano
JOURNALIST; WRITER FOR TELEVISION AND DOCUMENTARY FILMS
Cologne, Germany

To think that there is no anti-Semitism because the [German] state has an official anti-anti-Semitism[*sic*] policy should not be interpreted to mean that there is none. I received more than nine hundred death threats in the mail after some of my articles were published, or shows televised. This is a clear contradiction of such a policy and such a belief.

Two things kept some of us Jews in Germany after the war. First, there were people who helped us. What would become of them if we left? Second, although Hitler was defeated militarily, his spirit was not defeated. So we could not leave this land under such a threat.

German has always been my language. I make my living through this wonderful language and could never leave it. My thoughts and soul are expressed through German. Then, there are millions of people who think like I do, that Germany bears a great guilt, and that the criminals were not punished. I owe it to the victims of Nazi Germany to stay here and see that they are punished, that this crime not be repeated. These ties bind me to Germany.

Being Jewish is something I experience every day. Either from the outside, as a reaction from the others I come in contact with, or how I myself react in regard to these. The difference between me, with my experience in the thirties and forties, and the people I live with is always with me. Every day, there is something going on in this country to which I react as a Jew. Always. No day has gone by without some confrontation. For good and for bad. Between the two extremes of Germans—those who realize the guilt of Germany and those who are still reactionary and violent—there is enough room for play that allows for anti-Semitic ideas and actions to go unchecked.

People like me have two burdens. The first is the burden of events between 1933 and 1945. The truth is that the time that has gone by since 1945 has not cleared up anything. The second burden is what I call the second guilt: that it has been sublimated. No one wants to even talk about it. What is bad here is what keeps me here. Had I left because of this badness, I would always feel like a deserter. I don't know if every Jew thinks like I do. Not all Jews are such fighters like myself, and I don't blame them. After so many were destroyed physically and spiritually, they were unable to fight more.

During my life, I became more and more Jewish. When Hitler came to power in 1933, I was in high school. The first day, the students were separated into Aryan and non-Aryan. There were thirty-two Aryans and six non-Aryans. But my brother and I did not know what non-Aryan meant, so we stayed with the Aryan group. When we told our parents what happened, they told us we were Jewish, not Aryan. Up until that time, there was no sense of difference in our home. But from that day in April 1933, the separation, the isolation began. And it went on and on until 1938 when we didn't even look German any more. After 1938, the Nazis beat me into being Jewish. They beat it into my soul. And I can say that after surviving, I like being Jewish. Everything that happened after 1945 only made this feeling stronger. So I can say that I live as a Jew . . . in my fashion. Probably not typical or exemplary. I don't believe in God. He is a necessary invention by and for humans. So my Jewish feelings are not stamped by religious belief or emotion. I am a Jew in an un-Jewish way. I am Jewish in a political way. I don't belong to any of the Jewish congregations, but my talents and intellect are marked by my experience as a Jew. All my beliefs go back to 1933. One can say I was born at that time.

Gideon Greif
DIRECTOR, YAD VASHEM-TEL AVIV
Jerusalem and Tel Aviv, Israel

The main feeling I have is a sense of pride in being part of a nation which has suffered so much and endured, and has contributed so much to the world. That we still exist is a miracle. This gives me a sense of responsibility to continue, to go on living and contributing, to continue the heritage of such an ancient people.

For me, being Jewish means remembering, not always consciously, that you are the descendant of the sons of sons of Abraham, also of King Solomon, also of Rashi, also of Spinoza. This means that every generation must be at least as good as the former one, not less brilliant or less creative than the former generation of Jews.

Being Jewish means to be part of a nation towards which hatred is directed. It means to be always alert, to be always conscious, in any state, because I feel that my might, my physical existence, is not sure, even today, even after the Holocaust.

Then I would say that for me being Jewish is to believe that the Jewish people is the chosen people of God. If God had not set us apart, there would be no Jews in the first place. And if He didn't love us, we wouldn't have lasted thousands of years as a separate entity. We have been the main enemy of two big powers: the Catholic Church, which was the dominant church in Europe, and the most powerful country in Europe, Nazi Germany. If we overcame these two powers, it is because God loves us. And I feel that I belong to a people especially loved, by God; because we are not loved by people.

Remembrance is the value I live by. I'm not religious in the common way, but I feel my Jewishness. Remembrance means to fulfill the unwritten will of the Jews who were murdered. And that's what I do, twenty-three hours a day. I spread the knowledge of the Holocaust so that murdered Jews will not be forgotten. The Germans did not only try to destroy individual Jews, but also our culture, literature, heritage, tradition, and religion. Preserving all this is my task, although I do not keep Shabbat or the *mitzvot*. But because I strive to carry on what others tried to destroy, I see myself as a religious person.

Not even the Armenians were subject to a Holocaust. And other people have gone through discrimination and even destruction. But a mother whose interest is in the children of her neighbors is not normal. Your children, your family come first. There is a complaint that in the United States, the Holocaust has become a religion. I think there is nothing bad in this, because it is so Jewish.

The Jewish people must remain the most alert of all nations. When I'm asked if anti-Semitism will disappear, I say that the chances are very slight. After three thousand five hundred years of human history, this is the most permanent aspect. Rome and Greece collapsed, anti-Semitism remained. I have many non-Jewish friends, and sometimes I discover—and it's so discouraging—that in some corner of the soul, there is something very dark, something very unfriendly towards us.

Edith Hahn Beer
FORMER LAWYER (GERMANY); FORMER COOK (ENGLAND)
Now living in Netanya, Israel

Why don't you tell me what difference it made that I am Jewish? My parents, Leopold and Klothilde, were normal Viennese citizens, more Austrian than Jewish. Life promised to be lovely. In March 1938, Hitler's troops marched into Austria. My father was already deceased; my two sisters emigrated to Palestine. I stayed with my mother. I lived through several concentration camps, then returned to Vienna, living in misery through a period when no future seemed to exist for me. I saw my mother for the last time in April 1941.

On the advice of an SS officer, and with his help, I became Christine Marie Margarethe Denner, moved in with a German family near Munich, and met a Christian man who wanted to marry me. I took a chance and confessed my true identity, which made no difference to him. We married, lived in what was to become East Germany, and had a daughter. But I desperately wanted to be myself, to be the Jew I was born to be. Deep in my heart, even as I lied in order to survive, I wanted to live as what I really felt I was. In 1945, I went to the appropriate office to regain my true papers, my true identity. And whom did I see sitting behind the desk? The same former SS officer, who accused me of forging documents when I became Christine. I calmed him down by saying that probably there existed no authority that would prosecute me.

Under a Christian name, I had been able to study law during the war years, and I almost wound up as a judge during the Nuremberg trials. I declined at the last moment because I did not want to give rise to any suspicion of vengeance, which the people in Germany were talking about. The Soviet secret service wanted to recruit me, but I escaped to England with my daughter before the pressure became unbearable. Even then, events were against me. The English airline workers went on strike, and I had to wait in Germany for over two weeks before any airplane could leave. A kind German family, relatives of a friend, took care of us.

I believe in justice, not just as a lawyer, but mainly as a Jew. Life is not fair. We are commanded to make it so. I will never forget the people who risked their lives to save mine. Justice must apply equally to all. That is a value the Jews gave to the rest of the world thousands of years ago and it is still important.

Hanna Jordan
STAGE DESIGNER FOR THEATER AND TELEVISION
Wuppertal, Germany

There were many influences in our family during my childhood, Christian as well as Jewish. The Jewish part just seemed to be the more interesting. There was no question of a religious aspect. It was more a matter of spirit, an attitude towards culture, the arts, and towards life. The many Jewish relatives and relations with many other Jews formed a very strong presence that marked my upbringing and intellectual perspective. I do not identify with religious Jews, but with the intellectuals—Martin Buber, for example. This is one way that being Jewish made a difference.

It is strange that the Christian part of the family never took hold in me. I feel that I see the world through Jewish eyes. I am—this may seem strange—a lifelong member of the Quaker organization. You can say that I have one leg in Judaism and the other in Quakerism, but not as religion. There is a connection between the two. Once you remove all the impediments that humans put in place through religion, there remains a level of humanity, what I call the best in the world, with very much in common. No nationalism, no party affiliation.

The other aspect is Hitler's rise to power and the ensuing persecution. I was twelve when Hitler came to power and eventually went "underground" in order to survive. When I was fourteen years old, my parents sent me to an English school in Germany. This was the way the Quakers worked to save those Jewish children they could. The school was set up so as to minimize the religious aspect, in Germany, where religious education was obligatory. This opened my eyes to what the intellectual life could be like. For four years, school was a wonderful experience. Three quarters of the students were Jewish, in a Quaker school, where no religion was taught. But the spirit of humanism and intellectual challenge was there. After the war, most Jews left Germany, so even the little that was left after the persecution was gone. It was a big loss for me, personally. I married a non-Jew. I never fell in love with a Jewish man. To me, they all seemed like brothers. Too much like family members. I do not have real Jewish friends. I know several Jews here, but we are not friends. A group of us older women get together to discuss politics once a month. Twice a year, we celebrate a Jewish Sabbath. My best friend is Christian, and she arranges it.

My daughter was not given an active Jewish education. I put her in a Catholic school because that was the best one in the city. The nuns approached me one day to say—not in a bad way—that they could not answer her questions. She kept asking questions. When I explained her background, the priest was happy to hear that we are Jewish and was very obliging.

I don't know about my role in the continuity of Judaism. I only know that without Jews, the world would have no flavor. It would be like a soup without salt.

Michèle Kahn
AUTHOR OF BOOKS FOR CHILDREN AND ADULTS
Paris, France

To be Jewish today, for me, means to preserve as well as to transmit the sensitivity and culture of Judaism. Curiously, this feeling came to me gradually, and in close connection to my professional life. When my first books appeared, I had to decide on a pen name. Pseudonyms were in fashion. As a teeneager, I dreamed of becoming a writer named Anne Vanel. It sounded good, very French. But I realized that the selection of this name could be interpreted as a desire to hide my Jewish name. So I signed Michèle Kahn. I've had over forty books published, all for young people, none containing anything Jewish, autobiographical. I was happy to be an objective writer.

At around the age of thirty-five, I opened the Bible, which I thought I knew. The text seemed rather dry to me, and I had to go through great pains to find the beautiful stories told to me by the Jewish teachers of my childhood. In the bookstores, I couldn't find these stories in the religious books written for young people. All they offered were condensations of stories form the Old and New Testaments. After searching, I became reacquainted with the Midrash, which I had forgotten all about, and I threw myself into a presumptuous project: I would write my own Bible, a version intended for readers of all ages and denominations, in which biblical stories would be enlarged by details found in the Midrash. The motto for this book would be a verse from the Psalms: "Things that we have heard and know, what our fathers have repeated to us, from our children we shall not hide" (Psalms 78:3).

Writing these texts, through which I transmit my ancestral culture, which is also the culture of the Western world, I experienced a pleasure in writing that I never had before. Was I giving back to that little Jewish girl I once was the stories that she was born with and grew up with?

At the same time, I was interested in how my fellow writers were doing. As director of the Society for French Writers, I learned that there was a Jewish way of fulfilling duties rooted in French tradition. The day after the demonstration for Yossif Begun, I pacified my Jewish soul by informing the Writers Union in the Soviet Union that it is our aim to defend freedom of thought, so we could not sign the reciprocal agreement requested from us. I feel a rush of Jewish pride when the Society gives awards to Jewish writers and to translations of Israeli novels. When I was appointed president of the Authors Aid Commission of the National Center for Writers at the Ministry of Culture, I felt a

Jewish satisfaction in being able to contribute to the alleviation of social problems.

Last but not least, I feel that another part of my self wants to be heard, the woman that I have become. A woman for whom the question, "Where do I come from?" is shrouded in fog. In the effort to make me "really French, " my parents left me in the dark about their Polish history. I was a graft, a twig cut away from the original tree and planted in French soil in order to take root and become something new. I was marked by the terror of the Holocaust. My parents and I had to flee the Gestapo. My husband's parents were murdered in Auschwitz. A heavy silence, which I respect, hangs over this pain. But I needed to know about the circumstances in which I was born.

So I wrote a novel about a Jewish woman in search of her identity (*Hotel Riviera*, which was published by Grasset in 1986). Her parents had been deported by the Nazis. Then I wrote two novels—one for adults, one for children—in which I include true testimony about the Shoah. My book on a very little known episode during the Holocaust will soon appear: *Jewish Shanghai.*

"Do you consider yourself a Jewish writer?" a reporter asked me once. After thinking about it, hesitating a bit, I answered, "Yes." Whether I want it or not, I am a child of the Shoah. This knowledge never leaves me. At the same time, the more I advance in my career, the more it seems that the most interesting thing I can transmit and publish to Jewish and non-Jewish readers comes from my trove of Jewish memories.

As a writer in the Diaspora, it seems that my role is to testify to the history of the Jewish people, and thereby make my fellow Jews better known and appreciated. So I have the feeling that I am throwing myself into a search in which I am becoming myself and in which I sometimes find fulfillment.

As a Frenchwoman, I draw upon my Jewishness.

Oscar Klein
JAZZ MUSICIAN, "GREATEST IN GERMANY"
"Citizen of the world " living in Basel, Switzerland

Obviously it has made a difference. I had to leave Austria because I was Jewish. Other than that, I do not pray as a Jew nor attend synagogue. As a boy, I was always embarrassed by men who went around in funny costumes and boxes on their heads in order to pray. You don't need that.

I am grateful, perhaps that is a Jewish trait in me. I am grateful to Mussolini. When I fled Austria to Italy, I was not persecuted. Furthermore, I played jazz with Mussolini's son. We are friends to this day. When I play before audiences around the world, I mention these two facts: that I am Jewish and that I played with the son of Benito Mussolini, the son of a fascist dictator. He is not to blame for his father's actions. But he had to see his father hanged and beaten by the mob. He lives with this image every day.

Human relations are very important to me. The best jazz musicians are blacks, Jews, and Italians. We have all been persecuted and know how to identify with pain. Jazz came out of pain and poverty, just like Jews did. And then there's love; you have to love human beings. Doesn't Judaism teach that?

⌒⌘⌒

Abraham Lehrer
YOUTH LEADER, NATIONAL JEWISH WELFARE ORGANIZATION
Cologne, Germany

Living in Germany, one does not go around declaring that he is Jewish. Being Jewish is something I claim only after I know an individual well. My family lives in an area where there are no other Jews. And outwardly, we and our neighbors look the same. But they read about me in newspaper articles, and when they see me, they look at me out of the side of their eyes. Eventually they will ask me about how I feel as a Jew living in Germany. They know about Yom Kippur. Some even asked me if fasting on Yom Kippur is the first step to becoming a chasidic Jew who wears *payis* and a long black caftan, the kind of Jew they see in pictures. I assure them that it is not, and they feel better that no one will look different from them, that no one in the neighborhood will stand out as different. As a Jew in Germany, my attitude towards what we all see on the television news about Israel differs from that of my neighbors. To me, Israel is a living issue, not a philosophical matter. The Germans make a case of my being Jewish. To me, it is a very natural thing.

I am a quiet Jew. I will always try to find the middle way. Although

I am not Orthodox, my wife and I stress the holidays and the Shabbat at home. These are family times and we make sure we spend them together and with our extended families. Taking time for our children is important. When my daughter was preparing for her *bat mitzvah,* she wanted her speech to be special, different. She chose Tu Bishvat as a subject, the holiday dedicated to planting trees. We researched the Torah for all the laws and customs regarding trees, plants, and the earth. This early respect for nature among the Hebrews has been weakened through the ages and I was glad I could discover it with my daughter.

The Torah stresses love of neighbor. I think of this especially before Yom Kippur. So before I go to the synagogue, I make sure that if there is anything between me and someone else, I set it right before I start to fast.

----- ❧ -----

Helen Luksenburg
CONCENTRATION CAMP SURVIVOR; VOLUNTEER GUIDE TO GROUPS
VISITING THE U.S. HOLOCAUST MEMORIAL MUSEUM
Chevy Chase, Maryland

I am proud to belong to a religion that gave to the world the first and most ethical code by which humans can live—the Torah. It forms the basis for the activity of many governments in the world today. It is an ethic that does not apply only to Jewish people, but we, the Jewish people, have the obligation to live by it. This is a high-order responsibility which we assume. At the same time, I remain humble in the sense that I know of my modest place in the world, but also of its importance to others.

We, the Jewish people, are dedicated to the well-being of anyone who is oppressed. Our Torah and tradition is one of helping those in need. And our history of suffering is paralleled by our history of giving and solidarity with those who fought for their freedom.

It is painful to tell my life story, but I have to share this in the hope that what affected it so dramatically will not happen again. When I hear the stories of some survivors on record at the Holocaust Museum, I feel sorry for what some of them went through to hide their Jewishness. I could never pretend to be other than what I am. Even if being what I am means to endure repression or inequity. If I survive, then I survive as a Jew. I am not Orthodox. It took a long time for faith to come back. Faith comes back when you have children and you understand your responsibilities to our continuing as a special people who keep God's commandments.

As a European-born Jew who went through the experience of the coming to power of Nazism, I think that Americans, including American Jews, are naive. They believe that a Holocaust cannot happen again, and definitely not here. But it can. Some of the events I see and hear remind me of Hitler's time. Recent political events in Europe should make us more aware of the dangers of totalitarianism and fascism. There is a long history of blaming Jews when something happens that non-Jews don't like or that adversely affects them. To me to be Jewish means also to do whatever is necessary so that nothing like the Holocaust will ever happen again to us Jews or to any other nation.

I am a Zionist and a strong supporter of Israel. Israel is our legacy. Our children must cherish it and support it. A Jew does not live only for himself. Every deed reflects upon the others. Our standards are not a matter of convenience but of responsibility towards each other.

Max Mannheimer

JOURNALIST
Frankfurt, Germany

In all the stages of my life that I can recall, Jewishness defined me to the extent that at times I felt there was nothing left to define. But that would make Jewishness equal to destiny, and I know that as a Jew, I had to fight destiny in order to survive: to continue reading, writing, celebrating our holidays, helping others, and remembering the people around me who were slaughtered.

In Neutitschein, a town in Moravia not far from the border with Austria, I had no idea that to be Jewish was to be different. I began to grasp the difference between Christians and Jews during the Christmas holidays. In school, I always got smaller presents from the Christ-child, and I had the idea that he did not like Jewish children. The widow of the local rabbi explained to me that we Jews had a history of our own, much older than the one I learned about in school, and that the Christians should be grateful to us for having given them so much of what they claim to be theirs. It sounded good, but it could not make me feel better when my classmates yelled "dirty Jew" at me. In our town, Jews were considered good businesspeople and were respected for encouraging their children to study. To this dimension I added my attempt to excel in sports. Perhaps this gave me the physical strength to survive starvation and hard labor during years in concentration camps. But it was Jewish education that made a difference after the war.

I do not know to what extent wounds have healed. My wife was killed shortly after our wedding. Today, I can speak about reconciliation between Jews and Germans because I belong to a tradition that is not based on hatred. I can speak and write about remembrance because our history is based on remembering and honoring our dead.

David Markovitch
Prague, Czech Republic

"Be a good Jew and everything will be fine" turned out to be a joke for the few of us who survived the concentration camps. When you ask me what difference being Jewish makes to me, I can only think of our cemetery. Every name there lives in our memory. You cannot live only for yourself and for the moment. Being Jewish is part of being a community. We help and are helped, respect and are respected. The Jews who come to the Old New Synagogue are impressed that we maintain our traditions after all that has happened. Now they like our songs and customs. I don't think I could have survived without the hope that a new generation of Jews would carry on.

Arie Mellen
ENGINEERING STUDENT
Cologne, Germany

Here in Germany, Jews are seen as members of a minority, even if they are born as German citizens. Simply put, I am not a German according to the standards of the German people. This condition has marked my life. Germans expect me to act like a Jew, to think like one, regardless of how I personally think. If there is a question about Israel, they expect me to know all about it and to be able to answer their questions. They expect me to know the Old Testament from front to back. It is complicated to be a Jew here in Germany. If you decide to live according to our laws, you will always have a problem. You cannot socialize, because most of socializing in Germany goes on during Friday night and Saturday. It always involves food that a conscientious Jew will not eat. Even if you do not socialize, getting your meat is a complicated matter. There are no kosher butchers in major cities; you have to order your meat and *matzot* from Frankfurt, over one hundred kilometers away from here. At the university, exams are frequently held on Yom Kippur or on other days on which Jewish holidays fall. I tried bringing this to the attention of other students and the administrators, but they don't see why I should have a problem. It's not that they actively discriminate. They just don't understand why such issues are important.

The result of their attitude is that I decided to study Judaism to find out if it is worth being different. And the more I studied, the more proud I became that I am Jewish. I do not know how Christians feel about their religion, but as someone who tries to practice Judaism, I feel that there is something special there, something different in the way of regarding life and acting as a result of this perspective. Here I am a bit vague because I talk about a difference without defining this difference. Offhand, I can think of a sense of continuity that is sustained and nourished in the Jewish family.

I see no future for myself as a Jew here in Germany. I will probably go to Israel, where one can live like a Jew without complications, where I can feel at home.

Grazyna Pawlak
DIRECTOR, FOUNDATION FOR THE JEWISH HISTORICAL INSTITUTE
Warsaw, Poland

To be Jewish means to be conscious of the fact that one should live the ethics of Judaism. Many monuments were built to commemorate the victims of the Holocaust. There's nothing wrong with that. But to me, as a Jewish woman, life and how you live it is at least as important as memorials to those who died as victims of mass murder. Before the Holocaust, there were three million Jews living in centers of Jewish religious and cultural life: Warsaw, Lodz, Vilnius, Krakow. There were Yiddish newspapers and theaters and several publishing houses. There was a vibrant Jewish life in Poland. A museum commemorating this life is a statement regarding the difference that being Jewish made to people who contributed to the arts, sciences, philosophy, education, literature, as well as to religious life.

But Poland is also a country, not just our cemetery. And I want to show all the Poles, and visitors to Poland, how much Jews contributed to this land. Maybe they will learn that diversity is not a sacrifice or a blot on national purity, but a blessing. I am dedicated to this message because I am Jewish.

—◦◦—

Zalman Pinto
FORMER BUSINESSMAN; PHILANTHROPIST
Madrid, Spain

As Sephardim, we Spanish Jews always thought of ourselves as better than the Ashkenazim. As we resisted forced Christianization, we thought of ourselves as better than Christians, who wanted us to become like them, worshipping more than one God. We kept our Jewish soul, sometimes hiding our Jewishness, other times doing what we had to in order to just survive.

Now that we can again be Jews, we face a difficult challenge: Can we be what we are when no one is trying to challenge this right? To this question I have no answer. But I try my best to support every activity that shows the world something about our difference.

—◦◦—

David Solomon
PRAGUE, CZECH REPUBLIC

I lost my best years in the concentration camp, along with most of my family. Here in Prague, I live alone, trying to keep a connection to the Jewish community. At times I am frustrated by how easily people forget the terrible years of Jewish extermination. The rabbi says that slavery in Egypt was worse than the Holocaust. Comparing the account in the Torah with my experience, I doubt it.

Yes, being Jewish made a lot of difference in my life. All my non-Jewish classmates did well in life, became important businessmen, doctors, professors. Being Jewish means that I had to start all over again, with these two bare hands without fingers. Before we knew it, those of us who had to struggle were dancing at the first Jewish wedding, celebrated a *bar mitzvah*, and even got a *minyan* at the Old New Synagogue—all this under the communist regime!

Being Jewish means working hard, helping others, being honest, caring for your neighbor and enjoying the gift of life. I know that my Jewish songs and jokes and stories are part of my Jewishness. Will they survive after I am gone, like everyone else so dear to me? Look, this Old New Synagogue is still here after so many centuries and so much danger. So for me, being Jewish is believing that Judaism will not end with my end. Others believed in me to carry it on. I can only trust that others will do the same.

—◌◦◌—

Dumitru Solomon
WRITER
Bucharest, Romania

Since my childhood, I've been conscious of being Jewish. I come from a family that, without being bigoted, observed the holidays, kept the traditions, went to the synagogue, and spoke Yiddish at home and with the community members, even though they spoke Romanian with non-Jews in our city. I was also conscious of being a Jew during the fascist period in Romania, when we had to wear the yellow star of David; when I heard insulting remarks from adolescents of my age; when I had to take private lessons given by a Jewish lawyer because the Romanian high schools were closed to Jews; when my father was sent to do forced labor in German-occupied Russia.

The difference I felt was something imposed from the outside, connotations of oppression and humiliation. The feeling of humiliation and a vague inferiority went away after a while because the Romanian milieu in which I lived as a university student, and later as a writer, was never hostile towards me. At least, I never felt any hostility.

Anti-Semitism still exists in some parts of Romanian society. It is even part of post-communist politics. Jews have limited access to political positions and important cultural positions. No virulent anti-Semitism. I am well integrated into the major part of social and cultural life. I consider myself to be a Romanian writer, more precisely, Romanian-Jewish, not Jewish-Romanian, in the sense that all persons of goodwill, no matter what their religion or ethnic origin, aspire to universality. That is, universality seems to me to be one of the strongest Jewish values. My wish is that my message be understood by the contemporary world, Jewish and non-Jewish. I gave up the idea of being a member of an elite, of a chosen people. And I do not overestimate Jewish values. I am looking for new values and trying to offer, in all modesty, what I can offer on the spiritual level. I believe that I have inherited some of the defects of my people, to whom I have done nothing but to add my own personal shortcomings.

Guy Stern

DISTINGUISHED PROFESSOR OF GERMANIC LITERATURE
AND CULTURE, WAYNE STATE UNIVERSITY
Detroit, Michigan

The difference is that I feel a strong affinity with Jews worldwide. I know that no matter in what country I am, the local Jews and I have a common basis for emotional and intellectual communication. I know that other Jews accept me immediately as one of them. In Salonika, Munich, Leipzig, in any city in the United States. Being Jewish makes more difference to me, deep inside myself, than it makes to non-Jews. I have not been subjected to overt anti-Semitism.

Religion is not a deeply seated part of my Jewishness. I belong to a synagogue, but that is more in order to have Jewish social contact.

The matrix of Jewish ethics is marked by the religion these ethics come from. Although Jews have no monopoly on humanistic behavior, the profundity of this ethic is clearly distinguishable and differentiates the Jewish practice of justice and helpfulness from the practice of other religions or philosophies. The sense of family is also strong. I lost so many family members during the Holocaust that I am close to those who remain, no matter the degree of separation. I am close to second-degree cousins in Greece and Rome, a first cousin in New York, even to my wife's family.

There is no active reference on my part to any particular point of Jewish ethic in my behavior. My parents sent me to classes in Judaism as a child, but these stressed humanism—the *Pirkei Avot*, the teachings of Hillel and Maimonides—more than Torah and *halachah*. What I learned became part of me to the extent that when I act as a Jew, I do so instinctively.

I make a point of trying to deal fairly in my life and profession, sometimes to what may seem an extreme. As a writer, I am scrupulous about giving credit in the reference section to anyone whose work I mention. This may also be the source of an apparent contradiction: I am a professor of German studies. How can a Jew who lost family in the Holocaust, who observed a society that seemed the epitome of art and humanism murder innocent people, who interrogated murderers and who realized the extent of popular support of the Nazis—how can a Jew who went through all this find something to praise about Germany and its legacy?

The concept of *Bildung* (improvement through humanistic education) had a strong attraction to the Jews growing up in Germany between the two world wars. We filtered German culture through the Jewish ethic that had been shaped during the Age of Enlightenment. Many of us left Germany for America, where we distilled the best from the German cultural heritage, in keeping with the ennobling and creative Jewish ethos. In often night-long debates with German-Jewish exiles, I was more than once struck by the acuity and fairness with which they separated the valid from the invalid in German culture. In fact, we exiles have been in the forefront in representing the best of German culture, as Richard von Weizsäcker [former president of the German Federal Republic] recognized. We celebrated humanity. What could be more Jewish?

Jana Tesserova
DIRECTOR OF THE HEBREW SCHOOL
Kosice, Slovakia

After World War II, after the Holocaust, so few Jews were left in, or came back to, Kosice. Some of us, like my family, believed that our practices and way of thinking were important enough to carry on as we had for generations past. Those who survived, especially my generation that was born to Holocaust survivors, felt that we owed something to those poor people, to our direct forebears, to our parents. The *mitzvah* of honoring your parents was very important to me, and to my husband, all our lives.

I was lucky that I married a Jewish husband who shared my values. When the communists took over power in Czechoslovakia, many people decided that again it was dangerous to be Jewish, or at least openly Jewish. The Gentiles knew who was Jewish, we knew we were Jewish, but everyone kept his thoughts and beliefs to himself. Many Jewish families did not keep up our practices so that their children would not suffer or make innocent remarks to outsiders that could lead to trouble in a land run by communists. Many baby boys were not circumcised. Ours was. But even though a Jewish boy is not circumcised, he was still a Jew, to us and to the others.

We let our children know that we were Jewish and that they are, too. We kept the holy days, and more importantly, they kept us. I dedicated my life to educating the Jewish children in Kosice to the best of my ability under the given circumstances. My children are now grown and have been involved in the community and in helping other Jews.

But many young people are leaving now that there is the freedom to travel. We do not hold them back, just as our parents did not hold us back. I believe that to honor one's parents means to honor our continuity. You do the best you can for your parents and for your children so that there will be future generations of Jews.

Sabine Vogel-Krämer
PRIMARY SCHOOL TEACHER
Wermelskirchen, Germany

My father was Jewish, my mother German, so perhaps I do not fit the Orthodox definition of a Jew. But I was very close to my father; I was the replacement for the son he lost during the Shoah, and his only child after his second marriage. My father told me his story, and I identified with the victim. This somewhat alienated me from my mother. My father took me to the synagogue, but I received no religious education in Judaism. He had me take lessons in my mother's religion because he was afraid of what my life would be like as a Jew. We went to the synagogue together until he died, and before he died, he asked me to continue going.

My father taught me that I was not German, and I cannot feel part of a people who did what they did. Some Germans who are interested in the Holocaust formed a group to study what it means to be victimized. They told me that it is "easier" to identify with the victim, because there is no feeling of guilt to bear or to deny. However, the pain that comes with being a victim is not so easy to bear. I remember my father crying at night and yelling in his sleep. It is not easy to live with the fact of a Holocaust that was directed against you. You are very conscious of the fact that people can hate you only because you are different.

My husband—we are in the process of a divorce—is not Jewish. After my father died, he said I could stop going to the synagogue and start being a regular German. He told me how I was putting his life and the life of our son in danger, should another Holocaust come about. Now he is seeing someone he calls a *normal* German woman, not a crazy Jew.

So, these facts go into the difference of being Jewish. But these are negative aspects. I chose to be Jewish, to accept the Jewish way of life and its values, not just the music and history, but the values that guide our life. For example, we have many rules, but life is the highest rule. When life is in danger, these rules are suspended. Judaism exalts human life through its practices. It does not advocate that humans debase or humble themselves to an unnatural degree, as I perceive Christianity does. We are not to humiliate ourselves or to deprive ourselves, but to enjoy what God has given us. Our values are integrated into our daily actions, not relegated to one day through an act that is separated from living. This is especially true in family life. I also appreciate the chasidic songs of praise, the *niggunim,* as a way of lifting the soul to God. The Jewish soul is in constant dialogue with God.

CHAPTER SIX

———— ✎ ————

". . . You Shall Be Holy . . .

. . . as I am holy," God said to Moses and to the Hebrews liberated from Egyptian bondage. This phrase is often repeated after commandments are given for Moses to convey to the new nation. The answers included in this chapter express the authors' position that Judaism is defined primarily in relation to God and his commandments. The respondents consciously (and conscientiously) seek guidance from the Torah and the teachings of the sages in order to come closer to God and to the people with whom they interact.

David Aaron

RABBI; DIRECTOR OF ISRALIGHT
Jerusalem, Israel

Leading a Jewish life gives my life meaning because I feel that it places me as a word in a sentence in a chapter in a text that has been in the writing since before the written word and that is still in the writing. It also gives me a sense of a greater reality than what I perceive around me. A meaning of life that is greater than what I myself can conjure from what is around me, from what makes me "feel good."

Shabbat remains uniquely Jewish. Whereas other religions, other peoples, have a day of rest, Shabbat is more than a day of physical rest. It's not a day of rest in the sense of going to the beach. It's a day of spiritual reconnection to God, to family, to self. Shabbat, when celebrated in the *halachic* format, is unlike anything that the world offers.

I met a fellow one Sunday on an airplane—he was a born-again Christian—and we started a dialogue. What do you do? What do I do? He told me a little bit about his church and I asked him, what do you do in church? So he told me the format of the service on Sunday morning, about forty-five minutes long.

"Really? So what do you do in forty-five minutes?"

"The preacher gives a half-hour sermon, and for the other fifteen minutes we sing selected songs from a hymnbook. "

"What types of songs? Which ones do you sing?"

"Whichever ones the preacher wants to sing, that are related to the service, those are the ones we sing. What do you do?"

So I took out my *siddur* and showed him our prayer book. I showed him our daily morning service, afternoon service, evening service. The Shabbat service, morning, afternoon, evening.

"You have all this?" he asked, somewhat surprised.

And I realized even more what I have when I looked at his face, the admiration, almost a little jealousy, at not having such a spiritual format. I think that Jewish prayer, when we are immersed in it—a kind of a lost art—is very deep.

In addition, there is the concept of *mitzvot*. The Torah is not just a book of ethics—although it contains these—but of value. It is a book about achieving the status of *kedushah,* holiness. Before we do a *mitzvah,* we say a prayer. This makes it clear that the purpose of the *mitzvah* is to transform us into the status of *kedushah.* The prayer says that God has made us good through the *mitzvah.* He has not made us ethical through the *mitzvah,* or moral. There is a certain level to which the *mitzvah* guides one. If two people are walking down a street, and they see an old man who asks for money, one of them might be motivated from the ethical perspective to give money; the other from the perspective of *kedushah* to give charity. A similar act with completely different motivations. The Torah says, "You shall be holy for I am holy." We connect to God through *mitzvot*.

To me, all the *mitzvot* are like a dance. I can't say that I like one particular step because doing *mitzvot* is part of a whole dance.

———— ⌇ ————

Benjamin Benbuth
PROFESSOR OF PHYSICS, UNIVERSITY OF ROME
Rome, Italy

You ask me this question on Shabbat *Be-Shallach*, in which the miracle of the manna is told. In relation to this Torah portion, one difference Judaism makes is that we know that God will provide, but this does not mean waiting passively for divine intervention. Jews know that they must do their part in securing the gifts that God provides for us. Except on Shabbat. The miracle of the manna makes it clear that we must keep Shabbat in mind when we go out in search of manna during the week.

———— ⌇ ————

Eran Blajchman
RUSSIAN-BORN MATHEMATICS STUDENT
Cologne, Germany

In my case, being Jewish gives me a view of the world that is different from the one or ones that other peoples have: the idea of righteousness, in the first place. We must do what is right, correct, ethical. This is always very strongly emphasized in the teachings of the Jews. Another aspect is that we have a direct connection to God. There is no person or organization who comes between me and God. Finally, the family is very strong in Judaism. This may be a result of a history of persecution—the family was the only protective refuge—but a sense of family is still there.

Gabriel Chocrón
PROFESSOR OF ECONOMICS
Madrid, Spain

To me, Judaism is a unity of three points, something like a triangle: Land (that is, Israel), God, and Law. Some Jews tend more to a certain direction, while others try to keep a balance, which I hope I do. Progressing from total nonobservance to observance, I make a point of taking each of these points into consideration and practicing them in my life. I don't know what made me change direction in life. I was about to marry a gentile woman when the urge to study my history came over me. And I liked what I read, so I continued to pursue Judaism.

Let me give some examples of the difference that Judaism makes to me in view of the triangle I mentioned. Regarding the land: The Torah commanded Jews to plant trees when they arrived in the Promised Land. They were commanded to give the land a rest every seven years. I translate this to mean that we must respect the earth, to be aware of our role as caretakers of the land that God gave us. We also respect animals in that we do not hunt them and let them die in traps that maim them and kill them slowly, but slaughter them using a method that inflicts the least amount of pain. I honor one God, not a multitude of human beings that other humans decided to call divine. *Tzedakah* is the word that sums up all the laws. It means righteousness and justice. This is a commandment, not something left to choice or whim. This leads me to a type of political outlook that can be described as socialist in that I must look out for those less able to provide for themselves. I am not allowed to prosper while others go hungry or without food.

On a more personal level, Jewish family values are important. As opposed to Catholicism, in Judaism the unique relation between a husband and wife, which some people refer to as sex, is not considered original sin. It is incumbent upon the husband to give joy to his wife. There are mystical writings called *Hakitia* or *Haketia*—written in a language spoken in North Africa and called Isaquito (which is taken from the name Isaac)—that give explicit instructions on pleasing one's wife.

Stella Filler

MIME; SCHOOLTEACHER
Palo Alto, California

There is a saying in Spanish: "*Lo mamé.*" This means that I imbibed Judaism as a child imbibes milk at her mother's breast. I could never have been non-Jewish because Judaism is mother's milk to me. Therefore, a Jew will always come back to being a Jew. The mime Marcel Marceau, with whom I am close, never brought up the fact that he is Jewish during the course of his career. Now, in late career, he talks about it openly. Even my siblings, who are not religious, feel the need go to the synagogue for life's important events, such as circumcision, weddings, Yahrzeits. Although neither my husband nor I was Orthodox at the time of our marriage, we became so because of our children. One reason for this is because in Morocco, where I was born, a Jew was either Orthodox or nothing. There is no such thing as Reform or Conservative there. Another reason is that Orthodox Judaism seems more clear and consistent when it comes to raising children: Rules are rules.

The values of Islam and Christianity can be traced back to early Jewish law, with some reinterpretation, of course. A strong sense of collectivity, I believe, remains particularly Jewish. If one Jew does something negative, the whole community feels shame. On the other hand, if one Jew acts like a hero, all Jews rejoice for the whole of Judaism as well as for the one Jew. If an Irish Catholic does something great, only the Irish feel pride, not the whole of Catholicism. I also find that Jews abhor violence. They love to argue, even violently, but not to the point where they want to kill. This opinion may sound strange in view of conflicts in the Middle East. But Jews have to be pushed to the extreme before they react with violence. Killing is not a virtue. Given a chance for peace or violence, the Jew will opt for peace.

As for myself, I believe that the Torah teaches me to look into myself, to examine myself and my relation to God. As an Orthodox Jew, I must remind myself that God is always present, watching me. If I want to connect to God, I have to be mindful of my thoughts and actions. I want to be a happy person, and Judaism guides me in this direction. This can limit some of my actions. For instance, as a mime and an Orthodox woman, I perform only before other women and before children. But I am compensated by the fact that a certain value—female modesty and family purity—is preserved for my children.

Yaakov Fogelman
RABBI; MEMBER, MASSACHUSETTS BAR; DIRECTOR, TORAH OUTREACH
PROGRAM; EDITOR, *JERUSALEM JEWISH VOICE*
Jerusalem, Israel

Being Jewish means, to me, studying and following the laws and teachings of the Jewish religion as set forth in the Written and Oral Torah and accepting its claim, the essence of Jewish sacred tradition, to be the word of God. In that sense, I do not respond to the Torah only as a force that resonates within me, though it does, but, perhaps primarily, as the Law, the word of God, His guide for His image to follow with his free will. In the same way, I have to consider and regulate my life in the light of God's other "legal system," His laws of science and nature: gravity, nutrition, exercise, marriage, procreation, etc. I also have to take into account God's rules for societal life, how I act towards my neighbor, how to set up proper government, army, courts, social services, etc.

My teacher, Rabbi Dr. Joseph Soloveitchik, says that modern man makes a huge error in his basic approach to religion. He relegates it to the realm of the subjective and aesthetic rather than recognizing its essence in the realm of the objective and scientific. So I would assume that, if that same God of nature gave the Torah, a major component of it would be abstract principles that somehow lead to finely detailed behaviors, as in science itself.

In light of this, anything contained in the overall values and premises of the Torah regarding behavior equally affects my life every moment. In that sense, it makes me Jewish. Living in Israel is one of the bases of the law. Nachmanides, who risked his life to come here in his later years and renew Jewish settlement, stated that one cannot really fulfill the *mitzvot* of the Torah while living outside of Israel.

If I believed, like some breakaway modern Jewish denominations do (Reform, Reconstructionist, and most Conservatives), that the Torah does not come from God, that it is not permanent, but evolving and revolving, the Torah would not have such a tremendous effect on my life. It would be simply culture, not God's word. That's why I believe in the state of Israel, in what it should become, the center of living God's word in the light of His science.

Furthermore, one of the pillars of Judaism is that everyone is part of God's plan and a source of wisdom and knowledge. "Who is wise? He who learns from every man" (*Pirkei Avot*). So a very sensitive and articulate non-Jew may develop and teach some of the Torah's messages better than an underdeveloped Jew. I do not belong to the school that "over-Jews" it, that says everything that's Jewish is good and everything that's not is bad. That's heresy.

What is the source, the basis, of Jewish values? To emulate God as he reveals Himself in His Torah (we cannot ultimately know Him). He displays Himself as strong, powerful, and creative, as we, in turn, must be, to the limits of human ability. Kindness is another of His emphasized traits. There is a lot of kindness among non-Jews, too, but I believe that overall, Jews have been kinder, perhaps because it is also a *mitzvah*, even if one does not naturally have a kind disposition.

Avi Grun

INDUSTRIALIST
Quito, Ecuador

Though I do not believe that either morally, ethically, or intellectually the Jewish people are superior to the rest of the inhabitants or cultures that interact in this world, we, as a people, even under duress, have always subordinated our acts to the criteria of truth and justice. On a personal level, Jewish values embody "a superior reason to live" (to use Frankl's words), which constitutes a powerful driving force behind pursuing a fulfilling life. We do not possess the exclusivity of truth and justice, but have always acted according to them, even when the price to pay was life. We do not possess exclusivity to solidarity and commiseration, but practice it to the extent of putting in doubt the premise that egotism is the trait most characteristic of human nature. We are not the only ones promoting progress, but have led the way even under dire circumstances.

The difference in being Jewish is in the fact that we do not find any contradiction in leading a moral existence while pursuing the fulfillment of every facet of our human nature. The difference in being Jewish is that after all the suffering and hardship we have gone through, we can still wake up in the morning with optimism and no rage in our souls. The difference in being Jewish is expressed in the fact that no matter how tempting the transgression, we could always rescue the purity of our principles and the essence of our way of life and bequeath it intact to future generations. Above all, the real difference does not reside in the rationalizations we indulge in to justify our belief and conduct, but in the fact that we accept our tenets as cardinal directives to be followed and have made a historical pact to transmit them to generations to come.

I don't believe that there are any values upheld exclusively by Jews. But if continuity is the context of our dilemmas, then I would dare to say that truth, justice, and solidarity constitute the common denominators of the Jewish people throughout history and today. Truth and justice serve me as very strong guides. Solidarity, understood as commiseration, an act that extends beyond obligation, does not inspire my enthusiasm. I acquired these three notions and their practice at home, but I do not recall that my father, the theoretician of the family, ever emphasized the relation of these principles to either religion or culture. It was more a transmission of absolute values, edicts. Acquiring and consolidating principles came after I started my own critical reading. The significance of my adherence to these values is that being able to overcome temptation and to forgo eventual satisfaction is very satisfying and fulfilling on a personal level and enhances our standing as a group called to be something special and relevant in the world context.

Samuel Gutfreund
PHYSICIAN
Antwerp, Belgium

If I could choose an identity—Spanish, Russian, Polish, you name it—without having experienced being Jewish, I really don't know what I would choose. I respect Russia's great literature, Germany's great music. And I admire the values created by all nations on this earth. But being Jewish gave me something else that no other identity would have given me: a certain sense of destiny.

This is difficult to explain, but important to be aware of. There is something French in the paintings of the impressionists, as there is something Russian in Tolstoy and Turgenev, and German in Bach's and Beethoven's music. But the Jewish painters of French impressionism, like the Jewish writers of Russian literature and the Jewish composers of Germany have something else in their work. This is what I mean by the sense of destiny. They lived in a world to which they wanted to belong, and sometimes they were accepted. But they also belonged to a tradition that is only theirs and embodies values that others might accept, but not in the way I, as a Jew, bear them from my ancestors to my offspring.

The Ten Commandments changed the world in which they were first acknowledged. And they continue to define a human existence fundamentally dedicated to honesty, respect for others, willingness to help those in need, family life, education, and religious freedom.

ᴄᴠᴏ

Joseph I. Lieberman
U.S. SENATOR FROM CONNECTICUT
Washington, D.C.

To me, being Jewish means having help in answering life's most fundamental questions, such as, "How did I come to this place?" and, "Now that I am here, how should I live?"

My faith, which has anchored my life, begins with a joyful gratitude that there is a God who created the universe and then, because He continued to care for what He created, gave us laws and values to order and improve our lives. God also gave us a purpose and a destiny—to do justice and to protect, indeed to perfect, the human community and natural environment. In trying to live according to these principles, I am helped by daily prayer and religious rituals, such as observance of the Sabbath—a time to stop and appreciate all that God has given us. I also find strength and humility in being linked to something so much larger and longer-lasting than myself.

To me, being Jewish also means the joy of being part of a unique ethnic culture and reveling in its history and humor, its language and literature, its music and moods, its festivals and foods.

Being Jewish in America also means feeling a special love for this country, which has provided such unprecedented freedom and opportunity to the millions who have come and lived here. My parents raised me to believe that I did not have to mute my religious faith or ethnic identity to be a good American; that, on the contrary, America invites all its people to be what they are and believe what they wish. In truth, it is from our individual diversity and shared faith in God that we Americans draw our greatest strength and hope.

Aaron Marcus

GRAPHIC DESIGNER; DEVELOPER OF USER INTERFACES;
AUTHOR OF SEVERAL BOOKS ON COMPUTER-AIDED DESIGN
Emeryville, California

Every action as a Jew seems similar to ones done before, but it is different. It is like taking a step forward, then looking to the left and right and seeing parallel mirrors reflecting similar persons taking steps, replicated to infinity in both directions. Moving about in daily life, the Jew who has learned a bit of Judaism realizes that everyone is "typical" but still unique, that everyone operates within a web, a web of natural constraints, a web of humanity, and a web of Torah truths that gently, but firmly, and inevitably, lead us to right action.

Pesach and the Seder, as family rituals, are about celebrating the joy of being Jewish with family, friends, and especially generation. At my most recent Seder, I asked everyone present to remember Sedarim of the past. I felt we should be grateful for the pleasure of joining together in the retelling and hope for a future with many more Sedarim shared with family and friends.

Seth Margol
SOFER (SCRIBE)
B'nai Brak, Israel, and Orlando, Florida

Obviously, being Jewish is important, as it is the basis of how I try to live my life, that is, to understand the meaning of life and to live according to this understanding. If it were not for the fact that I was born a Jew, I might have pursued my initial desire to be an artist or a photographer. But life has more meaning than pursuing professional glory. If I were seeking what I presume to be TRUTH, then maybe I would have converted to Judaism, since from my point of view, that is where truth lies. For me, Judaism means everything because it is all-encompassing, if not directly from the Torah, then indirectly, including how things outside the Torah relate to it.

Diane Medved
PSYCHOLOGIST; AUTHOR
Seattle, Washington

Being Jewish is not something isolated from any other activity. Being Jewish is an infusion into every moment of every activity. This translates into an appreciation of every aspect of life. It is built into the Jewish system that every moment be recognized for what it is, where it comes from, and the opportunity it poses for us. And that's inclusive of the moment you wake up, to what shoe you put on first, to what you eat and how you eat it, and how you speak to your children, your peers, and your coworkers, throughout the day to the moment you go to sleep. And you thank God for the outlook you have and introspectively you look at how fulfilled you've been and how you've used the opportunity of being Jewish.

Michael Medved
FILM CRITIC; AUTHOR
Seattle, Washington

To me the advantage, the essence that one gathers from being Jewish in the 1990s is a sense of perspective. It's a perspective on continuity, a perspective on the notion that we are not the first people to face the questions and dilemmas that we all encounter in our lives; that other people face the same dilemmas.

Judaism helps put together coherent and effective responses to them. In fact, they are so coherent and so effective and so durable that it is difficult to escape the conclusion that they have an element of the divine.

Judaism also provides a sense of perspective on all of the activities of daily life, giving a spiritual dimension to very ordinary and mundane elements, including what we eat, how we work, getting up in the morning, tying one's shoes, and everything else that human beings do. Judaism also provides a sense of perspective through the mechanism of Shabbat, towards the distinction between what is urgent and pressing, and what is important and of enduring value. So for me, the essence of Jewish commitment involves all of those distinctions by which Jewish practice provides a deeper, richer, more meaningful perspective on the way we live our lives.

Arno Penzias
PHYSICIST; NOBEL LAUREATE IN PHYSICS ("BIG BANG" THEORY)
Murray Hill, New Jersey

To be Jewish means to me a way of reconciling, coming to grips with, in a manner different from any other, the ultimate issue: the world is impermanent, made up of perishable things. My religion allows me to come to terms with the finiteness of our existence, with my own finiteness. The only permanence is that of the divine. From here I derive all my precepts and my dedication to giving. If human beings were to decay, if they were to lose their identity, I would continue to give tzedakah. All my work and my entire life have been marked by this.

Charles Racimoa
BUSINESSMAN
Brussels, Belgium

My Judaism is strongly attached to the state of Israel as the center, the repository of Jewish thought and culture, and the home for all Jews. Here in the Diaspora, I think that Judaism still offers a higher ethical standard than that of other cultures. Even though many countries have adopted humanistic attitudes transmitted through the writings that the Christian world received from the Hebrews, the attitude towards this ethic is taken more seriously by Jews.

Ethics is elevated to holiness. It is a relation between humans and God, not just between one human being and others. I believe that the precepts in the Torah are adaptable to today's conditions when we apply them rationally.

Paul Rand

FOUNDER OF AMERICAN GRAPHIC DESIGN;
PROFESSOR OF DESIGN, YALE UNIVERSITY (DECEASED 1997)
Westport, Connecticut

Anything I can say about being Jewish would be speculation. All of my adult life I moved with Gentiles on an equal footing. There was really no difference between them and me. The rare occasions that I felt uncomfortable in the presence of strangers, I have managed to forget, or put in the back of my mind.

The only thing to which I can connect my being Jewish would be my obsession about being fair and honest in all my dealings, regardless of the consequences—perhaps to a fault. I pray every morning and evening because I feel that I must. This makes me different from mere animals. And this is also necessary: it is a sign that I realize that there are things more important than I.

Alfred Rosenthal

WRITER; PHOTOGRAPHER; HISTORIAN; FILMMAKER;
CHIEF PUBLIC AFFAIRS OFFICER FOR NASA
Silver Spring, Maryland

Judaism is a way of life, certainly more than a religion. It gives you ethics, strength, and hope. It is severe, demanding, and not easily forgiving. It is devoid of pomp and the promise of a hereafter. You live life now. You are being judged now. There is no intermediary. There is no escape.

There are lots of questions—the big WHY of the Holocaust. We shall never know the answer, but we must continue to live as Jews—to be an example and teachers of great values. And do so with humility. We do not need a crown or scepter. But we must never forget that often we are strangers surrounded by thoughts alien to us and often hostile.

Ursula Sabatzus
GUIDE AT THE JEWISH MUSEUM
Rome, Italy

Jewish makes a difference in that when I chose Judaism, I made a point of consciously observing the *mitzvot*. In saying that I chose Judaism, I should explain. My parents were assimilated and attended an Evangelical church. My grandmother was Jewish. My husband's case is similar, except that he was raised a Catholic, with an Italian father having some Jews in his family tree, and a mother born in the United States. We each converted for the same reason: When spirituality became important to us, we believed that Judaism presented the best form of pursuing a religiously conscious way of life. This choice affects where I work and what I can do. I work in the Jewish Museum in Rome so that I am free to keep Shabbat and the holidays. The Christians here cannot understand how important these are for a Jew. For instance, one of my sons is in public school, because the *yeshivah* cannot cover all areas of study leading to university. I have to explain to the school authorities why he will not eat the meat provided in school lunches, and why he will not attend school at all on Pesach. Some of the Christians sympathize, others just cannot comprehend why we insist on these things.

Of the six hundred thirteen *mitzvot*, I hold two especially dear. One is Shabbat, a day of rest that takes each Jew out of everyday routine and places us in another dimension, a higher level where worries do not come near us. And if they try, we know that the Shabbat supersedes these worries. Not even television is allowed to intrude on the peace of Shabbat. The other value is *tzedakah*, in its true sense of justice, righteousness, making right, balancing out what is not equal. What happens when you give money to the poor is that you bring their condition closer to the norm. Important for me is that in carrying out the *mitzvot*, you do it for yourself more than for others; you carry out what God wants you to do.

JEWISH: DOES IT MAKE A DIFFERENCE?

Joop Sanders

SECRETARY-GENERAL, ORGANIZATION OF DUTCH JEWISH COMMUNITIES
Amsterdam, The Netherlands

Being Jewish makes a difference in that I feel and enjoy solidarity with other Jews all over the world. It makes a difference in how I must live. I believe that it is incumbent upon me to accept the obligations that result from the covenant between God and the Jewish people, that is to say, living according to Torah and the Jewish tradition as interpreted by Orthodox rabbis who are—as far as possible—willing to integrate values of the modern world in Judaism. Finally, being Jewish means I owe support to the state of Israel.

René Samuel Sirat

FORMER CHIEF RABBI OF FRANCE; PRESIDENT OF THE
PERMANENT COUNCIL OF RABBIS IN EUROPE
Paris, France

To be Jewish means to be a witness for God, a bearer of hope. This I do by being faithful to the love of Torah that animated our ancestors, by being faithful to Israel, and to Jerusalem in particular. Being Jewish also means that I work unceasingly for peace and brotherhood among all creatures who bear God's image.

Study, solidarity with other Jews, and the belief that all humans are worthy of attention and help are the values that remain specifically Jewish and which I try to live up to. Fulfillment of the *mitzvot* and a sense of duty to all those who bear the divine image are other persistent Jewish values. And of course, looking forward to the time when "the wolf will graze with the lamb."

In France, at this time, there is a spectacular return to Judaism, manifested through a consciousness that community unity is one very strong fundamental value. Consequently, one must not do anything to push away those Jews who are "on the way," who have doubts, who do not perform all the *mitzvot*. I am very sad and very anxious when I see that chapels are being set up in the heart of our beautiful Jewish neighborhood. I am also very worried at the insidious growth of the extreme right in France. It is the duty of the Jewish community to react in due time and properly. We must never forget that Nazism came to power "legitimately" in 1933 in Germany. We must also be careful for signs of racism and xenophobia within our own community, and outside. Unfortunately, there are French Jews who are members of the National Front headed by Jean-Marie Le Pen.

--- οⁿᵒ---

Menahem Stroks

RABBI
Englishman living in Cologne, Germany

As a Jew, I have a sense of being different from others, even those who claim to believe in G-d. This difference means that I not only acknowledge G-d, but I consciously and conscientiously take it upon myself to fulfill His word, to live by the commandments that He gave us.

---οⁿᵒ---

Abraham Twersky

RABBI; AUTHOR
Pittsburgh, Pennsylvania

Being Jewish means to fulfill the mission assigned at Sinai: "And you shall be unto Me a kingdom of priests and a sacred people." Inasmuch as being Jewish essentially means being "a people of holiness," Judaism requires that everything that the Jew does be directed toward holiness. There is no dichotomy between what is secular and what is divine. Everything in life, including all physical activities, must be under the umbrage of holiness and directed toward the ultimate goal.

Jakov Vogelman
INSURANCE AGENT; CONSULTANT TO STEVEN SPIELBERG
IN THE FILMING OF *SCHINDLER'S LIST*
Los Angeles, California

One of the first questions a Jew will have to answer when he or she ascends to heaven is, "Have you been honest in business?" As an insurance agent and financial adviser, I want to deal with people in such a way that they feel that Jews are good people to do business with.

—◈—

Isak Wasserstein
FORMER BUSINESSMAN
Munich, Germany

As a Jew, not only do I believe that the Jews are God's chosen people, but I believe that Judaism presents the only way that one can be true to God.

—◈—

Abner Weiss
RABBI, BETH JACOB SYNAGOGUE
Beverly Hills, California

To be Jewish has always meant to live in a certain way and to have a certain system of values. What perhaps makes it much more important to be Jewish at this time are two considerations. Number one: This is a time when the family, the basis of the whole structure of society, is in deep trouble, and Judaism created the notion of family values. So in the point of view of a contribution to a society which is floundering, which has created an enormous amount of insecurity and uncertainty because of the undermining of the family, to be Jewish means to have something to offer, not only to one's own family, but to the family of man.

There's a second dimension as well: Judaism has always had a sense of mission to the world, not in the sense of converting other people, because we don't believe that we have a monopoly on heaven. Our sense of mission is based upon the notion of *tikkun olam,* which literally means "repairing the world." The Torah requires that we be a light unto the nations. That's done by individuals and individual families, and it's also done by creating a just society. And for that to happen, one needs to have a state, a political entity, which can enshrine and reflect these values.

People speak about the Judeo-Christian ethic. I believe that the notion of a Judeo-Christian tradition is a myth. Let me give an example: Judaism insists that the basis of society is law. "You shall pursue justice justly," in a righteous manner; the means and the end should both be just. Christianity says you should turn the other cheek. Now, it's my contention that no society has ever functioned on the basis of Christian love, and those that have succeeded have functioned on the basis of the Judaic ethic. And I would be willing to bet that if one examines those things which are commonly accepted by most civilized societies, one would find that they have not changed one whit from the Jewish ethic as stated in the Hebrew Bible. Bertrand Russell, who was a well-known atheist, a brilliant man, and a fine human being, suggested that one doesn't need a divine source in order to be an ethical person. Yet not one society has ever successfully substituted another ethic for the biblical ethic. Logically, you can argue that perhaps the old, the sick, and the weak are a burden to society. Hitler tried to argue that, and wanted to exterminate imbeciles and the people who were considered nonproductive. Not one social experiment that has gone against the Jewish value system has ever succeeded. And that makes it even more imperative that these values, which are commonly assented to but more commonly ignored, be supported by Jews, because they are essentially Jewish values.

My commitment is to a dual imperative: to sanctify the name of God by behaving in a way which brings glory to God, and also, for its own sake, to be a decent human being and open to other human beings in need. The Talmud asks: what is *kiddush Hashem?* How does one in fact sanctify the name of God? The Talmud provides its own answer: ". . . if a person buys meat and pays immediately; if a person sells and doesn't sell short, that is a sanctification of the name of God." In other words, to the extent that one immediately shows that one is a seriously ethical human being, one sanctifies God. And those are the values which motivate me as well. That's why when I lived in South Africa, I publicly protested against apartheid. Because to be Jewish means to be a sensitive, decent human being.

What can a rabbi offer to make the Jewish value system relevant to people who live in contemporary America? In the midst of all the materialism of Hollywood, in the middle of the plastic reality which is created here, there is an existential hunger for spiritual meaning. There is a feeling of emptiness. There is a sense that one cannot fill one's life simply by having activities which kill time. People want to be grounded in something which transcends them. They want to give meaning to their lives. This spiritual hunger exists and is more and more acknowledged in the psychology community, in the philosophy community, and even in the entertainment community, which is the window of opportunity for religious leaders. That's one thing which I do in southern California. I try and show how the Jewish path to piety with its tradition of meditation—and people commonly believe that meditation belongs exclusively to Eastern religions—that the Jewish path of piety, in which every act, from the act of eating to the act of going to the bathroom, to the act of buying new clothes, to the act of making a business transaction, each act is a springboard to the divine. I think that that kind of consciousness can fill the huge hole which the contemporary materialistic society has left in the souls of people who are searching for meaning.

Shoshanna Winograd

JUDAIC STUDIES STUDENT, BROWN UNIVERSITY
Providence, Rhode Island, and Palo Alto, California

If I were to rate the ten main influences in my life and on my life, Judaism would be on this list, close to the top. The life skills that I've developed—leadership, confidence, learning, to name some—all go back to the Judaism I was brought up with. My work in youth groups, environmentalism, building homes for people who can't afford housing, my studying to be a rabbi—all stem from Judaism. If it were not for being raised in a home in which my parents gave me a good sense of what being Jewish means, I am not sure what I'd be doing with my life.

The older I've gotten, the more observant I've become. My family is Conservative, and we always kept the holidays and a kosher home. Friday night was not one hundred percent traditional, but we were always together, always had the Friday evening *Kiddush*, and abstained from music, television, and phone calls. Naturally I went through my adolescent crisis and made a point of telephoning on Friday nights during that time. But now I am probably the most observant in the family. I still go through phases of varying degrees of observance, but always within the Jewish sphere. Judaism is bigger than myself, bigger than a physical country. No matter where I go in the world, there will be Jews and a Jewish framework.

The fact that Jewish laws, traditions, and values go back thousands of years gives them added significance and strength, in my mind. This gives me something to think about. Jewish values have spread to other religions, but values in Christianity or Islam have not penetrated Judaism. Learning to be a good person comes out of *our* tradition. It has been thought out for millennia. In Judaism, values are not things one might do, they are law. We *must* do them.

Kashrut is one example. At the university, I chose the kosher meal plan. There is a separate kitchen for preparing and getting our food, but none for eating it. We are able to sit with other students in the common dining room. Others ask me why I eat how I do, so I get a chance to explain the reasons for *kashrut*. This is also part of reminding myself of my Judaism in every aspect of my life. Judaism becomes a leitmotif for living life in a conscientious manner, asking yourself why you do each act that you do.

I want to be a scholar, I'm not sure whether this will happen by being a rabbi or by eventually teaching. I heard that the Orthodox are coming to accept female scholars. I know that I will find my place within our tradition, probably the Conservative tradition, which has plenty of room for women rabbis.

Josef Yakir
INDUSTRIALIST
Haifa, Israel

The main values that Judaism contributed to the Jewish people and to the world are represented by the high moral standard encoded in the Ten Commandments. Other laws in the Torah guide our behavior from birth to death: personal hygiene, generosity, charity, hospitality, land preservation, especially respect for other human beings. And I believe that I practice these values. However, living in Israel requires less observance on my part of all the minute laws that must be observed in the Diaspora in order to preserve the faith.

In my opinion, Israeli society inherited the sacred and blessed Jewish nation. The heirs of an old and widespread culture cannot afford to live an ordinary or low life, as represented by American mass culture, lack of self-criticism, and other bad habits that Diaspora Jews brought with them to Israel, such as involvement in crime, dishonesty, a careless attitude in respect to personal and public habits. These are the source of some of Israel's problems.

Absence of persecution (although it still goes on in some countries, like Syria and Iran) does not mean that danger for Jews is over. The festivals of Passover and Purim remind us of persecution and our longing for liberty. This is eternal and is reason for holding Jews together. The Holocaust is a reminder that even Jews who try to hide their identity cannot escape the danger of persecution.

CHAPTER SEVEN

"... How Deep His Judaism Lies Within"

At the beginning of the twentieth century, Western societies began to relax their prejudices against Jews and integrated them into the mainstream. Most of the respondents whose answers are placed in this chapter were born and raised during that time. As they were allowed to enter the mainstream, they abandoned their Judaism, or denied that it had any influence on their lives. However, a Jewish strain or attitude somehow shows through their work or acts as they relate to a human ethic transcending religious or ethnic identifiers. Paradoxically, the few non-Jews who answered saw more Jewishness in themselves than some of the Jewish respondents did. Rabbi Hochwald, whose answer opens the chapter, provides insight into this characteristic.

Abraham Hochwald

FORMER CHIEF RABBI OF THE NORTH RHINE DISTRICT, GERMANY
Antwerp, Belgium

It is a well-known fact that the Jewish religion and the Jewish people belong to each other. You can't separate them. So even a nonreligious person who belongs to the Jewish people has a certain contact, relation to his Jewish religion. Tradition is one of the foundations of Judaism. Every person who considers himself Jewish is connected to this tradition. So he cannot completely assimilate. That is a difference. So even if the person is not religious, he is attached to traditional values. I think this is the most important element in why a person continues being Jewish.

When a person accepts the principle that you should love your neighbor as yourself, there is no difference whether he is Jew or Christian. But I think that thousands of years of Jewish life have formed a sort of Jewish character that is more attached to this moral value than a Christian is. The Christian may theoretically and spiritually accept this principle of equality of man before God and assist other people who are in trouble. But we feel it stronger. For us, it is a part of our character. There are three elements in the children of Abraham: They have pity, they are modest, and they have a willingness to do good to others. These are the characteristics of a Jewish person, religious or not. It's part of our innermost feelings. And that makes the difference.

Every person who questions his Judaism, or who can see no difference between himself and non-Jews, does not realize how deep his Judaism lies within. This is made evident in certain situations, when he is directly confronted with his Jewishness. Even when he has hardly any contact with Judaism, he feels something. Then there are situations—for example, when a close relation dies—when he will react as a Jew. I believe that there are situations when someone's Jewishness comes out without his realizing it.

Madeleine Albright
UNITED STATES SECRETARY OF STATE
Washington, D.C.

When I found out that I had Jewish roots, I wasn't totally surprised. What did surprise me was the fact that my grandparents had died in a concentration camp. My parents never said a word to me, and I wish I had known about this earlier. Since I could think for myself, I always had a feeling of sympathy for the victims of the Holocaust. Now that I know it is part of my personal history, it means more to me.

—ಎಲ—

Janka Altschuler
Munich, Germany

Between Sin Gheorghiu de Padure, somewhere in Transylvania, and this Jewish home for the elderly in the center of Munich, I have accumulated experiences so contradictory that at times I wonder if being Jewish makes a difference or is the difference. I am one of the ten children of a rabbi's family of a small town still alive in my memory. Life was not easy. But the younger mind is impressed with our holidays, always celebrated with intense joy and a sense of sharing. Against this idealized image of a Jewish family comes the disappointment of many instances in which solidarity was lacking. We Jews are often depicted as a large family caring for each other. This might be true in many cases, but as among non-Jews, solidarity falls victim to apathy. Rabbis can be generous and righteous; they can also be corrupt and greedy.

It makes a difference that we survived against many tremendous odds. But there is no difference between a Jew taking advantage of other Jews and a non-Jew doing the same. It hurts when we are naive or sold on idealized images.

In my old age, I try to help others less fortunate than I am. But wouldn't I do this if I were not Jewish? At times I answer this question in the affirmative—good people are good people. At other times, I say that goodness comes from education, the tradition of being concerned for others. I am afraid that I will never be able to find the answer.

Jurek Becker

NOVELIST; SCRIPTWRITER (DECEASED 1998)
Berlin, Germany

Jakob the Liar is a Jew who always knows better. In the ghetto, he listens to a radio that does not exist and carries within himself the hope that will eventually lead him to his death. To hope against all odds makes a huge difference, especially if hope is connected to humor. I never felt comfortable being a Jew. This is why I frequently accept the role of the enemy, and play it out until I exhaust it. Call it a survival strategy or call it outsmarting. Many Jews live by this secret formula, which others interpret as impertinence. In *Bronstein's Children*, I used a phrase repeated to me many times, either as a compliment or as a reminder to the child who grew up in the Lodz ghetto: "The star suits you." I have no reason to deny it.

Louis Begley

ATTORNEY; WRITER; PRESIDENT OF PEN AMERICA
New York, New York

I am a Jew, not by choice but because I was born to Jewish parents. My Jewishness was a source of almost unbearable fear, considerable humiliation, and danger during World War II. Ever since the danger ended, knowing that I am a Jew has been a source of pride in the spiritual, intellectual and artistic achievements of Jews throughout our history and at present.

I have no doubt that being Jewish has had an effect on practically every aspect of my life and work. However, I do not spend very much time thinking about what it means to be a Jew. I prefer to think about what it means to be a man.

Adolf Burger*

TYPOGRAPHER; AUTHOR; LECTURER
Prague, Czech Republic

As a youngster growing up in Slovakia, I was a Zionist. So Judaism as a religion had no meaning for me from a very young age. After seeing children slaughtered and people used as experimental material by Dr. Mengele, God had no meaning for me.

If today I tell the story of what happened to me and to others as Jews, I do it on humanitarian grounds so that such atrocities will not be repeated. Whatever humanism Jews might have given to the world stopped being Jewish and is part of the universal heritage.

*[*Mr. Burger was one of one hundred forty Jews forced to produce counterfeit money, stamps, passports, and papers for the Nazi regime.*]*

—⌣—

Andrei Codrescu
POET; WRITER; COMMENTATOR FOR NATIONAL PUBLIC RADIO;
PROFESSOR OF ENGLISH, LOUISIANA STATE UNIVERSITY
New Orleans, Louisiana

While the general public does not identify me as a Jew, a number of nongeneral publics identify me as such: fascists (Romanian and American), the local JCC, which asks me for money every year, and a number of writers writing books about Jews. As for my own identification, I see myself as (1) human, (2) American, (3) Romanian, (4) Jewish. The only Jewish part of me I recognize as such is my uncanny ability to split hairs, due, I think, to a rabbinical gene formed in the sixteenth century. Also, I have been hypnotized by Chris Griscom and have had a birth-to-death vision of a sixteenth-century marketplace scribe who wrote letters for hire while composing (simultaneously) commentary in cuneiform.

My Judaism in America manifests itself only when challenged by the outrageous acts of fascists, such as the recent monument to mass murderer Antonescu in Slobozia and the rise of Hitler #2 in Russia. The first time my Judaism manifested itself was when I was ten years old in Sibiu. Two hooligans were pissing crosswise on a wall. When I passed, one of them said, "Every time we piss like this, a Jew dies." I then became conscious that not being a Jew has something to do with the way you piss. Also, I remember feeling awkward about being circumcised. America cured me; she gave me back my foreskin. It is important to me to remember these things and to maintain a reasonable defense against unexpected eruptions of anti-Semitism, which, given the times, can be expected to erupt with greater frequency. About assimilation I feel strongly: Everyone should assimilate. The best specimens are combinations of races and colors. The most beautiful women are Brazilian-Filipino-Jewesses. Nothing embarrasses me about being Jewish, though there is a kind of loud New York Jew that I can't stand. Of course, there are dozens of other types that give me the heebie-jeebies equally: fundamentalist Christian preachers, drunken rednecks, Romanian nationalists, obsequious academics. I feel good about being Jewish every time an anti-Semite bites the dust. I wore a *yarmulke* on the day neo-Nazi David Duke lost the election for governor of Louisiana.

I'm a writer and self-consciously proud that Jews are people of the book, but I'm not so crazy about the Bible, which is a pretty haphazard Jewish book, used mainly for beating Jews over the head with. I do believe, however, that most fundamental questions are moral. This may be Jewish or it may be biological. All people have a moral sense. I believe in tolerance and compassion, qualities found equally in Buddhism. I am proud of the radical streak of utopianism in certain Jewish writers, like Karl Marx, and equally delighted in the (more profound) anti-utopianism of Franz Kafka.

I have often wondered what it would have been like to marry a Jewish woman, and I have concluded that my mother was enough, and that I probably would have been fat by now. Maybe not. I'll never know.

Jacques Derrida

PROFESSOR OF PHILSOPHY, ECOLE DES HAUTES ETUDES
Paris, France

The being-Jewish and the being-open toward-the-future would be the same thing, the same unique thing as uniqueness—and they would not be dissociable the one from the other. To be open toward the future would be to be Jewish. And vice versa. And in exemplary fashion. It would be not only to have a future, to be capable of anticipation . . . but to be in relation to the future as such, and to hold one's identity, reflect it, declare it . . . .

[*From* Archive Fever, *translated from the French by E. Prenowitz, University of Chicago Press, 1996. Reprinted with the permission of the author. The statement was made in a discussion of Yosef Yerushalmi's book* Freud's Moses: Judaism Terminable and Interminable.]

Hilde Deutschkron

WRITER; LECTURER ON NATIONAL SOCIALISM AND THE HOLOCAUST
Berlin, Germany, and Jerusalem, Israel

Being Jewish makes no difference to me. It made more difference to
Hitler than it did to me, so I was persecuted by the Nazis. Today I
lecture on national socialism in Germany. The young Germans accept
me and my message, and I feel like one of them.

—⁂—

Alfred Eisenstaedt

PHOTOGRAPHER FOR *LIFE* MAGAZINE (DECEASED 1995)
New York, NY

We—my family and I, of course—were Jews, but we hardly went to
temple. Naturally, my father did, and sometimes he brought me with
him. My mother observed Jewish customs at home. I never had trouble
with being a Jew in Germany. I served in the German army, was
wounded, and received a medal—a kind of a cross—for bravery. I could
even work in Germany when the Nazis came to power. I had the documents that enabled me to work in Germany. Three years before
Kristallnacht, I left Germany for America.

I always said that I am Jewish. Everybody knows that. But I am not
a practicing Jew. Several Jewish magazines have interviewed me, especially during my last two or three exhibits. But I am not religious, I do
not keep the holidays. I did have a *bar mitzvah* when I was thirteen.
That's when I received a camera as a gift. Perhaps this is the main
difference being Jewish has made in my life.

David E. Fastovsky
PROFESSOR OF GEOLOGY AND PALEONTOLOGY,
UNIVERSITY OF RHODE ISLAND
Kingston, Rhode Island

My family lived in places where Jews were quite uncommon and I was raised to believe that being Jewish somehow conferred a separate quality on me. This increased my sense of isolation and alienation even more. But it also increased my sense of self. Most of our friends were Jewish—we didn't have many friends—so I learned that Jews hung together. A history of being a minority in all the places Jews lived only reinforced my assumption.

Looking out from my small circle of Judaism, I notice that our religion does not stress the hereafter nor have much of a punishment/reward philosophy as does the Christian majority which surrounds us. We are not promised bonuses for good behavior. Jews, it seems to me, celebrate life, which is now, not the potential rewards of a hereafter. Despite the latest events in the Middle East, I think of Jews as (perforce) a peace-loving people, a people committed to intellectual approaches and problem resolution, as opposed to the variety of other means that are commonly used by peoples throughout the world, even in our day. Our pursuits tend to be more mind-driven and less driven by earthly values such as acquisition of material goods or love of power. (I say "tend" because one can surely think of many exceptions.) The "golden rule" remains the arbiter of Jewish behavior.

While these values guide me invisibly and subconsciously through my daily life, those choices that I have made for my life—to become an intellectual, to play an instrument—are choices driven by the values I hold to be Jewish.

Milton Friedman

SENIOR RESEARCH FELLOW, HOOVER INSTITUTION;
NOBEL LAUREATE IN ECONOMICS
Stanford, California

Indeed, being Jewish has unquestionably affected my life. My wife and I have in fact always been conscious of being Jews, but in a sense have never lived as Jews. We have been in a generally secular environment throughout our lives.

Simona Fuà

SECONDARY SCHOOL TEACHER; DIRECTOR OF
ARCHIVES AT JEWISH SYNAGOGUE AND MUSEUM
Rome, Italy

My family is not religious and neither am I, really. Remaining Jewish is a matter of one's free choice. I do not know if my husband, should I marry, will be Jewish or Christian; therefore, I do not know in what religion, if any, I would bring up my children. Being Jewish in this part of Italy, in the type of work I do, presents no difficulties. My colleagues understand the way I pursue my religion.

Diane von Furstenberg

FASHION DESIGNER
New York, New York

I am not sure what being Jewish means to me. I am first a human being, then a woman and that seems to be most important. However, I am the child of a Holocaust survivor and that means a lot to me. My mother's survival was a miracle and I therefore cherish life more.

Jo Goldenberg

RESTAURATEUR; ACTOR
Paris, France

Each person is what he is. There is no difference. Just because one is born in a certain set of behavioral expectations, one is what one is more out of respect for the family and the education one receives. Later, when one feels like it, one becomes what one wants. In our day, people who want to be more religious become so. And there are those who reject religion. One must assume responsibility for one's own life, and for one's family.

Other people, down through history, have accused Jews of being cowardly, dishonest, because they perceived us as different. You know, the Christians believe that Jesus taught that people must love their neighbors, that they must turn the other cheek. But it is we Jews who have practiced this, before Christianity, and even more so since.

Being Jewish has made me different, and that has taught me to tolerate all differences. Here I see Jews who are from Tunisia, Ethiopia, Algeria, Turkey, from Russia, Bessarabia, Hungary, Poland. We are all different. One cannot say that we are the same. In France, there are people who come from Brittany, from Lorraine, from Provence, from Paris, from Normandy. They all consider themselves different. But for Jews, no matter what the differences in outlook, once one knows that another Jew is in danger, we help.

The holidays remain for me the only typically Jewish values. Why? Because the spirit of the holidays is to be strong in the family. When we celebrate the holidays, we get together, the family gets together. The parents pass the spirit of the holidays on to the children by living the holidays, by practicing all the aspects of the holidays. We talk around the table and recall our family history, as well as the history of the particular holiday.

Sir Ernest Gombrich

ART HISTORIAN; PROFESSOR
London, England

Like everybody, I had two parents, four grandparents, eight great-grandparents, and so on, resulting in the fact that, unless there were intermarriages among my ancestors, the number of my ancestors was one thousand twenty-four. Probably the majority of them were Jews. Since all this is wholly unknown and inaccessible to me, I can't claim that the fact that they were or I might be Jewish "means" anything to me. Only signs have meaning, not facts. I am the genetic product of my ancestors, that is all.

Katherine Graham

DIRECTOR, WASHINGTON POST PUBLISHING GROUP
Washington, D.C.

My father was Jewish and my mother was not. I was very close to my father and to his family, but he was not religious, and I am not. I don't think my Jewish identity influences my work and ethic, except perhaps as an inherited work ethic. I do not perceive any difference between myself as a Jew and my non-Jewish colleagues in how I approach my profession or live my life.

Kimberly Hirsh

HUMAN RESOURCES SPECIALIST AT
RADIO FREE EUROPE/RADIO LIBERTY
American living in Prague, Czech Republic

Being Jewish is part of the identity that my parents and ancestors bequeathed upon me. It is up to me to decide what part of that inheritance I want to take advantage of. "Different" is not the best word for explaining how I feel about being Jewish. It's a private identity, more private than the identifier "woman" or "American." If it comes up in conversation that I am Jewish and people want to know what that means, I am happy to explain. I like to share my Judaism that way. I am happy that people ask in a way that shows interest, not curiosity. I am a vegetarian, and people will ask about that, too.

The value of education is still very important to Jews, not just as a means to an end, but as an end in itself. My family comes from a modest background. My grandfather spent ten years to pursue an education. And I like it that women are encouraged to study. Of the other values and ethics that I have read about in the Torah and Talmud, I can identify with them, but I cannot say that these values came to me first through Judaism. While I believe that I have a strong sense of ethics that guide my life, I cannot trace them back to Judaism or even determine whether they are particularly Jewish. But I do know that my generation is more religious than that of my parents. We go to Israel and want to marry within Judaism. We are practically zealots!

Alice Kaprow
GRAPHIC DESIGNER
Newton, Massachusetts

My son Joey was four or five years old when we entered him in a day camp run by Combined Jewish Philanthropies. It was not a religious camp, but what with counselors from Israel, it had a decidedly Jewish emphasis. While we were in the car on the way to the camp, Joey asked me: "You're Jewish, aren't you, Mom?"

"Yes," I said.

"But you don't believe in God, do you?"

"No, I don't." My husband and I were always open with our kids regarding our feelings about religion.

"How can you be Jewish if you don't believe in God?"

Other than cracking up in the car right then and there because I had no good answer for him, I said, "I don't know the answer to that. Let's try to find that out together." And that's pretty much where I'm at.

For me, Judaism is a puzzle. I don't have a hold on it in order to sum it up and on that basis accept it or reject it. I wish I did. In the meanwhile, the question continues to create confusion. I grew up in a suburb of New York where a lot of people were Jewish. So I grew up with a certain way of life that I took for granted. It was not religious, but the Jewish element was there. Girls did not have a *bat mitzvah* celebration, and our Jewish education ended around age twelve. My husband, who as a male received more religious education, has a better handle on Judaism. That's why we raise our kids with a knowledge of Judaism. Not to force them in that direction, but to give them a basis for acceptance or rejection, as opposed to the vacuum I am in.

This is one reason we have a Friday night dinner. It is not a rule cast in concrete that we arrange our lives around this dinner. But I want my kids to know that there is more to Judaism than five holidays in the year. Before we had kids, my husband and I did not make this Friday night dinner part of our lives.

My parents raised me to be a rational and right-thinking person. They gave me values that might be based on Judaism, but you can say just as well that these values are based on history. I am not a student of the Torah, so I do not know which values go back to the Torah. This is not to say that my values are not based on Jewish principles, they were just never presented to me in that light.

Serge Klarsfeld
NAZI HUNTER AND DIRECTOR OF SEVERAL JEWISH PROGRAMS
DEDICATED TO THE HOLOCAUST
Paris, France

Scholars who reflect upon Jewish identity know what it means to be Jewish. I do not have time to think about such things.

Alan Levy
AWARD-WINNING AUTHOR AND JOURNALIST;
EDITOR-IN-CHIEF, PRAGUE POST
American living in Prague, Czech Republic

I have not been in a synagogue since my wedding on August 8, 1956, and I do not like to be known except as myself, Alan Levy, no titles, no adjectives. But this does not mean that being born Jewish has not made a difference. I recall my *bar mitzvah* in 1945, especially the fact that I selected the synagogue in which the ceremony would be held—one in which I would not be expected to sing.

It was in 1971, after the Soviets expelled me and my family from Prague and we settled in Vienna, that I started flying the Jewish flag. Viennese would ask if Levy was a typical American name. "Levy is a typical American Jewish name," I would answer. My wife and I sent our daughters to the French Lycée in Vienna because that was the only place they could fulfill the religious studies requirement by studying Judaism. All the other schools offered classes only in the Catholic and Protestant religions. In 1974, *Playboy* asked me to interview Wiesenthal. This interview was another vehicle that not only led to my writing a book (*The Wiesenthal File*) and winning an award for it, but also to my understanding the Holocaust as someone who was not there, so that I could explain it to others who were not there.

This much I can say about Judaism as a religion: I always accepted the Jewish explanation of God as the most sensible, in comparison to other religions. As for the rest, my Judaism is mainly a cultural thing. Early in my journalism career, people advised me to change my name to Leeds in order to be accepted as a journalist. But I was adamant. I figured that people would find out that I am Jewish, so why try to hide the fact? If you're born a Jew, the world will always find you a Jew. So be yourself as a Jew. Being Jewish is part of my fiber. It is not the most important part of me, but maybe it is.

Nevertheless, Judaism has given me a different outlook. As a Jew, I tend to be watchful, to "sleep with one eye open" because I am aware of our history as scapegoats. As a matter of fact, except for an incident in the army, and a run-in with the mayor of Vienna, incidents of anti-Semitism have been infrequent in my life. When the mayor of Vienna yelled at me that he had had enough of me and my kind, I realized that anti-Semitism was alive and well, in Vienna, at least. By the way, anyone who thinks of me first as a Jew and second as Alan Levy is an anti-Semite in my book. And of course being Jewish has made me sensitive to differences in general, to people who are not part of the majority. I am sensitive to ethnic slurs aimed at any group, not just at Jews, and to antifeminist put-downs. Last but not least, I think that being Jewish has impressed unity of family upon me and my wife. The husband knows he must be faithful; at least, I do. And I have been tempted!

Arthur Miller
PLAYWRIGHT
Wilton, Connecticut

Jewishness is complicated. It influenced all, or almost all, of my plays. I think the best answer I can give is to refer to half a century of play writing.

More than once . . . on crossing paths with some Ancient of Days, some very old man with a child's spirit, I would sense an unnameable weight upon our relationship, the weight of repetition of an archaic reappearance. Perhaps one of these is Gregory Solomon in *The Price*, another, the silent Old Jew in *Incident at Vichy*.

As a young man learning about religion, I noticed a certain disinclination to explain anything rationally that might impinge on the sacred. I found religion classes to be boring or meaningless. The Hebrew teacher who came to our house a few days a week, this bearded ancient taught purely by rote.. . . . when I spoke a passage correctly, he called me a *tzaddik*, a compliment whose cause I understood neither then nor later.

I had been taught how to recognize danger—even where it did not exist—but not how to defend against it. . . . But the more overtly Jewish memories, in fact, are suffused far less with fear and flight than with power and reassurance: sitting in the lap of my long-bearded great-grandfather Barnett in the 114th Street synagogue, his basso voice resounding in my ears as he prayed, swaying back and forth and moving me with him like a horse on a merry-go-round. Naturally, I could not read Hebrew, but he would keep turning my face toward the prayer book and pointing at the letters, which themselves were magical, as I would later learn . . . it was frightening at times, and totally movingly male . . . in some osmotic way, it was my great-grandfather I would strive to imitate as a writer though he died before I even started school.

The Jew in me shied away from private salvation as something close to sin. One's truth must add its push to the evolution of public justice . . . I was striving toward a salvation of religious superreality that did not, however, depart the conditions of earth, a version of avoidance of evil that would thrill even atheists and lead them "upward" and perhaps shame priest and rabbi into realizing how their "spiritualizing" of raw life had made a trifle of religions. The more excitingly true a character or dilemma was, the more spiritualized it became.

[*Adapted from* Timebends *(Grove Press, 1987), in which the author refers to his Jewish upbringing. Reprinted with the permission of the author.*]

Lee Montague

ACTOR
London, England

I am an actor who has been fortunate to have been able to pursue his chosen career for some fortyfive years. And the reason (or rather one of the principal reasons) for being an actor was that, as a Jew, I felt it imperative that I had to express inner turmoil and emotions which I believed I felt because I was Jewish. As I got older, I saw non-Jewish actors playing Jews (and why not? I had been playing non-Jews most of the time), but there is an indefinable quality which Jewish actors bring to playing Jews. A sense of rebirth? A sense of history? The art of self-mockery?

I feel particularly responsible for trying to continue certain traditions and beliefs, although I have moved away from my parents' beliefs (they were Orthodox; I am a member of the Liberal Jewish synagogue). I cannot cut myself off very easily from their traditions and values. I am forever conscious of the Holocaust. I am not quite sure what being Jewish means, but I will not discard my Jewishness, which, I suppose, simplistically means trying to lead an honest, decent life: "Respect the stranger, for you yourselves were strangers in the land of Egypt." I am aware that many, many millions who are not Jewish are trying to do this very thing. But that is not a bad thing, is it?

Daniel Pinkwater

AUTHOR
Hyde Park, New York

How would I know if being Jewish makes a difference if I've never been otherwise? I know there are cultural differences, even among Jews from different countries. What these peoples have in common is their Judaism, which is a religion, not a system of ethics.

As a writer, "Jewish" is not an identifier I go by, even though my wife once remarked that all the characters in each of my seventy books are Jewish. I don't do this trying to make some point, I just do it. I pick on Jews and make fun of them.

I have found it my preference to deflect the question of Judaism in regard to my art. When I go to a town to talk about a book, Jews come out, in a kind of show of solidarity. But I decline invitations proffered to me as a Jewish author. It pleases me that there is a measure of Yiddishkeit in me, but it's not an identification mask. I am an American author, a Buddhist author, but I refuse to take my place in literary history as a Jewish author.

Neither am I clear that there are such things as "Jewish" values. I identify values with the people who impressed those values upon me, my father, in the first place. And one that he impressed upon me was this: Try to help other people when you can. I know this exists as doctrine in other religions—Islam, Buddhism, Christianity, even animism, which predates Judaism.

Sophie Scheidt
FORMER ADMINISTRATIVE ASSISTANT

Walter Scheidt
FORMER LEGAL LIAISON FOR THE SOCIAL SECURITY ADMINISTRATION
Hollywood, Florida

We were both born in Germany before World War I and had a very good childhood there, even though we came from religious families and went to Jewish schools. Other than that, we never noticed any difference between us as Jews and the non-Jews around us. And we still do not.

Robert Schopflocher
FORMER BUSINESSMAN; WRITER.
Buenos Aires, Argentina

My book *Wie Rab Froik die Welt rettete* (How Rabbi Froik saved the world) is as much as I will ever be able to say about being Jewish. Born in Fürth in 1923, I ended up in Argentina in 1937, bringing more German than Jewish culture with me. As I started agricultural training at the Jewish Colonization Association, established by the renowned

Baron Maurice von Hirsch, I realized that my life would take a turn that nobody in my family left in the land I had fled could have imagined. Argentina was meant to be a place of refuge, not my homeland (or *Heimat*, as my family would say). I myself never expected that late in life, after working so many years and in several capacities in my new homeland, I would find my way back to my Jewish roots through a novel written in German.

My life took a strange detour, as did the life of the main character in the book that discusses what makes Jews the way we are. The rabbi with whom I identify is by no means your traditional Orthodox man, rather a person who lives a tradition that each Jew inherited and lives by, sometimes without knowing why. I was glad to discover how deep my Jewishness lies within me and how it affects how I think and what I do. Writing in the language of the people who wanted to exterminate all of us, I discovered how the German culture shaped a specific type of Jewishness, and how Jews responded by contributing to the German culture. This story is repeated in every culture around the world in which Jews have lived.

David Mayer Selby
JUSTICE OF THE SUPREME COURT OF NEW SOUTH WALES
Sydney, Australia

Does being Jewish make a difference? To whom? To me? To my way of living? To the way others regard me? Whatever the inference, I think the answer is no. I can only refer to conditions in Australia, more specifically to a part of Sydney where neighbours don't care if one is Jewish, Christian, atheist, or Calathumpian. If I were to ask them if a certain value were specifically Jewish, most of them, and most Australians, would ask, "What's particularly Jewish about that?"

Tamara Shamson

TRANSLATOR
Columbus, Ohio

My vision of Judaism is typical of a pretty large circle, if not the majority, of the intelligentsia of Jewish origin born and shaped in the Soviet Union. I doubt whether I can call us "the Jewish intelligentsia," because the majority of us were not brought up in the Jewish tradition.

In my understanding, Judaism has three components: (1) it offers a myth of how the world is arranged and where the human race came from; (2) it carries the early history of our people (though wrapped in legend); (3) it gives us an ethical code. For me, the first of these components has long lost its viability. In my vision, its supernatural origin was an early attempt to explain the world and our place in this world.

The second aspect provides us data on our cultural roots and our early accomplishments; it gives a sense of our collective family tree. This knowledge is important for a self-consciousness in every nation. For our people in the Diaspora, it has gained a still greater importance, for it instills a sense of pride and helps us withstand all kinds of prejudice on the part of the non-Jewish milieu. To me, this part of Judaism, broadened with the notion of our nation's accomplishments through the centuries and up to the present time, is an important part of Jewish education. I can't say, though, that such a kind of national awareness is something distinctly Jewish. Every nation seeks it. But for us it probably has a more acute meaning. I know Jewish people from Russia who say that the Jews are the smartest, the most talented, the most righteous, the best of all nations on earth. I can't share that view. Examples of greed and treachery committed by our forefathers can be discovered even in the biblical stories. In my vision, both good and bad manifestations of human nature depend on the individual and his/her upbringing, not on the national or ethnic origin.

Now about the moral code: I consider this aspect of the Jewish law as the ever viable value of all mankind. Though it was first formulated by our sages, it transcends ethnic and religious divisions and is (or should be) ingrained in the ethics of every nation. Not to mention that the Ten Commandments are equally honored by Jews and Christians alike. I presume that those ideas are universal for all the nations of the modern world and do not see them as being exclusively Jewish.

I prefer to stress what unites people, not what separates them. There has been so much bloodshed, so much national hostility of all kinds, that building bridges and seeking a common ground seem to me more appealing ways of approaching cultural and religious differences, whenever possible.

I respect our rituals, yet I don't feel an inner need to observe them myself. They just have never been a part of my life. The same situation seems to be typical of the majority of Jewish intelligentsia in the former Soviet Union. I was raised in the home of my mother's parents. (My parents and grandparents lived together in the same small apartment, a typical Soviet scenario.) My grandparents weren't religious. My grandmother was a suffragette. She had gotten an education in dentistry, but quit working in order to take care of her children. My grandfather was a professor of law, a man of learning and a convinced agnostic. He knew Hebrew, Latin, and three modern European languages. I remember him tuning the radio to the broadcast from Israel and telling us in Russian what he had heard in Hebrew. He knew Jewish culture and closely followed all political developments in Palestine, yet there were no typically Jewish traditions in our home. It was an assimilated (emancipated) home, where people were appreciated for their deeds and knowledge, not for their genes or pattern of life.

Can the faded traditions—I do not equate tradition with value—be restored under more favorable conditions? I don't see this happening in our midst, among our friends from Russia. The only exception is the gastronomic side of the Jewish holidays, but without the holidays' rituals. I am the same way.

Jonathan Shiloach

PIONEER; COFOUNDER OF KIBBUTZ SHAMIR
(AT AGE EIGHTY-FIVE, HE STILL WORKS THERE EVERY DAY)
Kibbutz Shamir, Israel

My immediate family was very integrated in German society before Hitler came to power; but we never felt totally part of German society. By the time Hitler became leader of Germany, we knew we were not part of German society. My uncle, who believed with all his heart that if he acted like a good German, other Germans would not harm him, stayed in Germany and died in Theresienstadt. As a family, we did not keep many Jewish traditions. What my brother and I learned about Jewish religion and tradition came from living among other Jews. Before 1933, I joined the Jewish *Werkleute* [Work People] movement and became a Zionist. We learned all the trades that the future state of Israel would need in order to prosper. My brother joined the Jewish Boating Association. He was never a Zionist and eventually emigrated to the United States. Our group eventually emigrated to Palestine and we settled in the Golan Heights, in an area once known as Scorpion Hill. Back in 1935, it was covered with rocks. Today, it is covered with grass and trees and our homes, factories, public buildings, barns, and farms.

As opposed to people who talk about values, we here on the kibbutz live them through our work, our working on the land and for each other, sharing all that we make and earn, sharing responsibility. We shared the same bunkers during Arab invasions after the state of Israel was declared. We shared guard duty when our kibbutz was less than one hundred meters from the Syrian border. But whatever I have done, I have done it as an Israeli, not as a Jew.

I am connected to the land and do not follow a religious way of life. In the year 2000, there is no need to live as one did two or three thousand years ago. We study Torah on the kibbutz and teach it to our children. It is our history, after all. My wife and I recently visited Jordan and were excited to see the places mentioned in our Torah, in our history. The Torah tells us where we came from. But our future is with the land as it is today.

Kibbutz Shamir was established as a communal kibbutz. We were one big family and we took care of each other. Family life was always strong with Jews, for some reason. Maybe because of being surrounded by strangers in the Diaspora. Jewish family life is still closer than gentile family life.

Herbert A. Simon
PROFESSOR OF COMPUTER SCIENCE AND PSYCHOLOGY;
NOBEL LAUREATE IN ECONOMIC SCIENCES
Pittsburgh, Pennsylvania

Before I can answer what it means to me to be Jewish, I must define in what sense I am Jewish. There is both a genealogical and a socioreligious aspect to the latter question. My father's entire family, the Simons and the Bernays, were German Jews who had lived in the Rhineland for at least several centuries, and perhaps much longer, occupied as wine merchants and vintners. My maternal great-grandmother, born Dahl, was a Catholic from Bavaria who married a Jew, Alexander Goldschmidt, from Prague. Their daughter (my grandmother) married into the Merkel family in St. Louis, a family of Lutheran piano builders who came from Cologne. We retained contact with the Goldschmidt relatives, some, but not all, of whom remained Jewish, but my mother's other relatives were Protestant. So by Jewish rules of maternal determination, I guess I am not a Jew. By the rules promulgated by the Nazis, I definitely am. They would not have rejected me as fuel for their ovens.

Now the social side of it. Although my paternal grandmother maintained a kosher home in Germany, my father expressed no religious preference of which I was aware and participated in no religious groups or rites. His friends and associates were mostly business and professional colleagues and acquaintances, a few Jewish but most not. Of the few families in the neighborhood with whom we exchanged visits, several were Jewish but others not. Our middle-class, mainly skilled blue-collar neighbors were mostly Protestant, some Catholic, and a very few Jewish, and we did not live close to the principal Jewish community in Milwaukee, my boyhood home.

At the same time, my father always identified himself ethnically as a German Jew, and certainly took no steps to avoid any professional or social disadvantages that might have accrued to his Jewishness. Although we had no nonwhite friends or acquaintances, I conclude that this was because there were no such people in our neighborhood or in the professional groups that my family was part of. I certainly could not attribute their absence to any prejudices that I heard expressed or implied by my mother or father, and I acquired no ethnic prejudices from them, but rather a strong antipathy to such prejudices. In our home, blacks were Negroes (in the 1920s and 1930s), not "niggers"; the Italians Italians, not "wops"; and the Poles were Poles, not "Polacks." I played with the Russian Jewish girl who lived next door for a few years. (My German grandmother, visiting us, was scandalized by this, and I was scandalized by her prejudice.)

My mother maintained a nominal Christian affiliation, mainly liberal Congregationalist, during most of her life, although it was only in her later years, long after I had left home, that she attended church at all regularly. At times she expressed the belief, with some bitterness, that my father's Jewishness had hurt his engineering career, but the anger was directed towards those who she thought had exhibited the prejudice, not towards his Jewishness. She sometimes felt, with what basis I do not know, that she was rejected by the one family of my father's relatives who lived in Milwaukee because she was not Jewish.

While I was quite small, my elder brother picked up some anti-Semitic sentiments from school friends, and as a result was sent off to the synagogue for a few months of Sabbaths to reflect on his heritage. That is the only religious guidance (if that is what it was) that I recall either of us receiving from our parents. The upshot is that the decision about what being Jewish would mean to me was left up to me. From my high school years on, I was certain that I was an atheist, and still am. That did not prevent me from regularly attending the Congregational Church (with which most of my school friends' families were affiliated) and the meetings of the Christian Endeavor group associated with it. During the monthly communion services, when all Christians were asked to rise, I remained seated. Although I was not particularly Jewish in appearance, on any occasion where it made a difference, I made my Jewish ethnicity explicit. I did not want to "pass." At the same time, I acquired a deep distrust for the claims of superiority that any ethnic group, one or another, might make. I also acquired a belief, which I have never lost, that morality has little or nothing to do with formal religion.

My basic attitudes about being Jewish were firmly established before I reached adulthood and have not changed. I am American of Jewish origins and a member of the human race. My wife and I have long been members of the Unitarian Church because it provides social solidarity with others who are mainly liberal in their social views, as we are, and tolerant of great diversity in beliefs about theology, cosmology, and religious rites. (I attend church services only occasionally, finding more satisfaction in devoting Sundays to my scholarly work.) I do not see myself as belonging to any special group in society, certainly no ethnic group, and for many purposes I regard my highest loyalty as being owed to the human race rather than a national affiliation. In short, I am an assimilationist, but with no strong feeling that others who don't wish to assimilate should change their ways.

All of this sounds like sweet reasonableness, and I would give a very wrong impression of myself if I concluded without describing some of the ways in which I can and do feel very strong emotions relating to my Jewishness. First, I am very proud of my heritage in the way that most people are proud of their heritages—the vintner ancestors in Ebersheim, the craftsmen in Cologne, the goldsmith in Prague, and the farm girl from Bavaria who married him. I am especially proud of their diversity, and most especially of their ethnic and religious diversity. They seem to me to symbolize the family of humankind. I am proud that love for a Protestant girl of Scottish and German ancestry led me to continue this demonstration of the practicability of diversity (miscegenation is the technical term) and to procreate two more generations who have brought some Oriental blood into the stream. Surrounded by ghastly ethnically motivated events in Bosnia, Rwanda, Sri Lanka, India, the Middle East—the list is endless and does not exclude the United States—I derive from this family history a certain very guarded hope for a better future.

Second, the occasions when I regret my Jewishness—and there are some—are the occasions when I see Jews exhibiting the same ethnic insanity that we have suffered as the result of anti-Semitism. There is no place in my imagined future world for "chosen people." I confess that I am unable to sit through a Seder ceremony celebrating the victory of a vengeful deity visiting, on our behalf, all sorts of atrocities upon the men, women, and children of the "others." The Exodus is Bosnia all over again (or vice versa). Less horrifying, but poignant enough, I feel a great sadness at the increasing influence of Jewish fundamentalism, with its ethnic exclusiveness, in Israel. The value of Israel to the Jews and to the world disappears to the degree that Israel becomes another demonstration of religious exclusiveness and intolerance, even intolerance towards liberal Jews.

Third, my reason does not govern me so completely that I can, or want to, suppress or deny the exuberant joy I felt when "we" whipped the Arabs at the time of the partition, and in the three subsequent wars. My people showed themselves to be tough and smart, two qualities that I admire. Irrational and inconsistent? Definitely, but perhaps no more so than cheering for "our" Pittsburgh Pirates.

So I am deeply thankful for my Jewish heritage. By permitting me, while growing up, to be always conscious of my position as a member of a tiny, and sometimes hated, minority, it taught me the essentiality of tolerance to human survival, and it made me acutely aware of the much more severe inequities visited upon other minorities in our society and the need to work to end them. By handing down to me a tradition that places a high value upon learning, it opened up an exciting career in science that has given me marvelous pleasure and satisfaction. And by transmitting this heritage to me in a way that allowed me to select what was best in it, and to reject the parts I found unbelievable or ethically questionable, it has made me the most fortunate of heirs.

Reeva Slutzkin
Lusaka, Zambia

Being Jewish does not make any noticeable difference in my daily life or in my social life. Although I do take pride in the enormous courage my people have shown through centuries of sorrow and persecution. I also appreciate the moral culture that has been refined through suffering down through the centuries. But this is not a matter of religion to me. One does not have to be of any particular religious persuasion to have a sense of value. These come with believing and belonging to a group one identifies himself with. Guidance to one's fellow man is essential to life. Is this solely a Jewish value?

Steven Spiro
SOUVENIR SELLER
New York, New York

I was raised as a Jew. We didn't go to school on the Jewish holidays, I had a *bar mitzvah*, and I went to Hebrew school. We were taught that all other people hate us, the typical stereotype that a Jew grows up with. But it all means nothing to me now. It makes no difference to me if I'm Jewish or not. I don't practice my religion and I don't identify with the state of Israel. The only difference being Jewish makes is that I make sure to see Cecil B. De Mille's movie *The Ten Commandments* when it's on television.

Andrei Strihan
PROFESSOR OF AESTHETICS
Tel Aviv, Israel

Does being Jewish make a difference? No! To be Jewish means first of all to be a *mensch*. This is what marks the Jewish soul more than customs and form of worship. My father took me to the synagogue on the holidays, where I listened to the droning of old men as they said their prayers and was bored to death. But on Yom Kippur, the wonderful coloratura of the cantor awoke me from my lethargy and carried me to heaven. While the traditions that my family did keep brought me into the fold of the Jewish community, I did not actively pursue a Jewish identity. Not even during the time of forced labor in World War II, when racial and ethnic discrimination hit me with its full force, did I seek refuge in a Jewish identity. Inside me I wanted to be like all the people, free of any stigma, so I tried to stamp out my Jewish origin. One way was to change my family name, make it more Romanian, which I did in 1946, after liberation by the communists. What a delusion! The ideology I believed in so much, because it stressed the equality of all people, proved to be a lie, enhancing ethnic differences even more than the former society had. I came to believe that it was normal that a member of the majority receive all the benefits, and get the better jobs, whether he deserved it or not. This led to a type of conviction, humiliation, self-effacement, that is, it led to the attitude that a slave must have.

Over twenty years ago, after my son had emigrated to Israel and I was fired from my job, my wife and I also left Romania. I felt that at last I could be my Jewish self and live free of discrimination. Another illusion! This time, I faced discrimination from those who called themselves Jewish, a religious discrimination that is totalitarian in nature. Whoever does not fit the religious mold is not really Jewish. After more than twenty years in Israel, I cannot understand how people who have been the victims of horrible intolerance, persecution, and humiliation make other people go through the same things.

That is why I prefer to think of myself not as Jewish, but as a member of the human race, a citizen of the world.

Edward Teller

PHYSICIST, "FATHER OF THE NUCLEAR BOMB"; DIRECTOR EMERITUS OF THE LAWRENCE LIVERMORE NATIONAL LABORATORY
Stanford, California

There were five Hungarians who made an important contribution to American national security [John von Neumann, Leo Szilard, Eugene Weigner, Theodore von Karman, and Teller himself]. Jokingly, it was said that we are not Hungarians, but Martians. I claim that these five people did quite a lot in America's war effort. And even more afterwards. What you may not know, or perhaps you do: all five are Jews. However, I do not claim that Jews are more clever. It was clearly conveyed to me, early on, not in words but through behavior, "You are a Jew. That means you will experience prejudice. So if you want to get anywhere, you'd better be much better than everybody else. If you do a really good job, you will get over." I grew up with this conviction, that I had to do really well to get anywhere. Also, all five of us—incidentally, our families were not really religious—had to study abroad because there were severe limitations in Hungarian universities placed on Jewish students.

My wife is of the same class as I, except her family had converted to Christianity. This made no difference in her life. I don't think being Jewish made a lot of difference to me personally. It made some, as I already stated. Our children—we have two children—know that they are Jewish, but I don't think that I have transferred to them any feeling that on account of being Jewish they are at all different. And they look, I think, at the whole question of being Jewish as not something terribly important for them. After all, it is not comfortable to be different from other people. I would rather ignore this difference if I could. And to the extent it was possible, I did. Of course, it made a difference to me in that when Hitler came to power, I had to leave Germany. That is why I and the other four "Martians" landed in the United States.

Niels Bohr, probably the greatest physicist, is supposed to have said that monotheism is the best approximation to atheism. And I see a lot of monotheism practiced by Jews, if you know what I mean. The point is that the Jews have a God who has one very important property: nothing must be known about him. The high priest sees him once a year, but never reports what God has said. There is one God, and he is responsible for the laws, for every detail. Not only can you have no pictures of him, not only does he not have a beard, but nothing should be known about him. He is a very good approximation of not existing at all. I claim that the Jewish religion, by believing in one God and not naming any of his properties, has come as close to atheism as possible.

I'm not an atheist. I'm only a person who asserts, with emphasis, that he knows nothing about God. And that furthermore, to know nothing about the God of practically nothing is a very Jewish tradition. We have no pictures of him, we do not discuss his properties, we do not talk about his story. Only when we need an authority on which to base laws, we say, "On God's authority." Other than that, we know nothing. And with this, I am emotionally in agreement. I don't claim to know, I don't believe I can know, anything about God. I don't even know that he doesn't exist. To which I can add that I don't like to talk about things I do not know.

Georg Stefan Troller
SPECIAL CORRESPONDENT FOR ZDF (A GERMAN TELEVISION STATION)
Paris, France

Everyone knows I am Jewish, so I am Jewish. Does being Jewish make a difference? We are all the result of our genes, upbringing, circumstances, history. I am marked by my Viennese-Jewish birth, early anti-Semitic experiences, Germanic romanticism and poetry, emigration, service in the United States Army, my Paris home, my marriage to a German wife, my two daughters (I speak French to the one, English to the other), my television and literary work for postwar Germany, and other things besides. I am also marked by the murder of so much of my family in the Holocaust. I am marked by "looking Jewish," and as long as Jews are not persecuted again, there is nothing wrong with that.

I am Jewish the way I am Austrian, American, a father, a filmmaker, a writer, a lover. I don't feel that there is anything predominantly Jewish in me, nor in any other Jew, for that matter, unless they were brought up that way or made to suffer for it. I don't think there are any particular Jewish traits—at least I can't find anything in myself that I do not find, in this or that admixture, in any of my non-Jewish friends or acquaintances.

I am not proud of being Jewish or ashamed of it. I am neither particularly happy about it nor sorry. It's just one of the many things that went into the construction of my life. A challenge. A damned nuisance. A stimulus. A thorn in my flesh. Like innumerable other challenges and thorns.

I don't think Jews are "different."

Being Jewish has enriched my life, has made it difficult and interesting. It's simply something I have learned to live with, like this damned necessity right now to read Rimbaud till three in the morning.

JEWISH: DOES IT MAKE A DIFFERENCE?

Mischa Uralsky
JAZZ BAND LEADER
Bremen, Germany

I have made music, jazz, for over twenty years. Before that, I played traditional Russian music and, in between, Yiddish music, the type we play at weddings, *bar mitzvah* parties, and other occasions when we are *freilach*. It makes no difference to me that I am Jewish, but it makes a difference to me that others are. I talk to them through my music. I feel more Russian than Jewish, but a special kind of Russian, with more salt and pepper in my blood, and with the *tallit* [prayer shawl] to survive. Half my band is Jewish, although none of us lives like a Jew. But we care for each other. And when we feel a Jewish soul in the audience, no matter where, in a little town in Russia or a bigger city abroad, our hearts beat a different beat. For those who do not believe that this happens, I can only say, "If you were a Jew, you would know what I mean. Even if you eat pork, like I do, and do not fast on Yom Kippur, which for some reason I myself do not understand, I do."

Judith Urbanova
INTERNED IN THERESIENSTADT AT THE AGE OF TWO; WAITRESS AT
THE KOSHER RESTAURANT OF THE PRAGUE JEWISH FEDERATION
Prague, Czech Republic

There is no difference. There are good people and bad people. My husband was a Christian and a very good person. My children were raised as Christians.

What Hitler did not destroy of Judaism, fifty years of communism did. I just happen to be here at the community restaurant, where I work as a waitress, because a Jewish Federation now exists in Prague. And I go to the synagogue on the holidays.

Corinne Whittaker

COMPUTER ARTIST; EDITOR OF *DIGITAL GIRAFFE*, AN INTERNET MONTHLY
Carmel-by-the-Sea, California

The question touches a central nerve in me. Being Jewish, as I grew up in Connecticut, certainly did mean being different. There were Jewish schools, Jewish country clubs, Jewish quotas (ten percent at the Ivy League schools then), and Jewish holidays. It meant the wrath of an eastern European grandmother if my doll was used as the infant Jesus in a first-grade play. It meant being under constant pressure to conform to the ideals held up by a less-than-ideal but nevertheless demanding extended family organization. It meant that difference was branded on your soul at every turn. It meant a passionate desire to find out what lies on the other side of that difference, and then to deny all differences, in terms of organized religion anyway.

But here is a real personal irony when it comes to difference. I am an artist. I discovered that I have a rare genetic disorder, Gaucher's disease, which is concentrated in Jews of Ashkenazic descent. And it has been discovered that a disproportionately large percentage of Gaucher patients are artists.

Edmund Wolf

WRITER; JOURNALIST
London, England

If running away from what a person was born as can qualify as what makes my life different because I am Jewish, this would be my answer in a nutshell. It doesn't make me different from many others I know or about whom I read. Maybe this is what Jewishness is after all—an attempt to free oneself from a powerful set of assumptions and expectations only in order to find out that this is not possible after all.

I was born in Rzeszow, not far from Krakow, the place so often mentioned in connection to its Jewish population and culture. But mind you, it was not Poland, it was part of Austria at the time of my birth (in 1910). That I became a German writer, or more precisely a writer whose language of choice was German, has a lot to do with this historical reality. In Vienna I discovered the beauty and charm of the theater. My first play was performed when I was twenty-two years old, still a student! And while my life did not necessarily help me pursue my passion for play writing, I am still a playwright deep in my heart. I am neither the first nor the last Jewish playwright. There are many who are better, or at least better known. But I think that it has something to do with my Jewishness that I like theater. Jews love to debate, and love to do it for the public.

But it was not to be. I had success; I wanted to forget who I was. But in 1937, I immigrated to England. Where else if not in Shakespeare's country would somebody in love with the stage find a better place for pursuing his calling? As the war started, I discovered that even a Jew who escaped from Germany out of fear for his life could not escape the destiny of remaining an alien. I was interned and sent to Canada and freed only after the PEN Club intervened.

Back to my Jewishness. I continued to search for ways to reconcile my Jewish background, the Western culture to which Jews contributed so much, and the religion to which I did not want to submit. Probably this reconciliation never took place. As much as I desired to find a place in German culture, I was not allowed to. But still I respect it, and I hope that after the experience of the war, we all learned something. I wish being Jewish had not kept me from a career in the theater, but I know that without my Jewish heritage, I probably would have been less attracted to it.

Henri Wolf
GRAPHIC DESIGNER (*VOGUE* MAGAZINE); PHOTOGRAPHER
Long Island, New York

Vienna was my birthplace, a city where many different nationalities lived. Probably I would not have become aware of my Jewishness if we Jews had not been forced to leave when Hitler came to power.

Yes, I am aware of Jewishness. Especially of the consequences prompted by Nazi Germany. But I see these as a technicality. To be thrown out of the country of my birth was quite an experience. But in all honesty, being Jewish had little influence on my work or life. I never think about being Jewish. Sure, during a history of almost six thousand years, one generation of Jews inherited qualities from another. I have friends who are aristocrats, and the five hundred years of history of aristocracy makes a difference. In good and in bad. The values inherited by Jews from their precursors reflect the struggle for survival. Having faced antagonistic forces, Jews developed survival strategies, which Jewish intelligence reflects.

—cͨᴠᴐ—

Hana Zantovsky
TRANSLATOR; MEMBER OF PEN
Prague, Czech Republic

It is hard to say whether being Jewish makes a difference in my life. I married a man from a feudal Czech family that goes back to the Middle Ages. Mine is not an unusual case. My family has intermarried for three generations. My mother was Jewish, and so was her family. My father came from a Catholic mother and a Jewish father. A woman from America once asked a group of us Jewish women why we didn't choose to marry Jewish men. Simply put, after the war, there was no choice. Do not misunderstand me, I hold my husband in great respect. He knows a lot more about Judaism in Bohemia and about Judaism in general than I do. And he helped many Jews during the war and afterwards.

I never denied my Jewish origin. And I can identify with Jewish tradition, but in a Central European context, which means cultural, not religious. I recall my grandmother on my mother's side, who was the last one in the family who held strongly to Jewish traditions. I remember from my childhood that after the fast of Yom Kippur, the family would have a large dinner at her home. But Easter and Christmas were spent with the Christian part of the family. These holidays had their own poetry and have remained in my memory.

Hitler brought back some of my Judaism. After the war, I studied Torah in order to understand my background. I have given much thought to pursuing my Jewish identity. I am often invited to and participate in memorials held for Jewish communities in the Czech Republic and in secular celebrations pertaining to Jews and Israel.

Of course, my Jewishness makes a difference in my world view. It has given me a greater sensibility to how people treat each other. I have a certain reserve with people in that I wait to see how they react to me as an individual and as a Jew. My Jewishness also led to an interest in other peoples, even through the world of books. That is why I am a translator. And I tend to be a moralist, especially in the area of modern sexuality. In this day and age, however, I try to hide this side of me.

My values are mostly humanistic, influenced by Jan Masaryk. If you exclude the Ten Commandments, I could not think of any particularly Jewish values. In the Czech Republic, the intelligentsia tended to be philo-Semitic, so their values were in harmony with Jewish values.

⸏

Rafael Zeligman
NOVELIST
Munich, Germany

Some people would condemn me as a *yored*, a person who failed or gave up. Only because I left Israel to return to Germany. I am a Jew whose language is German and whose culture goes back sixteen hundred years. This synergy is what makes the difference in my life. My parents emigrated from Germany to Palestine in 1934. When they returned to Germany after the war, I entered school here as an illiterate and failed miserably. But I managed to become a writer, and not a bad one. As a chronicler of Jewish life in postwar Germany, I was embraced neither by Jews nor Germans. I am driven by the Jewish obsession of contradicting—the idealized image of the Jewish victim, the idealized image of the new German with high moral standards.

It is not that I try to sit on two chairs at once, I try to sit on no chair and still remain comfortable. After my first novel, the Jewish press in Germany accused me of being a *Nestverschmutzer* [equivalent to one who airs dirty laundry in public, but the connotation is much stronger in German, almost equivalent to slanderer]. And why should I support the appearance of contrition that many Germans show? They go through the motions of regret for their actions under Hitler. But after flirting with the romantic Israeli kibbutzniks, they discovered the Palestinian cause: the victims of their victims. When I wrote about this, the Germans were not happy. But in my role as a writer, as an outside observer of the world I live in, in other words, as a Jew, I do not have to please, but to confront people with their own duplicity.

Moshe Zimmerman

PROFESSOR OF SOCIAL HISTORY, HEBREW UNIVERSITY
Jerusalem, Israel

To me, being Jewish does not make a difference; being Israeli makes a difference. "Jewish" is an identifier for people living in the Diaspora, in Europe, North Africa, the United States, and in other countries. I identify with the land, the nation. I am not religious, so the values I have are common to all humanity. Sure, they are written in the Ten Commandments, but they have been enlarged upon by philosophers and social scientists who are not Jewish, but mainly European. I do not have this romantic notion of the Jewish people, which developed during the Diaspora in Europe, as long-suffering and enduring, despite hardships, because they remained true to their tradition. Israel presents us with a new reality, a new measure of identity. We have to live for the future.

Fred Zinnemann

FILM DIRECTOR
London, England

A person's character is his destiny. The line comes from Robert Louis Stevenson and pretty much defines my credo. And this is my answer to your question. Sheriff Kane in my film *High Noon* answers the question even better: "I am the same man, with or without the star." In Vienna, where I was born; in Paris, where I lived when I was young; in Berlin and in Los Angeles; and now here in London, I can only repeat the same words. I am in sync with Jewishness through my work, but I did not want to let my Jewishness become my destiny.

CHAPTER EIGHT

—— ⚭ ——

Repairing the World

T he respondents whose answers constitute this chapter emphasized their commitment to making the world a better place for all its people—Jew and Gentile. They also acknowledged that the ethic or motive underlying their actions derives from the teachings of Judaism. It is no surprise that many of these respondents have pursued careers in politics or law.

Bella Abzug

DIRECTOR, WOMEN USA, WOMEN'S FOREIGN POLICY COUNCIL;
U.S. CONGRESSIONAL REPRESENTATIVE FROM NEW YORK, 1971–1977
(DECEASED 1998)
New York, New York

It is my Jewish background that drives me to be active in political life, the life of the people. Not just Jews, but oppressed people from all walks of life. First as a congressperson, now as a spokesperson, at the United Nations and on a national level in the United States, for women's rights here and all over the world.

Walter Annenberg

COMMUNICATIONS MAGNATE; PHILANTHROPIST
Rancho Mirage, California

For every advantage one has in life, one has at least the responsibility of balancing that with the less privileged.

Alexander Bergman

LAWYER
Riga, Latvia

On Ludzas Street I can still hear the voices of the people killed in the winter of 1941. Here, at the wall of the old Jewish cemetery, the frozen corpses were piled on top of each other. About twenty-eight thousand people were shot in the Rumbula woods. If you could survive as a Jew after that moment, you were marked by your Jewishness. We might not be better than others, but we have suffered more. Suffering makes a difference. As a lawyer by training, I have committed myself to fight suffering—not only Jewish suffering, everyone's.

Norma Brier

EXECUTIVE DIRECTOR OF RAVENSWOOD, A JEWISH CENTER
FOR PEOPLE WITH LEARNING DISABILITIES
Middlesex, England

From a personal viewpoint, being Jewish means I have a commit-ment to a minority group of people who have been oppressed in the past and who have continued to reestablish themselves in society and remain major players in it, especially in regard to business, the arts, media, etc. In regard to organisational life, I am particularly interested in the care and education and support of people with learning disabili-ties (mental handicap) and their families, and here again, similarities abound. A hitherto oppressed group of people, often scapegoated by communities, who have the potential to reestablish themselves, but require a great deal of championing and support to do so. I see a link between the Jewish perspectives and the work involved here, and par-ticularly feel that the Jewish learning-disabled group are a double mi-nority and therefore would easily fade out of sight and out of mind, if organisations like Ravenswood did not exist to constantly keep the needs of these special people in the hearts and minds of our supporters and other statutory bodies.

While I do not believe in offering a Jewish way of life as a panacea to people with learning disabilities, I do believe that religion and cultural background ensure the uniqueness of each individual. The Jewish cul-tural environment offers a variety of tastes, smells, and sounds, part and parcel of helping people with learning disabilities.

In Judaism, not only the Ten Commandments are important, but also the gifts that each individual brings to the community. Sadly, there is in Jewish life a sense of high expectation for Jewish children. People with learning disabilities can often feel devalued, and it is a poor com-ment on the Jewish community when such people are considered with shame and guilt.

The values that guide me personally are the ones that encourage us to think of people in terms of what they can do, as opposed to concen-trating on what they cannot. These are the values of respect for the individual, equality, dignity, and practicing my beliefs as opposed to just talking about them. It is good to be Jewish and to be part of a group of people who have held the value of human life sacred. It is important, however, to keep in mind that the goals of high achieve-ment and financial and material reward are not alternatives to the val-ues of respect and of *tzedakah*.

Alexandre Bronstein

COMPUTER SCIENTIST

Palo Alto, California

My Jewishness has been reinforced from without and from within. From without because the world is still full of *un*official anti-Semitism. Just take a look at the Internet for good old-fashioned incitement—in multiple languages—to murdering Jews. From within comes the most powerful drive, though. Once you become convinced of the existence of God, and once it seems plausible, although uncomfortable, that the Torah is His will, it becomes hard to remain intellectually honest and not act Jewish—in the old-fashioned way. Emotionally, I feel several thousand years of ancestors who were beaten, tortured, and murdered so I could be Jewish. It is hard to throw that away. In the final analysis, it's physics: I am a Jew, just like a stone is a stone, whether I like it or not. My practice at this point becomes simply a matter of intellectual honesty or internal consistency.

Jews still have—more so than other groups—a passion for a world free of human suffering. And perhaps even more Jewish is our irrational conviction that it will happen. We also hold to the mandate to develop our intellect as much as possible, and, paradoxically perhaps, a mandate to ignore our intellect when God says so. That's the ultimate act of "being a witness to God." I do this every time I tie my left shoe before my right one—and I have a Ph.D. in theoretical computer science from Stanford University! What I do for a living—high technology and mathematics—is not directly related to my being Jewish, except for the ultimate goal I hold dear: to reduce human suffering.

The mandates Jews have from God get me back up every time I fall down, emotionally and otherwise. If I could play back thirty-six years of life-tape, I could say that Judaism has guided many if not most of my actions: from giving all my childhood savings—not much at age twelve—to send to Israel to help during the Yom Kippur war, to giving money to the same beggar week after week at the age of thirt-six. And a zillion other daily decisions and actions in my marriage and family because "that's what a Jewish husband/dad does."

Michael Cernea

CHIEF SOCIAL POLICY AND SOCIOLOGY ADVISER, WORLD BANK
Washington, D.C.

My identity as a Jew has had a profound influence on my life, my values, my behavior, along two most essential dimensions: self-perception and perception by others. Why? For one thing, I nearly lost my life because of my Jewish identity during the famous pogrom in Iasi, Romania, in June 1941, when some ten thousand Jews were murdered in cold blood, simply because they were Jews. Just for being Jewish, twenty members of my own family were exterminated in camps in Transnistria during the Holocaust. For decades afterwards, I endured "hot" and "cold," overt and covert anti-Semitism, raw and violent or refined, pernicious and hypocritical. This, of course, is only part of why "being Jewish" has made a huge difference to my life. But this experience has been intense—and definitional.

From early childhood, my parents set me on a path of learning. They enabled me to study the Torah, the commentaries, and the writings of the prophets, forever shaping my mind and my sensitivity. This too was, and is, definitional. All this made me ponder early in my youth about matters of personal and collective identity, about "multiculturalism" *avant la lettre*, and about existence in a pluralistic society. I even had a passing belief that broader social concerns could override individual identity. But I soon learned what a sad illusion that was.

I feel a deep and quiet pride in being heir to the culture that has given humankind the ten moral commandments, and so much more. Because many of my ancestors paid with their lives for their faith in, and respect for, their Jewish heritage, maintaining this heritage, enriching it if possible, and passing it on is a commandment intrinsic to my existence.

As far as values are concerned, is retaining a monopoly important? I would emphasize outer- rather than inner-orientedness. The fact that many other cultures have embraced and internalized values originating in Judaism is infinitely more important for defining Jewish values and their contribution than the values that might have remained today specific to Judaism.

Important distinctions occur in how values are practiced, not just declared. My sense is that "solidarity in need" has been, and remains, a core practical value of Judaism. While not exclusive to Jewish culture, it seems to me that this sense of communal responsibility is harbored and practiced by Jews more intensely than in many other cultures that I have come to know, cultures which are strongly permeated by individualism. I cannot forget the beauty and force of a moral injunction that I learned in my childhood: *Shlach lachmecha al p'nei hamayim* . . . "Cast your breadloaf on the water's surface; the waves may carry it to a distant shore where a hungry one may need it."

From my very early experiences, I developed more than an abstract appreciation of the Jewish value of social justice: I grew with a thirst and a driving need to act myself to help bring it about. Because I believe in the transforming power of ideas, I have also spent a good part of my life writing about the values and ideas I hold dear. Fortunately, during the second half of my professional life I have been able to influence not only ideas, but also the channeling of significant financial resources towards more equity in this world, towards the reduction of poverty, towards realizing social justice.

Perception by others, as I said earlier, reinforces Jewish identity and culturally constructs it. I felt it to be a great tribute to my Jewish identity when non-Jewish colleagues at the World Bank publicly traced my choices and positions on social policy and moral issues, during decades of international work, to my Jewish identity and personal history. The decades I invested in the causes of the powerless and forcibly displaced people and refugees, in fighting impoverishment, have led to tangible results in many countries. And within both illuminist and "engineering" traditions, I have placed great faith, and a lifetime of work, in trying to apply social science, social knowledge, sociology, and anthropology to the rational conduct of public affairs, to "putting people first," to promoting social betterment.

We are links in a long chain. In an immediate family and intergenerational perspective, little else can equal the gratification of seeing how fruits ripen on the tree: how my children have learned and absorbed these values, how they cherish their identity, and how in turn they are nurturing these high values in the minds and hearts of their own children.

Alan Shawn Feinstein

BUSINESSMAN; PHILANTHROPIST (LOUIS FEINSTEIN SCHOLAR-
SHIP FUND, INSTITUTE FOR PUBLIC SERVICE, PROVIDENCE COLLEGE;
WORLD HUNGER CENTER, BROWN UNIVERSITY)
Cranston, Rhode Island

The responsibility to do all I can to see that the world is a better place when it comes my time to leave it than it was when I arrived.

David Finn

CEO, RUDER & FINN, PUBLIC RELATIONS CONSULTANTS;
PHOTOGRAPHER; WRITER; PAINTER
Washington, D.C.

In my family, being Jewish has always meant devotion to study and commitment to ethical behavior. As a child, I worried that this treasured heritage might be obscured when my father, a writer, decided to change our family name from Finkelstein to Finn. Proud as I was of my father and his writings under the name Jonathan Finn, I dreaded that people would think we wanted to hide our Jewishness. My mother dealt with the problem by laughingly calling ourselves the Finklestein-Finns. My way has been to identify the higher priorities of my life ever more strongly with Jewish values.

This has been particularly true in relation to the Jewish ethical tradition, an approach to life that I absorbed from my uncle Louis Finkelstein, the former chancellor of the Jewish Theological Seminary. When weighing the moral consequences of business decisions, for example, the Ethics Committee of our public relations firm seeks knowledgeable counsel to guide our thinking. I will always remember how some years ago a professor at the Seminary helped us make the decision to resign the sizable Greek tourism account after three colonels seized power and installed a military dictatorship.

Other elements also lie at the core of my Jewishness: the life cycle that our traditions—such as circumcision, *bar* and *bat mitzvahs*, weddings, and *Kaddish*—and holidays represent and recall. My wife and I have been married forty-eight years, and I want our ten grandchildren to know that one reason our life together has been so fulfilling is our sense of being part of the Jewish people.

[*From* Why Be Jewish? *Reprinted with the permission of the American Jewish Committee.*]

Ruth Bader Ginsburg

ASSOCIATE JUSTICE OF THE U.S. SUPREME COURT
Washington, D.C.

"Justice, justice shalt thou pursue" are the words I keep on the walls in my chambers. The late Supreme Court Justice Arthur Goldberg said, "My concern for justice, for peace, for enlightenment, all stem from my heritage." I am fortunate to be linked to that heritage. The Jewish tradition prized the scholarship of judges and lawyers. As anti-Semitic restrictions were lifted in various countries, Jews were drawn to the legal profession. In the United States, law became the bulwark against the injustices that Jews had experienced in many lands and for countless generations. As opposed to keeping and enforcing law and order, which is what the lawmakers of the Third Reich did, Jewish jurists used the law to extend equal rights for others. I hope that in my years on the bench of the Supreme Court of the United States, I will have the strength and courage to remain constant in the service of the age-old demand.

[*Adapted from Justice Ginsburg's address to the Annual Meeting of the American Jewish Committee, May 1995. From* Why Be Jewish? *Reprinted with the permission of the American Jewish Committee.*]

Laurence Gratiot

CRIMINAL LAWYER
Paris, France

It is my Jewish heritage that compels me to seek justice, even for those who are accused of heinous crimes.

Walter Homolka

RABBI; HEAD OF GREENPEACE, GERMANY
Munich, Germany

It's not important how one becomes a Jew. It's important what he makes of being Jewish. Many Jews do not base their Judaism on religion. But for me, the religious aspect is the nucleus of being Jewish. Judaism is a house with many mansions. Orthodox pretensions to being the only true Judaism make me sad, because as a people we are united by the very variety of our existence.

Ion Ianosi
PHILOSOPHER; UNIVERSITY PROFESSOR
Brasov and Bucharest, Romania

There's no point in retelling the misery we Jews went through during the fascist period before World War II and during the German occupation. I lived through it by immersing myself in literature and essays, mainly by French authors. When the liberation came, I welcomed it full of optimism for the future. I embraced socialism. In the utopia I had constructed for myself, complete equality of all people was adequate compensation for earlier frustrations. For this, I was willing to surrender whatever remained of the family assets. Even when the communists expropriated our large house in the center of the city, I did not want to emigrate, like many of the Jews and Germans did. I was never a Zionist, and if I had emigrated to Israel, I probably would have lived on a kibbutz.

As a university professor, I never thought about what it meant to be Jewish, especially in a country with a decreasing Jewish population. I never idealized the Jews. I was a Romanian-speaking cosmopolitan, living under a nationalistic-communist dictatorship. But as a Jew, I was lucky: certain positions were closed to me, positions that might have led to taking advantage of the system, like so many did. So, despite some outward conformity, I was able to keep my honor.

In 1974, my book on the prophet Jonah was published. In 1994, another book on Jewish and Christian biblical sources. In 1980, 1989, and 1995, I was able to have my memoirs published, in which I discussed my Jewishness. I am one of the "people of the book," with all that this entails. Messianic utopias fascinate me, even the ones that have failed. I am a prodigal son of a bourgeoisie to which I shall never return. What remains for me to do? To go ahead educating a second generation of intellectuals at the university. To visit friends. To take care of grandchildren. To listen to music. To read and reread books. And to write, for as long as I am able.

Anna Landau
INSURANCE AGENT
Antwerp, Belgium

It is not only the past from which we Jews extract our self-definition. I know how much—some think not enough—talk takes place
about the role of the Jewish woman. People want to tell us that we
Jewish women are blessed by the role given to us. I, for one, think that
the blessing is in the role we play in family life, in the community, and
in society. My Jewishness means that I was encouraged to study and
that my ideas did not go unnoticed. It also means that I was given responsibilities early on.

All Jewish organizations are for me a chance to be active in fulfilling
my role as a Jew. In particular, the women's organizations are a very
stimulating environment for learning more about tradition, but also
about what we can do in this world of conflict, pain, unequal opportunity. If what I do makes a difference in the world—my little world of
family, friends, community, and my business—this difference represents the effects of trying to live like a Jew.

Egon Lansky
SENATOR, NATIONAL PARLIAMENT
Prague, Czech Republic

My background, my childhood, was marked by Nazism, the Holocaust, World War II. I was in a number of concentration camps and
was liberated from Theresienstadt. In my adult life, the consciousness
of being Jewish brightened my horizon and broadened my perspective
on humanity. I realized that I shared a culture with others around the
world. However, there is very little that I can call "religious" about
this consciousness, although I do grasp the connection between the
Jewish religion and its culture, even the religious connection between
Judaism and Christianity.

Judaism still has, in my opinion, very strong values centered on the
family. The Italians and Greeks, for example, also value the family, but
the Jewish family bond has a different root. Centuries of living as outcasts in Western societies has given the value of family a different accent. Family was a matter of survival.

Education also remains a strong Jewish value. Jewish parents will still do all in their power to help the children get a good start in life. This, too, must be seen against the background of social acceptance as a minority. Jews choose those roads to social acceptance through professions such as law and medicine, professions that were closed to them due to the *numerus clausus* practiced in universities throughout Europe.

If there are any other Jewish values that I practice in my life and work, then they remain on the unconscious or subconscious level. All the values and knowledge that I have of Judaism are part of my general outlook. I cannot point to any particular value or custom that guides me. In general, the Jewish outlook on humanity has the greatest impact on my decisions and actions, especially regarding the question of human rights. I try to be visible on this question, for example, by my stand in favor of granting civil rights to the Gypsies here in the Czech Republic.

Tom Lantos

U.S. CONGRESSIONAL REPRESENTATIVE FROM CALIFORNIA
Washington, D.C.

Although both my parents were Jewish, I feel that I am more of a passive type of Jew. Being Jewish means being committed to a legacy of caring social activism, and the possibility of creating a better and more just and compassionate social order. Being a Jew also means being committed to Israel. For me, Israel is the most significant aspect of Judaism, now and in the future.

Tony Leon

LEADER OF THE DEMOCRATIC PARTY; MEMBER OF PARLIAMENT
Cape Town, South Africa

Growing up as a Jew in the Diaspora, in particular in a country with a very small but cohesive Jewish population, has undoubtedly made a difference. Although I attended non-Jewish primary and high schools

---

in Durban, South Africa, I did have a very rudimentary Jewish education in the form of *bar mitzvah* lessons and so forth. At my school, I was made acutely aware of the fact that I was Jewish, being one of twelve Jewish boys in a school of five hundred (essentially Methodist in denomination). I think Jews were regarded as having certain characteristics, mainly negative. The extent to which Jews conformed to or rebutted the stereotype determined what sort of existence one had.

In my political life, where, in the parliament of South Africa there are few Jews, my Judaism has not been a particular issue, although sometimes it is used by opponents to make a hostile or negative point. For example, "Jews are rich" or "Jews are capitalists." These are particularly pejorative concepts with the very strong trade union movement in South Africa, with which my party and I have political differences.

Among the values that are Jewish-specific are close family ties, the value of education, the concept of justice, and liberal notions of the freedom of expression and movement. Many of these concepts grew out of biblical injunctions, such as those of the prophet of social justice, Amos, and out of the circumstances of the Diaspora. In respect to South African Jewry, which came from the Pale of settlement in tsarist Russia to escape pogroms and religious persecution, social justice is of prime importance and has spilled over into daily and communal life. They have certainly informed my own political agenda and personal beliefs. These concepts are no longer unique to Judaism, having been taken up by other groups and religions. Social justice and personal responsibility are the values of prime importance to me.

—⁕—

Carl Levin

U.S. SENATOR FROM MICHIGAN
Detroit, Michigan

What difference does being Jewish make? Education is critical to us as a people. It is the path our grandparents and parents charted for success. We cannot sit by and watch the government cut education programs.

Our dream has always been social justice. Our forebears organized their way out of sweatshops. We cannot sit by and watch newer immigrants, who sweat in the fields rather than factories, be exploited. Responding to injustice is central to our integrity as a people. By fighting for justice, we reaffirm our past and redeem our future.

Yehudi Menuhin

VIOLINIST (DECEASED 1999)
London, England

Being Jewish is the privilege and the burden of belonging to perhaps the oldest literate, moral, and religious heritage, unbroken in its continuity, far more durable than any national sovereignty has ever succeeded in lasting.

Being a Jew means constantly to remember—from biblical history and the Pharaohs to the Inquisition and Hitler—and to be prepared for the recurrent repetition of such events until the Jews can teach humanity, as did so many of our prophets, including Jesus and those who followed, that any persecution based on religious, racial, or national motives can only spell continued tragedy and suffering, continued injustice for all peoples.

Persecutions have grown in size and scope with the growth of nations and their illusion of omnipotence and sovereignty and coincide with the most effective expressions of false superiority—predatory greed, prejudice, and hate masquerading under a "holy compulsion," a crusade, a "mission." As a Jew, I must guard against playing their game and be true to the Ten Commandments.

Being Jewish means to learn to project oneself and to hold out the hand of friendship at the very same time. It is very difficult to treat one's enemy as an imminent friend, yet it is essential for a true Jew to learn this and to teach it.

Alfred Moses

U.S. AMBASSADOR TO ROMANIA
American living in Bucharest, Romania

I had the good fortune of being raised in an Orthodox home in which Sabbath was a day of prayer and rest, the holidays were days of joy, and *kashrut* was strictly observed. When I became a teenager, I felt more and more that these observances took time away from enjoying good all-American sports like baseball and football. However, Hitler, the Holocaust, and then the establishment of the state of Israel awakened me to the fact that Jewishness was most important to me.

While external threats to Judaism have diminished in the United

States, Jews are questioning the reason for continuing as Jews. I tell young people that Judaism has the task of uplifting humankind through living the ethical and moral principles that are part of our covenant. It is this dedication to repairing the world that motivated my practice as a lawyer, my public service as special assistant in the Carter government and as ambassador to Romania, a country I first came to know through helping Jews and others to get out from behind the Iron Curtain. In all these endeavors, the teachings of the Torah and Talmud have been my inspiration.

[*From* Why Be Jewish? *Reprinted with the permission of the American Jewish Committee.*]

—— ⌀ ——

Stephen Rhinehardt
JUSTICE OF THE SUPREME COURT OF CALIFORNIA
San Francisco, California

A person's basis for reasoning goes back to his background, of which religion is a part. It can be organized or it can be a question of cultural background. Being Jewish does not necessarily mean that one adheres to the religious aspects of Judaism. One is born Jewish if the mother is Jewish. Even one Jewish parent can color your experience. Certain things come with being born a Jew. Traditions, values, and attitudes are transferred through a kind of osmosis, even if they are not actively taught.

Growing up in New York City during a time when anti-Semitism was accepted social practice made a difference in my formation. Religious or not, a Jew was reminded that he was Jewish when he came up against discrimination, so I relate strongly to this. But the Jewish outlook instills respect for intellectual pursuits, which led me to read a lot as I grew up.

Values in Judaism are probably more a matter of degree of feeling than any specifically Jewish value. Jews emphasize things that other religions or other philosophies do not. More than any other group, Jews are consumed with a sympathy with human problems, human rights, and justice. These are part of our history and heritage. We believe that the less fortunate deserve to be helped, even if this means that the state should do it. Helping the less fortunate is not based on an individual act of charity. It is a social obligation. As opposed to other religions concerned more with the hereafter, Jews believe in making this life better.

Being a judge is not science. A judge has to rely on all his knowledge and wisdom in deciding a case that is more than routine application of a law. For example, how does one define "fundamental rights"? In addition to a knowledge of history, sociology, philosophy, and some science, a judge relies on the ideas that he learned throughout his life. In my case, this includes my experience as a Jew.

—◌◦◌—

Helen Suzman

MEMBER OF PARLIAMENT
Sandton, South Africa

During my years in Parliament as an opposition member of the apartheid government, I have been the recipient of many anti-Semitic remarks, but I cannot claim that this antagonism in any way influenced me. What I can say is that many of the values to which I have always adhered could be closely correlated with the Jewish ethos, or to be more specific, to the *Ethics of the Fathers*. These values include consistency, principles, rule of law, and simple justice.

—◌◦◌—

Shmuel Trigano

PROFESSOR OF SOCIOLOGY; DIRECTOR, SCHOOL OF JEWISH
STUDIES, ALLIANCE ISRAÉLITE UNIVERSELLE
Paris, France

In our day, the Jewish experience acquires greater meaning because it is faced with a serious test on which its soul and existence depends, in which it must put its authenticity to the test. The reason for this is specific to Jewish history. After an exile of twenty centuries and endless tribulations, and since the creation of the state of Israel at the end of the Shoah, Judaism renewed relations with the world outside it, with history. It is no longer "protected" by exile. Indeed, if the "return to Zion" is the beginning of the realization of a messianic hope (and one can think of it as such since nothing like it has occurred for twenty centuries), it is now that the veracity and credibility of the Jewish experience is at stake. Perhaps we assist at the conclusion of millennia of waiting.

The reason for such a situation is also universal. We live at the end of modernity, the collapse of its ideals and notably of the ideal of unending progress and of man's omnipotence. This universal crisis restores to the message of Israel all its importance. This is not a rhetorical affirmation. The Jews have lived modernity with intensity and passion; they were among its principal actors. The Shoah definitively shook this experience and obliges Jews to revisit modern civilization, to make a *cheshbon ha-nefesh*, to recognize and analyze their failures and successes. That is why, on meeting the challenge of the crisis that confronts them, they can also face the challenge of the collapse of modernity. It is upon their ability to face these challenges that the present and continuity of the Jewish message depends, as well as the very existence of the Jews. Today, this ability is far from evident. My conception derives from the hypothesis that the message of Judaism still has meaning and is even unique; and it has been exhausted neither by Christianity nor by modernity. Is it possible for our generation to find in the words from Sinai answers to the great questions of contemporary society? This hypothesis inspires my philosophic work. To find the answers is possible only through a heroic effort, and not at all from the passive appreciation of the Jewish heritage. The Word from Sinai houses unique solutions to contemporary dramas (in politics, society, for couples and for individuals) or at least an original way of posing the questions that these dramas give rise to.

Among the original contributions that make Judaism so relevant is a conception of time that escapes the fatal cycle of birth, apex, and decline, and a vision of the world as unfinished, in the formative process. The individual human being is supposed to take part in the birth of the humanity given to him by the Creator. In the social domain, the model of alliances that link individuals through giving and sharing also opens a new conception of human relations, where unity hovers but does not settle, allowing for the uniqueness of each one to be manifest without making an attempt at social bonds, but without ignoring them either. In the multiplicity of the world and society, the contemplation of the One is possible because man sees himself distinguished by his undertakings and by his existential investments. The society outlined here is altogether different from consumer society.

Judaism is also a civilization of the Book, the example of a society at the center of which is the text, inventing a social space and time entirely different from the institutional centralism of modernity and more of a bearer of a future for cybernetic society than the state model.

Judaism is animated by a conception of the divine that generates intellectual clarity and spiritual enthusiasm, far removed from the magic and mystery that are the lot of many religions and contemporary religiosities, a God who manifests Himself through a text and allots liberty to man, a one God in whom all values unite without annulling one another.

The confrontation between Judaism and the crisis of modernity is an occasion to put to work an epoch that is greater than modernity, to blaze the trail of a new adventure in human civilization. Within this configuration the currency of the message of Sinai will come about, on the condition that a new creativity be developed, that a new commentary adequate to the demands of the twenty-first century be elaborated.

In the opinion of many, the Jewish people is the oldest among humanity. Its members speak almost the same language and worship the same God, live in the same symbolic structure as in antiquity, despite the considerable developments that Judaism experienced. It is testimony to the origin of a humanity that is today disoriented and lost. This people itself, nevertheless, has not escaped this perplexity, but it has in itself the resources of its long memory. Dispersed among all civilizations and all peoples, it constitutes a sort of inner people of humanity, a vault of resonance in which all the echoes of the world are heard.

I remain Jewish through faith in such an experience and through belief in the veracity of moral consciousness inaugurated with the departure of Abraham from Ur of the Chaldees. I am deeply persuaded that Jewish existence plays a role in the fate of humanity, even when the Jewish people forgets its calling. This engagement is not purely individualistic. The alliance forged by Abraham and confirmed by Moses is a bond that still unites contemporary Jews with the past, but also and especially with the future and with hope, with divinity but also with humanity. To be Jewish is the synthesis of affiliation and of alliance. Today, we must rediscover this dimension of alliance in a Jewish condition that too often remains at the level of ethnicity. The stake of Jewish destiny is not played solely in relation to other nations, but also in relation to the Jews themselves. This is the most burning question today, which will decide their relation with the world and the resurgence of their spiritual calling.

CHAPTER NINE

---◦◦◦---

"The Interesting Traditions Are the Ones We Stick To"

This chapter consists primarily of responses from Jews who look to tradition as the main expression of, or connection to, Judaism. Tradition is defined in a variety of ways: as *mitzvot* given in the Torah, as holidays and customs shaped and re-shaped through time, as vital guides for living subject to reinterpretation in order to meet changing circumstances. Other respondents included in this chapter stressed their awareness of Jewish history and the importance of carrying it forward.

Benjamin Almasanu

STUDENT OF VETERINARY MEDICINE
Bexley, Ohio

Being Jewish means that I am part of a distinctive religious and cultural heritage that provides me with a link connecting me to my people down through the ages and with future generations of Jews. Judaism also provided me with many of the values I hold dear: a sense of family, a sense of justice, a sense of what is right and wrong. Although I do not follow all the traditions of Orthodox Judaism, its basic rules serve as guidelines for me to follow. While the Jewish law contains clearly defined rights and wrongs, it also provides for flexibility in that there is room for inquiry and debate.

Judaism is especially significant in my life because it emphasizes that although individuals may choose their own destinies, much in human life remains unintelligible and uncontrollable—influenced and controlled only by the will of God.

Orna Attias

DANCER
Israeli living in Cologne, Germany

As an Israeli, the word "Jewish" has no meaning for me. I cannot separate being Jewish from being Israeli. I do not see anything different about being Jewish because in Israel, Judaism is the standard, the way of life.

I was born into a traditional, that is, observant, family and was raised according to the commandment "Honor your mother and father" and everything that goes with obeying authority. These traditions tell me who and what I am, and where I am going. But I am not Orthodox, I do not live my life thinking about each thing the Torah says. I know that I will have a traditional home and pass on the Jewish traditions to my children: the holidays, lighting candles.

And I will teach my children that they have the right to choose. My parents never forced me to keep certain laws of the Torah or teachings of the prophets. The Torah was presented to me as the law of liberty, and to me, this is a great value.

Josh Backon

PHYSICIAN
Jerusalem, Israel

Jewish is part and parcel of my identity. It gives me a focus. I know what's expected of me and what my response will be to a given situation.

—⁓—

Tomas Böhm

PHYSICIAN; PSYCHOANALYST
Lidingö, Sweden

My Judaism gives me a very concrete feeling of history, destiny, and belonging to a group. I live in Sweden because my parents had to escape from Austria before World War II. And they lived in Austria because they and their families had to escape from Hungary and Poland at earlier times in history.

But instead of sharing a heritage of persecution, I search for the positive values in being Jewish. In Sweden, this means having different values regarding family, education, history, international relations, food, and religion itself. For me, the most Jewish characteristic is tolerance of differences. Judaism is not a missionary religion; you don't try to convince other people to be followers. Also, our history endows us with sympathy towards minorities, marginal groups, and persecuted groups and individuals. The other values—family, tradition, etc.—are not Jewish in the same way that tolerance is. Other peoples have strong family values and strong ties to a national or ethnic tradition. The values that guide me have to do with being both inside and outside, trying to tolerate and integrate differences.

Hanna Brodt

OWNER OF REAL ESTATE COMPANY
Munich, Germany

When I was a child growing up in Silesia, there was a clear-cut division between Jews and non-Jews. I did not understand why, it just was. I lived in fear knowing only that I was a stranger, I did not belong to Poland. My family was nonassimilationist, and to this day I would not want to be a Gentile. But today, in Munich, I live in among Gentiles, I deal with them. When I moved to a very good address in Munich, the neighbors welcomed me. To this day we remain on friendly terms, even though I am an observant Jew. I have no more fear.

Although I run a real estate business, I am, and always have been, a *Yiddishe mama*. The *Yiddishe mama* is still different from the non-Jewish mother. She is responsible for passing religion and tradition to her children by maintaining a Jewish home. She sets the mood for the home.

Himan Brown

PIONEER IN RADIO DRAMA; TELEVISION AND RADIO PRODUCER
New York, New York

My parents were not religious, so I did not have a strong background in Torah, although charity was an overwhelming force in my life. But I celebrated my *bar mitzvah,* and the entire cultural life at home was Yiddish: the daily Yiddish newspaper, Yiddish music, and of course the many traditional Jewish holidays which were celebrated more for their traditional values rather than their religious significance. My world was Jewish and not until I was finished with grade school and had to go to a high school outside the neighborhood did I realize there was another culture.

The Yiddish theater was flourishing. It was really the Yiddish theater which had a tremendous influence on my life as a Jew. Jewish drama, humor, comedy, music were never taken for granted. In 1937, I began to create and produce for radio and film endless dramas relating to all that was happening in the world.

There is no question in my mind that the emotional drive which makes all my efforts work is my commitment to the Jewish ethic. The Talmud and the Old Testament have served me well.

All the surveys which are being made show that Jews are being assimilated in one way or another. Jewish identity and Jewish continuity are sorely threatened. Now I am producing a number of dramas for radio to address this issue. I hope my efforts will help.

∞

Esther Fisher
KINDERGARTEN TEACHER
Hamburg, Germany

Give thanks before eating. Honor your elders. Be with one another for one another. I remember these lines in the Hebrew and they protect me from assimilation and give me the energy to live like a Jew in the Diaspora and to pass our heritage on to the Jewish children living in the Diaspora, in this case, in Hamburg. This is what moved me to start a Jewish kindergarten in this city with a sizable Jewish community. I teach the children to look out for each other, not just each one for himself.

∞

James O. Freedman
PRESIDENT, DARTMOUTH COLLEGE
Hanover, New Hampshire

The Jewish sages taught, "Make your home a regular meeting place for scholars; sit eagerly at their feet and drink their words." Being Jewish means many things to me, but none more important than being part of a tradition of scholarship and learning. Perhaps that is why I became a teacher, seeking to extend that tradition by following the talmudic observation, "When you teach your son, you teach your son's son."

My father was a teacher, and our house abounded with books and conversation about ideas. Our pantheon was peopled with intellectuals—our rabbi, Freud, Brandeis, Einstein, and Salk—whom I admired as following in the footsteps of Isaiah, Hillel, Maimonides, Rashi, and Buber. And so, as I matured, my search for my most authentic self was ineluctably linked to my identity as an intellectual, and that identity was inextricably linked to my sense of myself as a Jew.

For my parents, education was of preeminent importance. I attended Harvard in the mid-1950s, an experience that confirmed everything my parents and my Jewish upbringing had inculcated in me about the joys of learning, even as it provided but a handful of Jewish academic role models. Only when I arrived at Yale Law School, where the faculty included many Jews, was I able to meet Jewish scholars whom I could emulate.

I dearly wish that my father, who confronted anti-Semitism in finding his early teaching positions, had lived long enough to see the installation of Jewish presidents at numerous Ivy League and Big Ten universities. Only during the 1980s did American society come of age in recognizing Jewish scholars as academic leaders. At Dartmouth, as at other American colleges and universities today, the significant texts of the Judaic heritage are studied alongside the classics of Western culture.

[*From* Why Be Jewish? *Reprinted with the permission of the American Jewish Committee.*]

Ethel Fuchs
HOMEMAKER
Antwerp, Belgium

The neighborhood in which I grew up in Montreal was Jewish, and I never realized there was a way of life different from Judaism, in its varied aspects. My parents were committed socialists, my father almost communist, so to be religious meant to be primitive, inferior to the enlightened humanists. When I married and moved to Europe, I was told to keep my Jewishness to myself because of a fear of anti-Semitism ingrained in those Jews, my husband included, who went through the Holocaust. But as I started to get involved in the social scene with non-Jews, I learned that being Jewish usually aroused their curiosity, mainly because it was something different. But I myself could never realize in what way I was different. As a mainstream Jew, I met the more religious Jews through my husband, who is more observant of tradition. I had a chance to realize for myself what characteristics irritated my parents, but I also discovered a richness of tradition that I feel should continue. That is why I am happy that our children worked and studied in Israel and are pursuing a Jewish way of life.

Michael Gertler

ATTORNEY
New Orleans, Louisiana

Some of the values of Judaism are so strong in an individual that one can almost believe that they are genetically transmitted. Moral traits, such as helping the victim, the underdog, the powerless, are very strong. The sense of family, which is the beauty of Judaism, is especially strong.

Perhaps it is exaggerated to say that such traits are in our genes, but in my own case, it seems that way. As a child, I did not study the Torah. My father kept to the traditions, attended Shabbat services and High Holiday services. We did not keep the religious practices. Only when I got older, thirty to thirty-five years old, did I feel this yearning to learn about religion, which is more than identity. And after my father died, I said *Kaddish* at morning and evening *minyanim*.

It seems to me that different aspects of Judaism played their roles at different stages of my life. As a child, the family influenced what direction I would take in order to have a constructive life. My early maturity was marked by a kind of ethical monotheism, in which the societal element was strong, the responsibility of setting a good example that would reflect well on Judaism. Now that I am older, I feel a strong need to perpetuate both religious practices and values, to support the synagogue, and to show the younger generation—my own children included—why I feel that Judaism is worth perpetuating.

Monty Hall

TELEVISION GAME SHOW HOST
Beverly Hills, California

My Jewishness is important to me, and keeping its traditions alive in my family and in my community is a top priority of mine. I belong to two temples, assisting them with their fund raising, and have encouraged my children to join and participate. Am I a religious Jew? Not in every detail. But I am an emotional Jew, a traditional Jew, a Zionist, all the while being a devoted citizen of the United States. I find there is no conflict here. If you are a good Jew adhering to ethical principles, you will be a good citizen.

Jacob Hassan

ECONOMIST; PRESIDENT OF THE THE JEWISH COMMUNITY
Seville, Spain

Jews are no different from other people. But being Jewish makes a difference to me. It means Sephardic culture and the Sephardic form of Judaism, which we have maintained during five hundred years of expulsion from the land that formed this culture. But the main difference is *Adonai echad*, "God is one." I affirm this every day, here in this very Catholic country. And my children affirm this belief also.

Clara Karmely

CORPORATE LAWYER
Los Angeles, California

Being Jewish binds me to a history and culture. There are things that I do that were done two thousand years ago and are done around the world. I am the daughter of a Holocaust survivor who was born in Poland and who lived in Munich, Germany, after the war. His traditions, which did not make life easier for him even after the war, were passed down to me. But I am not Orthodox, as he still is. I came to Germany to celebrate Passover with him because he had a heart attack, and I don't know when I'll see him next.

The attitude that learning is something to pursue is probably a singularly Jewish value, although the more I know of other cultures, particularly the Oriental, I find that this value is shared by others. Then, there is the notion that we are all responsible for one another. This can be good and bad. When need arises, there is always some group a Jew can refer to. But there is the way we react to bad Jews—a crook, for example. He reflects badly on all of us, or at least each Jew seems to think this way and cringes inside. I do, when I hear about or read about such cases.

It is hard to pinpoint any specific Jewish value. So much is intrinsic when you are raised in a certain atmosphere. You take a lot for granted. The fact that men must be more active in religious services is one value I can live with quite comfortably.

Edward I. Koch

ATTORNEY; FORMER MAYOR OF NEW YORK CITY; FORMER
U.S. CONGRESSIONAL REPRESENTATIVE FROM NEW YORK
New York, New York

I am a Jew by birth. I continue to identify through personal choice. I am not an observant Jew, but I believe in God and I do attend synagogue on High Holidays. I believe that it is important for Jews—who are less than one-third of one percent of the world's population and less than two percent of the U.S. population—to identify publicly through cultural and religious activity with the Jewish nation. It makes me proud to know that we have continued on this earth for so long and have contributed worldwide in a positive way, notwithstanding our small numbers and efforts to destroy us.

It is important to transmit pride in our heritage to the children. If it means ridding oneself of one's Jewish identity, assimilation is, indeed, bad. If it means maintaining one's identity but absorbing the culture of the larger society as well, there is nothing wrong with it. I was raised to be compassionate towards others irrespective of whether they were Jewish or not. I hope that my personal achievements serve as a role model for others, Jewish and non-Jewish alike.

My advice to posterity is to remember all who came before us: those who suffered; those who gave the world monotheism; those who gave the world cultural contributions, uniquely Jewish; and most important, to remember that in the United States, we urge people to never forget who they are and to retain strong links with their traditions. That applies across the board to blacks, Hispanics, Irish, Italians and all other groups and to us as well.

Pavel Kral

Prague, Czech Republic

Nothing has made a greater difference in my life than being Jewish. This consciousness resounds in my moments of happiness, of sorrow, my pain, and my laughter. Shabbat, our New Year, all our holidays are times of remembering that we are a large family. We are the soul of the world, even when the world has no heart for us.

Tomas Kraus
EXECUTIVE DIRECTOR, FEDERATION OF JEWISH
COMMUNITIES IN THE CZECH REPUBLIC
Prague, Czech Republic

Religion in Bohemia and Moravia, the two lands making up the Czech Republic, was never a priority in public life. The majority of Christians were not religious, and Jews in pre-World War II Czechoslovakia were to a great degree assimilated. This is important because it had a bearing on the aftermath of the Holocaust: Some survivors were confirmed in their disbelief; others became religious, to the extent possible under communism. Since anti-Semitism is practically nonexistent here, Jews are not made to feel different in their public lives.

On a personal level, yes, there is a difference. There are some national traditions that I do not take part in, that I cannot feel part of. While Christianity is taken lightly here, the public holidays have heavy Christian overtones, even though they are celebrated more as pagan festivals. Family life is different. I am one of the few who is a child of a couple that survived the Holocaust as man and wife. I am also one of the few Jews in Prague who can claim to have a Jewish mother.

Although my parents made a point of keeping a traditional Jewish home, I cannot today point to any values I practice that are specifically Jewish, although I am sure there are some. For over fifty years, we could not study Judaism. We knew we were Jewish and went to the synagogue on the holidays. At home, my family celebrated the holidays. My values are the same as all human, democratic values. I was raised in a democratic tradition that goes back to pre-World War II Czechoslovakia. "Love your neighbor," which comes from Judaism, reappeared in our land after the Velvet Revolution. Now, our community is reforming and gaining members. We can study Judaism. What we do here at the Federation may be the essence of Judaism in that we are creating the atmosphere for learning Torah and Talmud so that we can discover what it means to be a Jew.

Jacob Kuperminck

HEAD OF THE JEWISH LIBRARY AT THE ALLIANCE CENTRAL, PARIS
Paris, France

If one really ever asks himself why he is Jewish, I suppose the answer would be, "out of respect for one's parents." If one asks himself why he remains Jewish, or what makes him remain Jewish, then it's because he has found something to commit himself to. In my case, it is a combination. I am Jewish by birth and remain so out of respect for my parents and history. But I am also a Jew by choice.

The respect for knowledge and the tradition of education make a decisive difference to me. Also the intellectual dimensions of questioning, submitting no matter what to discussion. There is openness to different ideas, a respect for other ideas. The philosophy behind our laws demonstrates a respect for other persons who are different, who are not Jewish. My parents came from Poland, immigrants to France. My grandparents were also immigrants, foreigners in Poland. Such a history lends a certain sensitivity towards the outsider, towards the one who is different.

Maurice Levy

DIRECTOR, PUBLICIS-LE DRUGSTORE
Paris, France

You have asked me an extremely difficult question. Everyone asks himself "What am I? Where do I come from? Where am I going?" These are life's fundamental questions. These questions are even more complicated when one is Jewish.

In the first place, I believe myself to be a human being, without reference to what one believes or believes in. Personality is based on what one receives and what one acquires. Is Jewishness transmitted through centuries and millennia of Torah study and study of Kabbalah and other texts? Or is it acquired through family and environment? I do not know how to answer these questions.

If it is a matter of acquisition, that means that the difference is practically a result of education and what others think. This answer seems too simple for me.

What difference does it make to me that I am Jewish?

Raised in a traditional home, having a mother to whom religion was very important, I did not even know that other religions existed until I was six years old and came up against the names that my classmates gave me—from *sale juif* [dirty Jew] to every name one can think of that had to do with money, greed, dishonesty. This led me to ask "Why?" And I have never found a satisfactory answer.

But after all is said and done, I can say that I was never really troubled about being Jewish. I lived and worked without having to face any insurmountable obstacle, and often benefited from the help of many strong personalities that I met in my personal and professional life, who had no ties to my family. I think that my name helped me. *Levy* is almost a caricature, a stereotype. In France, there could not be a more Jewish name. My background is clear from the start, and my position regarding others is clear. And this helps me to overcome any problem.

I do not know if there is anything about my behavior that is typically Jewish. Even raising the question reveals a sort of racism. Are there Jewish values that are necessarily better than other values? I do not know.

But there are Jewish traditions, which my grandfather inculcated in me with since my childhood, and which are essentially Jewish but also held by other religions. First, there is the human ethic, how one acts regarding his neighbor, respect for the other, for his person, for his morality.

There is also the morality of human relations, an interest in the other, a deeply human approach to all types of relations, even professional relations.

There is the incessant questioning, permanent doubt: Have I done enough? Have I done well enough? Can I do better?

There is this obsession with what others think: If the other thinks it is bad to be Jewish, I will excel and overcome him, force him to respect me, even to admire me.

Then there is this tendency to cover up a minority status by claiming that one belongs to the chosen people, the people of the book. The people that are made to suffer in order to measure the ability to resist. To be subject to destruction in order to see if they can rise up again. And again, and again.

In my everyday life none of these questions poses themselves, nor do I refer to them. Nevertheless, I feel that I lead my personal life and professional activity guided by some very simple ideas:

First, respect for the other. This is probably the most important.

Then, a little sentimentality, or humanity. This is dangerous in business, but too bad.

Also, a lot of curiosity and creativity, to be where one does not expect to find me.

I do not know if I have religious feelings, even if I am one of those traditional Jews who likes to fast on Yom Kippur and celebrate Pesach with the family.

Above all, I have the feeling that I should not be one who passes through this life on his own, but that I have a duty to transmit something. I am a connection between a past and a future. I am the future of my parents and the past of my children. I have the exalted duty of providing them with comfort, well-being, and preparing them for life, but above all to pass on some rules of conduct that will make them into a connection, a witness between generations that a certain idea of humanity should be perpetuated.

—◦◦◦—

Miriam Marbé
COMPOSER (DECEASED 1998)
Bucharest, Romania, and Amsterdam, the Netherlands

On one hand, I feel a very strong attachment to my family's ancestral roots. On the other hand, I am extremely open to and interested in other cultures. I am happy to discover the essence of wisdom in tradition. And I am happy to be the bearer of an experience that goes back for millennia, and which I have transmitted to my daughter.

For a long time, prudence dictated our behavior, that is, we have had to keep silent while behind the Iron Curtain. Now that the danger is less—although it still exists, it does not frighten me—I am still hesitant because I do not know what the future will bring.

Whether being Jewish has made a difference more than being a woman or more than having been born in Romania, I cannot say. These aspects are intertwined and hard to disentangle, and they have to be seen in the light of other aspects, such as strength of character, degree of talent, the country in which these are developed, a spirit of complicity with a given situation, etc., etc.

Robert Merrill

BARITONE WITH THE METROPOLITAN OPERA
Upstate New York

My folks came to this country from a small town outside Warsaw, got married there and lived in a tenement. As I was growing up, I heard a great deal about the problems and the persecution they went through in Poland that prompted them to leave. I heard these stories of survival, and tradition, and strength to survive. My mother had a beautiful voice and her brother was a cantor. Their father sang. I kept hearing this, too, as a young man. When I sang Tevye in *Fiddler on the Roof,* I finally understood Tevye's character, because he went through the same things. He was from a small town. He fought his poverty through humor and by quoting the Bible. It was a great lesson for me, and it carried over to my personal life. We went through the Great Depression, two world wars. The courage to survive, to keep going was always there. And it helped me all my life.

To survive, Jews developed a sense of humor, even about themselves. The humor also gave strength. It certainly helped me. I inherited this humor from them.

It's not just a cultural thing. The religious aspect is important to me. I've never worked on Yom Kippur. I didn't always go to temple on Yom Kippur, but it's, how do you say, inborn, it becomes part of our genes, our inborn character. A very interesting thing happened to me. When I was going to make my debut in London, at the Royal Opera House—this was many years ago—the date was booked seven to eight months in advance. A month before I had to be there, I realized the date fell on Yom Kippur. So I called the man in charge, Rudolph Bing of the Royal Opera, and I told him, "Look, I've never worked on Yom Kippur. It's a tradition, so if you could change the date. . . ." Well, they did. It was quite a thing to do, because the night after my debut came a ballet, the night after, another opera, etc. They had to turn back the entire thing. The newspaper editorials in London were fantastic. They said they admired Robert Merrill's courage and devotion to his religion. "We'll no doubt show up at his performance," they said. So I was reviewed in all the papers.

My family goes to synagogue almost every Yom Kippur, especially to say the prayer for our parents. Of course, every time I hear the *Kol Nidre,* I get tears in my eyes.

I have children and grandchildren. My son married a non-Jewish girl. However, they had a Jewish wedding. They broke the glass, which I think is another fabulous tradition. She turned out to be more Jewish

JEWISH: DOES IT MAKE A DIFFERENCE?

than my son, and I think it's wonderful. My daughter married a Jewish man, and they don't go to temple or *shul*, but they are very conscious of the fact that they are Jewish. For Chanukah, my four-year old grand-daughter lights candles. She doesn't know why. Her parents tell her that it was a festival of life and survival. But the memory, the feeling is there. They never really leave.

I feel sorry for people who forget their Jewishness. And when they get older, they're concerned about death and join temples and become quite religious. I know several people who are quite well known in the arts who turn to religion because they're concerned about death. I don't think we should be concerned about what non-Jews think of you. We don't have to flaunt Jewishness, but feel it. And practice being a *mensch* with everyone. I had non-Jewish friends who have passed away and I've participated in masses at St. Patrick's Cathedral for them. At one time, Cardinal O'Connor announced to the people that "Robert Merrill, a devoted Jew, is here. And we admire him immensely for coming down and participating in a mass for his dear friend who passed away."

And of course, we should never forget our devotion to Israel. It's something we should be conscious of, that we have a Jewish land. I've been there many times, and sung Italian opera there. I've sung all over the world, but the Jews in Israel brought with them, from wherever they came, a love of music and art. So that when you perform at the Frederick Mann Auditorium in Tel Aviv, you have to do it five times. The auditorium has only two thousand seats, but ten thousand sub-scribers. So you have to do a performance five times. How much more Jewish can you be than that?

------cvo------

Margareta Molnar
OWNER, ORTHOPEDIC SUPPLY STORE IN MEA SHEARIM
Jerusalem, Israel

Being raised as a Jew in Transylvania gave me a strong sense of be-longing to the Jewish people. My husband and I came to Israel for two reasons. We were not religious but we wanted to prevent our children from becoming integrated into Romanian society. We did not want them to marry non-Jews. In Romania, intermarriage means the end of being Jewish. The family is a very strong Jewish tradition and value. It ensures our survival and continuity. It cannot be explained; it is something we grow up with and feel deep inside. In Israel, we feel secure that Jewish family life will be preserved.

Berry Nahmias
HOMEMAKER
Athens, Greece

As a survivor of the hell of Auschwitz, I feel even prouder of being a Jew. So I try every day to cry out and tell my personal story at universities, schools, and writing about the Holocaust. I suppose this is a big difference that being Jewish has made in my life. There are also our laws. No matter who else has adopted them, the Ten Commandments remain specifically Jewish. Tradition transmits these and the other values of Judaism. Being Jewish is a different and private way of living and maintaining Jewishness. Through our holidays and life celebrations—circumcision, *bar mitzvah, bat mitzvah,* marriage—all these bind us and guide us and enrich our lives.

It is said that a person is considered Jewish if he has Jewish grandchildren. I have the honor of announcing that I have two granddaughters at Tel Aviv University.

Peter M. Oppenheimer
PROFESSOR OF ECONOMICS
Oxford, England

Judaism provides me with an extra dimension of identity in the Diaspora, an identity that contains spiritual, cultural, and social elements. What I value most about my Judaism is family cohesion, which is centered on at least some degree of religious observance.

Jodi Padnick

COLLEGE STUDENT

During a trip to Spain as a high school exchange student, I realized that being Jewish made a difference to me. As the first Sabbath drew near in Barcelona, I longed to be with other Jews. Sitting in a small synagogue among and listening to the melodies of the prayers, I felt a kinship with these individuals. The once thriving communities of Jews all over Spain were thrown out of the home they had known for centuries, just like my ancestors were in other parts of Europe. The spark of my deepening awareness of Jewishness was struck.

I have gradually developed the spiritual side of my Jewishness through the holiness of the Sabbath and its unique power to renew my spirit. Judaism has strengthened my bonds with family and friends. It challenges me to get involved in society and its problems. Because of the commitment to help others that Judaism entails, I feel a partner with God in the ongoing creation of the world.

[*From* Why Be Jewish? *Reprinted with the permission of the American Jewish Committee.*]

Estrella Sarfatí

MOTHER OF FIVE AND GRANDMOTHER OF TWO
Seville, Spain

Although this does not sound modern, I would do everything in my power to help my family, because if there is something that is Jewish, it is the understanding that the family is the nucleus of Jewish life. Here is where you learn what it means to have children, how important a good name is, and that you are respected for maintaining traditions. From birth to death, family life is a greater teacher than any university in the world. And I am happy that our family continues the traditions we inherited. But here is where I begin to worry when I think about the future. More and more families are coming apart, and the value of holding to each other no matter what . . . is being replaced by a sense that it is better to live so as to avoid sources of trouble to oneself.

Miron Haskelevitch Shichman

CIVIL SERVICE EMPLOYEE, HAIFA MUNICIPALITY
Haifa, Israel

Family is very important to me as a Jew, even though my family is not religious (except for my older daughter). When my wife and I first applied to emigrate from Kishinev, she was worried that it was an attempt on my parents' side to come between us. Since I felt strongly that a man and wife are one, I put off emigration for sixteen years, until she was convinced that the step was right for us as a family. In addition to this, I feel that helping one's fellow, where one works and in the community, is also an important Jewish value.

In the Diaspora, people speak about Jewish values. Here, in Israel, we live them.

Steven B. Silvern

CURRICULUM AND TEACHING ADMINISTRATION
Auburn University, Alabama

Our synagogue is very small and is located in rural Alabama. We do not have much money, and we do not have much in the way of decoration. Instead of a throne for the Torah to rest on, a child from the congregation holds it until it is returned to the ark.

Some time back, I was lecturing to a university religion class about Judaism. One of the students asked, "It seems like there are a lot of laws and requirements to be Jewish, not to mention being a minority. It must be easier to be a Christian, so why not just convert to Christianity?"

As I pondered my response to her, I was struck by a memory. I remembered being in *shul* on Shabbat mornings. Our *shul* had the *minhag* of a child holding the Torah until it was returned to the ark. Frequently, I was that child. I remembered sitting in a chair that was much too big for me and having a very large, heavy Torah pressing down on my chest, on my heart. I clutched it tightly to me so that it wouldn't fall. The soft, furry velvet of the mantle rubbed warmly against my cheek. The odor of the parchment filled my nose. It was so pungent that I could literally taste it on my tongue. My ears and mind were filled with the melody of the chanting of the *haftarah*. Each and every one of my senses was being touched by the Torah—not just once, but many times during my childhood.

Today, as I think of the importance of Judaism to me, I think of the weight of the Torah on my heart. I related that story to the student and asked, "How could I not be Jewish?"

As I finished the story, I placed our Torah in the arms of the younger brother of the *bar mitzvah* and vowed that we should always do so, and never purchase a throne for our Torah. I looked out onto the congregation and one of the Christian guests of the family was weeping openly. After services, he approached and gave me a giant hug. His only words were, "Now I understand."

I don't know if I answered your questions, but I repeat mine: "How could I not be Jewish?"

⌀

Emil Sivob

BULGARIAN-BORN ECONOMIST
Seville, Spain

Being Jewish does not make a difference to me. The fact that my mother was Jewish does. My father was a Bulgarian Christian and our home was not at all religious. So I hold to my Jewish heritage out a feeling of closeness that I had towards my mother and what I learned from her. Maybe this is why I feel that family is important in Jewish life. When one is a stranger in a foreign land, as I and my family are, one tends to keep close to the family and to do those things that are reassuring and eternal. I try to observe the Jewish holidays, like Purim, which we are celebrating this evening. My mother described them to me, and I tell my children about them. And I hope they will remember and carry on at least the little bit that I do.

Morris Smith

FORMER MUTUAL FUND MANAGER
New York, New York

I left my position as manager of the largest mutual fund in order to dedicate myself to pursuing two values that Judaism holds dear: family and the study of Torah. The practice of Judaism and the study of our religious tradition have guided me in conducting my personal and professional life. The Torah has the power to enhance our relationship with God and humans. Ethics and religion are seen as one. Judaism preserves authentic values and morality that go back thousands of years and which prove themselves during an age of "popular" culture in which standards change from month to month.

[*From* Why Be Jewish? *Reprinted with the permission of the American Jewish Committee.*]

Leyla Speker

JEWISH ROOTS COMMITTEE IN TURKEY
Istanbul, Turkey

Being Jewish means to share all the values meant to improve the human being morally and spiritually. It is enjoying taking part in a rightful and just society, taking pride in belonging to an ancestry that cherished these values, developing love and compassion for others, and aiming to reach that very goal set for me ages ago. Our tradition is the very essence of spirituality. While taking pride in belonging to a nation that first acknowledged the existence of one almighty God, I know that had it not been for our tradition, stubbornly transmitted from one generation to the next, we could not survive. Enjoying Jewish social life and identifying with Judaism on a social as well as spiritual level are special to me. To give an example: Who can enjoy a Seder at Pesach alone, with no child around the table to transmit the Haggadah to? It does not make sense. Jewish family life is very important. Keeping the warmth, equity, and humanity alive within the family is particularly Jewish. That is where our survival strength comes from. Our religion is uniquely family-oriented. Let us keep it that way.

As a Jewish mother, I believe that observing the Shabbat is of primary importance. In a world where all sorts of religions and trends bring pressure to bear on Diaspora Judaism, Jewish education at home can do marvels to keep us together. Of course, making *aliyah* is another issue through which one can solve the problem of pressure towards assimilation. But transmitting Judaism is mainly a home issue, no matter where we live.

Zipporah Stern

TRAVEL AGENT
Brussels, Belgium

Judaism and the history of the Jews affect my thinking and behavior. When I look back at the Holocaust, I have to think about why it happened. Before I put a *mezuzah* on the doorpost, I have to think about possible consequences for my home and business. How I dress, the hours that I work, the Shabbat, when I do not work. All these things make a difference in how I, as a Jew, think and regulate my life.

The Christians and Muslims took over the easy laws of the Torah: Do not murder; do not steal. But the Jewish attitude towards the Torah is different. We think about what we do and why we do. This might sound ponderous, but it is not. Take Shabbat, for example. It is a day of rest and peace. No matter what may be troubling me and my husband, or if we have a misunderstanding, Friday evening he comes home from the synagogue and he has to tell me *"Shabbat shalom."* And we have to forget every bad thing and live Shabbat. In my business, I have to run it by the laws of our tradition, which means, be honest in business.

Francine Szapiro

CO-OWNER AND MANAGER OF GALLERIE SAPHIR
Paris, France

The privilege of being Jewish is interwoven with that of being a woman. This dual status also entails responsibility. Jewish women have been an influence throughout our history, directly and openly, but more often behind the scenes. Here in France, a woman was the director of

---

the Jewish Council, and Simone Weil is well known for her role in the French government. In my own way, as director of an art gallery, with my husband, we try to make Jewish contributions to the history of art better known. We do this also by living our traditions. For instance, our galleries are closed on Shabbat.

Judaism contains a sense of history, culture, and tradition, with specific values that I really feel are worth maintaining and transmitting. Our history makes a big difference. After all that the Jews as a whole, and each Jew as an individual, have suffered, we become more receptive to the suffering of others. Our history gave us an extra dose of humanity, because of all the persecutions we have been through. When I think of my own Judaism, I think of a solidarity with other Jews and the desire and duty to continue for our own sake. We are the bearers of values that are worth transmitting. And I do not think that other people, outside of Judaism, have the same sense of transmitting values like the ones we have and gave to the world.

Gil Tayeb
Paris, France

Jews who developed in an Arab culture full of Muslim fervor are probably more intense in their concern for preserving the values, the traditions of our people. I do not mean to make these Jews sound more special than Jews in other parts of the world, but to explain why the large majority of us are dedicated to maintaining a difference as opposed to nullifying it through assimilation. Everything we inherited from our parents and grandparents is important: rituals, ways of acting with non-Jews, survival strategies, and the determination to remain Jewish against all odds. For me, this means dedication to the community of Jews. Now that I live in Paris, I represent those Jews who found a new home here and make sure that our special identity adds to the variety of Jewish life here.

Allie Toledo

PRIMARY SCHOOL TEACHER
Waiuku, New Zealand

Family, heritage, and a sense of identity are very important. A sense of tradition in a country that is only one hundred fifty years old and still has a British colonial feel to it is hard to come by. As New Zealanders, we find it difficult to remember ANZAC Day. ANZAC Day is commemorated on 25 April, the anniversary of the landing of soldiers of the Australia New Zealand Army Corps at Gallipoli during World War I. As Jews, we never forget the Passover that occurred thousands of years ago.

Alan Veingrad

FORMER NATIONAL FOOTBALL LEAGUE OFFENSIVE LINEMAN
Dallas, Texas

Most meaningful to me is Judaism's strong emphasis on family and celebration, which my parents passed down to me and my brother. My warmest memories are of Passover Sedarim, when family and friends would sit at the table and retell the story of our liberation; and of Chanukah, another celebration of freedom.

I knew that my wife would be a Jewish woman. When a new Jewish family moves into our neighborhood, my wife and I welcome them to our home for a Shabbat meal. While our traditions link us with the past, our daughter, born three years ago, is our link to the future of Judaism.

[*From* Why Be Jewish? *Reprinted with the permission of the American Jewish Committee.*]

Margers Vestermanis

HISTORIAN
Vilnius, Lithuania

This little museum of the Jews of Letonia tells everyone who visits what a difference it made to our ancestors to be Jewish. It is the past, I know, but it displays the force and motivation that have kept us alive for over two thousand years in the Diaspora. It makes a big difference to me, a historian by training, to preserve this spirit.

Beate Wyhler

CONSERVATIVE RABBI IN OLDENBURG AND BRAUNSCHWEIG
(FIRST WOMAN RABBI ORDAINED IN GERMANY SINCE BEFORE
WORLD WAR II)
Oldenburg, Germany

It is a mistake to assume that persecution has held the Jews together. Persecution has had an important role in our history, but it is not the reason that we kept together. We have kept together because we believe that the Jewish people have a covenant with God, a covenant with two partners. One of them is God and the other is the Jewish people. As long as we stick to the covenant as a people, we stick together and persecution cannot do us any harm.

This holds true for today also, I hope, when outright persecution is nonexistent in Europe. Today, there are different forces compelling Judaism, and Judaism reacts to these by reinterpreting what the covenant given at Sinai means and what God wants us to do. This is the very nature of Judaism, the very nature of the covenant, which requires every single person to think for himself or herself what it is that God wants from them. We get different results of how to observe the laws, and how to obey the commandments.

Judaism is a system of social justice, as we can read in the Torah and in the Prophets. There are many Jews who are vegetarians, because they think that the way animals are raised today is not kosher; or they don't eat food produced in a politically incorrect manner. This is how they interpret the Jewish understanding of social justice. And I have no hesitation in claiming that their consideration for animals is a Jewish value.

Family life, even though it has undergone severe changes in the last generations, is another outstanding aspect of Judaism that is still highly esteemed. One example is the whole *chavurah* movement, a New Age movement, in which people try to form new groups of *chaveirim* and to organize services and celebrations and Jewish programs. That is a movement which started in the United States, and which came out of the 1970s. It meets the challenges that families face. In most communities, there is a high number of one-parent families. The high esteem which the family enjoys in the Jewish tradition has found a new interpretation. This refers back to the Jewish penchant for reinterpreting tradition—so that we don't have to throw it away. A husband and a wife, both with children from earlier marriages, get together and build a new family, and they share each other's children. Sometimes several one-parent families live under one roof in a big house; and they make up one big family.

Probably the most important, enduring value we have is education. There is a saying in the Talmud: "I have learned much from my teachers, I have learned more from my peers, and I have learned most from my students." There is another saying in the Talmud: "Even if you have only learned one letter from the Torah, there is somebody who doesn't know it yet, and with this person you share it." That basically makes every Jew—even if he or she knows very little—a potential teacher. The sages of the Talmud said that studying is as valuable a *mitzvah* as all the others put together. Learning becomes a form of worship. I think that's a most phenomenal concept: to take a book, to meet with a friend, to study together, and to find new meaning for your lives. For me, this is study and learning as a form of worship, and this is one of the two very great concepts that Jewish tradition has offered the world.

The other one is Shabbat. Shabbat is an extraordinary, very powerful concept. It is not that the Jews kept Shabbat, but that Shabbat kept the Jews. Shabbat is not only a day of rest, but a day of social equality—because Shabbat is for you as it is for your children and for your servants, even for your animals and for the strangers that happen to be in your house. The servants, the slaves, had a right to claim Shabbat. If you ask me, this is political gunpowder for people who are not used to the fact that one day of the week makes us all equal. The interesting traditions are not the ones some or all Jews have given up—such as polygamy or the test of jealousy. The interesting traditions are the ones we have stuck to. Shabbat is one of them; and Talmud Torah is the other.

Conservatives indeed follow tradition, but a very important aspect of tradition is that it needs to remain dynamic. Once you give up the dynamic within our tradition, you're dead. We live in the twentieth century, not the seventeenth century. Take the role of the woman in the community. With traditional means, there are ways of interpreting, or of accepting, that the role of women has changed drastically, particularly in this century. So in a Conservative *shul*, we can have a fairly traditional service, but one in which women can lead services and women can be called to the Torah and be counted in the *minyan*.

Here is an anecdote that proves my point about dynamics or death: I lived in Germany for a year, and I *davened* in a nonegalitarian *shul*. I had no other choice, but still I insisted on putting on my *tallit*. One man there said that if you start to allow women to be called up to the Torah, that would be the beginning of the end. So I said, "I understand you are arguing on the basis of tradition. Well, there are three cornerstones of tradition. Do you keep Shabbat? Well, he said, you know, it's difficult. Okay, number two, what about *kashrut*? This, too, was difficult for him. And yes, it is difficult here in Germany, but it is possible. Number three, what about the tradition of family purity? It may be none of my business, but does your wife go to the *mikveh*?" And the fellow could only walk away. So, who was keeping the tradition—the Orthodox or the Conservative? The stagnant or the dynamic?

The holy days are another example of dynamism. Maybe many Jews do not observe Shabbat, but they certainly observe Pesach. This applies to most of the United States and Europe. And it is interesting to notice that if someone decides to observe only one Jewish holiday, it is Pesach rather than Yom Kippur. I find that very remarkable because Pesach is a holy day of liberation; it is the very core holiday of the Jewish tradition. The exodus from Egypt, liberation from enslavement by God's hand. And if we keep that one memory alive, then we are in good shape.

Gad Yaacobi

AMBASSADOR OF ISRAEL TO THE UNITED NATIONS (1994)
Israel and New York

There is only a personal response to the fact that one is Jewish. First of all, I would not be an Israeli were it not for the fact that I am a Jew. Beyond being Israeli, however, I am Jewish. In my mind, this means to identify with and represent the very best of Jewish heritage and culture:

the striving for excellence, justice, and brotherhood, as stated in our Bible, "Justice, justice shall you pursue," and "Love your neighbor as yourself." Jewish values are important for maintaining Jewish continuity, more so in the Diaspora than in Israel. Yet in Israel, as well, we have to pass along its meaning to our students and children. Their worth as Jews plays an important part in creating their worth as human beings.

—ঌ—

Rosalyn Yalow
NOBEL LAUREATE IN MEDICINE (1977)
New York, New York

Jewish tradition emphasizes learning—learning for the sake of understanding and perfecting our world, and learning for its own sake. Through the ages, we Jews have taken pride in being known as the "people of the book" and have carried our Torah and our traditions with dignity and affection. Even in the face of persecution and dispersion, and often denied access to centers of learning, the Jewish people, never satisfied with conventional answers, have always valued intellectual inquiry and continued to honor wisdom and learning.

Moreover, being Jewish means to me having a deep attachment to family. I grew up in an era of tightly knit families which shaped our values and world view. Today, the family, including the Jewish family, is said to be an endangered institution. It is time for us to rededicate ourselves to strengthening Jewish family life. Surely this is our best investment in the Jewish future.

Finally, Judaism represents a great synthesis of universal and Jewish values. For me as a Jew, there need be no conflict between science and religion. Moses Maimonides, philosopher and commentator on *halachah*, also graced the world of medicine. He is a role model of living in two worlds—Jewish and universal—and of making them one.

[*From* Why Be Jewish? *Reprinted with the permission of the American Jewish Committee.*]

Haroun Yashayaee

CENTRAL JEWISH COMMITTEE
Teheran, Iran

The history of the Jews in Iran goes back thousands of years, to the first Diaspora. The graves of Esther, Mordechai, Daniel, and Habakkuk are in Iran and the Jewish community takes care of these. It also maintains a hospital, a nursing home, nursery schools. There are also schools for youngsters, but the majority of Jewish youngsters attend public schools. While schooling is open to all, even non-Muslim students, Jews are limited regarding the course of study they can pursue. And up to a certain level, there is no limit on the type of work or profession a Jew can pursue. This is all I can tell you.

CHAPTER TEN

---cᏰ꜄---

The Networked Jew

Two years into the preparation for this book, we addressed our inquiry to some of the many Jewish groups active on the Internet regarding topics pertinent to Judaism. In addition to the original questions, our e-mail asked respondents to state their opinion regarding the influence of the new technology on Jews and Judaism. It was not an attempt to capture the new flavor of the interaction among Jews facilitated by networking, but rather a desire to point to a new medium for self-identification. Between the time we transmitted our inquiry and the publication of this book, Jewish presence on the Web has increased considerably. The habit of forming networks of support predates the global model of today's world by more than two thousand years. In order to survive, Jews came up with a "worldwide web" that kept independent and far-flung communities spiritually connected. Communication among them, in a variety of forms, was of utmost importance in preserving Jewish vitality under extremely varied circumstances. In view of this history, we can only say that it is no wonder that Jews take to the Internet like ducks to water!

Jim Egolf
RABBI
Jackson, Mississippi

I come from a family of converts in which religion never played a strong part. Yet, for some reason, when my father began to get involved in Judaism, I knew that I had found my home.

For most people the involvement in Judaism comes either by birth or by association. Most Jews by choice make their choice in the context of a wider community. My family made their decision in the middle of southern Alabama. We would drive eighty miles to Temple Beth-El in Pensacola, Florida, to attend religious school. My identity was further buttressed by many summers at the Henry S. Jacobs Camp in Utica, Mississippi, where several people, including the director, impacted my life and my Judaism.

The *mitzvah* of being a good person (having a *shem tov* [good name]) is crucial to living. Too many times in the community where I grew up did I see "good people" profess their belief in their faith, then act as if God had built only their house of worship and not the rest of the world. Thus the piety practiced and sometimes feigned in the pews was not to be carried out into the rest of the world.

Today there is a move towards making Judaism more introverted. The argument that we should only take care of our own is gaining momentum. I believe that this is a dead end street. We should be learning Judaism to then be a light unto all nations. If we are too focused on ourselves, then we run the risk of burning the wick. We are to be strong within ourselves in order to be the example to the world. What kind of an example can we be when we are only self-centered and only care for our own? Where does it say not to oppress just the Jewish orphan and the Jewish widow? Are we not also commanded to care for the stranger in our midst? And does Judaism not teach that the righteous non-Jews also gain a place in the world to come?

Thus the difference is that Judaism demands of us a balance which keeps one eye looking at our own house and another eye on the world. Being a Reform rabbi, I stake my belief that modern Judaism has a message not just for Judaism, but for the entire world. That message is something which must be fostered and set free to make the difference; otherwise, we are leaving the wider world, thus forsaking our responsibility to carry out the mission which Scripture demands of us, namely, "Seek peace and pursue it." We are the light of that peace, and without Judaism, all may wish to pursue the peace, yet without the light to find their way, good intentions will be wasted.

"Jewish: Does it make a difference?" is not the question. For me the question is "Jewish: Does it make *the* difference?" Yes—*amen v'amen*.

―✦―

Paul Freedman
England

Judaism is an important *part* of who I am. I feel that there is enough freedom within Judaism for a theology that I am comfortable with. It is not doctrinal in the way I perceive many other religions. Mostly, I feel that Judaism is "right for me" and therefore am quite happy for other religions to be "right" for other people. I don't think anyone has a monopoly on Truth, and it is dangerous when someone believes they have.

I do not live in a large Jewish community, but it is large enough for a synagogue and so synagogue attendance is a significant way of expressing my Jewishness. Nevertheless, I have found the Internet unique in its ability to put me in touch with other Jews around the world.

Judaism seems right for me now. I also think it is part of a bigger picture. I am occasionally struck by the international spread of Jews and, perhaps more importantly, the historical chain of Jews reaching back thousands of years. To be part of that chain is humbling, exciting, and holds a responsibility for the future. Without Jews, the world would get along just fine, but it would be all the poorer for that loss. I have a problem with being "the chosen people" and am still trying to understand what it means. But I do believe that the Jewish people are a significant part of human history.

Having been around for so long, Judaism has become a very amorphous and complex thing. I, a Western European Jew living at the end of the twentieth century, share something with Jews from Australia, India, Iraq, Russia, South Africa, and Ethiopia. Putting my finger on what I share is not easy.

Joel Gluck
Rhode Island

When I was growing up, I wanted nothing to do with religion, especially Judaism. I grew up in a very Christian neighborhood and felt different and just wanted to blend with the status quo. I wanted to finish Hebrew school, have my *bar mitzvah,* and get out. This unfortunate attitude continued until I began graduate school.

While in graduate school, I was the victim of anti-Semitism. My apartment door was painted with swastikas and vulgarity. It hurt a lot. However, what hurt me and confused me even more was that the fact that the person who did the damage was Jewish! Since that incident, I felt I needed to be more connected.

I began going to services, just the High Holidays at first, but it was a start. I have always been interested in music and began studying Jewish music. I began singing with a Jewish choir in Philadelphia and it was this that really got me interested in Judaism. I have since begun studying more, and now I can say that I am a practicing Jew. My wife and I go to services every Shabbat. We both sing in the choir; I am a cantorial soloist, I conduct a Jewish choir, and I sing with a professional Jewish choir from Boston. I wish my childhood rabbi and cantor could see me now. Boy, would they be surprised! As for my childhood temple phobia—presently, I am on the board of trustees at my temple, on the board of the Brotherhood, and am in the temple building at least three to four times a week. Some change, huh?

The difference that my religious practice makes in my life is especially evident during the summer months. Our temple Shabbat services are more low key, less involved, more congregant directed. This makes a major difference in how I pray. Although the same liturgy is recited, it doesn't feel the same. I guess what I am trying to say is that temple life makes a major difference to me. I feel less whole during the times when I can't get to the temple—especially for services.

Peter Haas
San Francisco, California

To me it doesn't matter how *halachah* defines Judaism. If a person feels Jewish, and does some of the things that characterize most "observant" Jews, then I consider that person Jewish. This thought does, however, require the following additional comment: Doing some of the things that characterize observant Jews is, to me, a prerequisite because that's not only what we Jews have in common, but also what, in some ways, sets us apart from non-Jews. These characteristics should include some of the following (unless there are some very extenuating circumstances):

- attending services on High Holidays (or staying at home and praying the same prayers)
- being familiar with the Jewish Bible, and aware of the history of the Jewish people
- observing some of the customs and holidays of Judaism
- having Jewish friends
- belonging to a synagogue and/or a Jewish community center
- financially contributing to Jewish/Israeli causes
- feeling a bond with the land of Israel
- feeling that the history of the Jews is the history of your own family
- believing in most of the ethical values of Judaism

The Internet will certainly facilitate learning more about Judaism and about each other. But, in the final analysis, I don't feel such impact will be profound. What will affect *Am Yisrael* profoundly, in my estimation (and not in a favorable way!) is the effect of intermarriage and assimilation.

Cory Michael Lebson
STUDENT
New York, New York

To me Judaism is a protection against a very large world, in which one can feel lost. It's a way for me to structure my life and it forces me to take time and reflect, to observe Shabbat and the holidays, and to be able to spend time with my family and friends. I believe that the Jewish concept of family is somewhat unique, as well as the Jewish concept of completely taking a day of rest on Shabbat.

Judaism also gives rights to women that don't exist in other parts of society. It also seems to inspire youth in a way that other religions are unable to do. I believe that Judaism has a special ability to help in all aspects of life. Jewish mysticism is also very fascinating to me.

As technology increases, people will turn more toward religion, all religions, to escape from technology every so often. However, I also believe that the Internet is an excellent medium for maintaining Jewish connections, especially in remote locations.

David M.
Stockholm, Sweden

Absolutely, being Jewish makes a difference! The traditions, beliefs, values, family relations, friendships, and education are a way of life quite different from the Swedish way of life. All in all, somewhat warmer. We teach our children to ask questions, not to be quiet. Of course, *tzedakah* is especially a Jewish value.

The quest for education, for information, is also an outstanding trait. In this respect, the Internet provides so much information that I think many more people will learn a lot about our Judaism, whether that is their intention or not. But I don't think it will make Jews more Jewish.

Diane Romm
REBBETZIN; WRITER
Bellmore, New York

As a rabbi's wife [*rebbetzin*], I can say that being Jewish matters a great deal. I have just published a book called *The Jewish Guide to the Internet,* which is an attempt to show people the wealth of information of Jewish content on the Net, and where to find that information. I think we are standing on the brink of what can be truly monumental developments in the way Jews "congregate." Resources of the Jewish world can reach people who never had access to them, people who might never set foot in a *shul* but in the privacy of their own home, just out of curiosity, might look at a Jewish source.

JEWISH: DOES IT MAKE A DIFFERENCE?

Michael Scheinberg

MEMBER OF JEWISH CAMPUS SERVICE CORPS
Princeton, New Jersey

My family stressed Jewish values and ideals in a way that fit us all very well. We would have Shabbat dinner as far back as I can remember. We went to synagogue regularly. I went to Jewish day school for thirteen years, and my education complemented my family practice. I joined a Jewish youth group and was involved in Jewish activities in college. Now I work at the Center for Jewish Life at Princeton University, where I try to help students connect positively to their Jewish heritage.

At the beginning of 1996, I met a student who came to a discussion group about Yom Kippur. When we spoke individually, he told me that he was a Jew for Jesus, that he had just recently "seen the light." He told me his story, how he had felt very lonely as a student. He was never involved in one of the many Jewish communities here. His best friend, a born-again Christian, confronted him, saying that he was missing Jesus from his life. He found solace on the Internet, checking out the Jews for Jesus website, and started using it as a crutch. The response time to him was quick. He found a virtual community—and fast!

The Jews for Jesus website was beautiful, more so than any of the Jewish sites at that time. Luckily, we have come up to speed for the most part. We now have a website, Jews for Judaism, the countermissionary organization that often combats Jews for Jesus. This is one of the reasons I see the Internet as a supplemental community for Jews. People who are looking for this supplement will find it. But the Internet cannot shake hands with someone, wish someone *"Shabbat shalom,"* invite him/her over for coffee or lunch.

I work in a field called Jewish engagement, which, like any outreach Jewish involvement position, requires individual attention to Jewish people. It is also a personal resource for them at the individual level. If the Internet can connect people in a more independent setting, that's fine. But with many people, there is no contact like the individual face-to-face kind.

Ben Shneiderman
PROFESSOR OF COMPUTER SCIENCE, UNIVERSITY OF MARYLAND;
HEAD OF THE HUMAN-COMPUTER INTERACTION LABORATORY
Baltimore, Maryland

In the book of Isaiah, God instructs the Hebrews to "build a road, clear a path, cast away all stumbling blocks from my people's path." These imperatives to create, to pursue new directions, and to repair the world (*tikkun olam*) are ancient Jewish themes, and after 2,700 years they are still inspirational.

Some people scan the Torah and *haftarot* looking for an inviting path of inspiration. But ancient sacrificial rites and an imperial God offer little comfort in our scientific age. However, some passages, such as "Love your neighbor as yourself," and later rabbinic interpretations can lead us past the post-Holocaust stumbling blocks to hopeful paths within the Jewish community. The theme of responsibility for the future will be even more important than in the past, reflecting the greater impact we have over our environment, society, and technology. We have the power to control population and manage our nonrenewable resources. But we must act wisely.

The liturgy tells us that God and humans jointly engage in the process of "renewing daily the works of creation." Rabbi Mordecai Kaplan, founder of the Reconstructionist movement, writes that "We might gear our own lives to this creative urge in the universe and discover within ourselves unsuspected powers of the spirit." We are reminded of our creative powers in the verses we read when called to the Torah. We bless God for "planting within us the life force of the universe." Kaplan continues: "There can hardly be any more important function for religion than to keep alive this yearning for self-renewal and to press it into the service of human progress."

I believe that a renewal movement based on responsibility for the future can invigorate our feelings for Judaism and how each one of us deals with contemporary concerns to overcome the sense of frustration and powerlessness. We live in complex societies that are enriched by technology and extended by medical treatments, but challenged by deterioration of communities, feelings of depression, and threats to our planetary environment. I see three hopeful paths in need of clearing. The first path begins with the biblical sources on agricultural practices and leads to environmental protection. Exodus (23:11) promotes agricultural planning and responsibility: "The seventh year you shall let your land rest and lie fallow." Another verse requires farmers who harvest crops to leave corners of their fields for the poor. Elsewhere the

Torah limits destruction of trees even during war. And talmudic stories revolve around the wisdom of old men planting trees for future generations. Environmental concerns are still greater today. Arthur Waskow describes Reb Zalman Schachter's concept of eco-kosher within which synagogues should be built to be energy efficient, crops should be raised with minimal use of pesticides, and organizations should use recycled paper. Waskow's promotion of eco-kosher practices has made them a growing activity within Jewish renewal organizations such as P'nai Or and other *chavurot*.

A second path leads to responsibility for the social ecology of our communities. Isaiah impels us "to unlock the shackles of evil, to loosen the thongs of the yoke . . . to bring the poor wanderer home. When you see the naked clothe them." In modern times, our concerns for social justice encompass the fight against crime and drugs, the need to limit child and spouse abuse, and more.

A third path leads to responsibility for use of the widely promoted information technologies. Jews are known as the people of the book, and they are already becoming the people of the electronic book, the Internet, and the World Wide Web. I think if Isaiah were alive today, he would tell us to "build a road, clear a path, and spread the information highway." We can promote universal access to information technology by developing low-cost computers and designing for ease of access by diverse communities and handicapped users. While the cyber-*shtetl* will always be less intimate than face-to-face meetings, it can foster personal contacts, encourage constructive communication, and establish new communities. Parents and teachers can guide children to appropriate information technology and caution them about excessive use and cyber-porn, while instructing them in netiquette (network etiquette). We want to teach kids to surf the Internet, but more importantly, we want to teach them how to make waves. I expect my students to apply their computing skills to creative team projects that benefit others outside the classroom.

Each positive act is a contribution, even small contributions are valuable—they make a difference, they inspire others, and they reaffirm that we have a choice.

Joanna Spinner
Waterloo, Ontario, Canada

I went to Jewish schools until I graduated from high school. Obviously, this fact affects my outlook on Judaism in that I have studied about the religion, the people, and the culture through history, Bible studies, oral law/tradition, and literature and poetry. I was born in 1975 and met my first non-Jewish friend in 1993. I am not "religious" at all—I do not keep the Sabbath nor do I go to synagogue every week, but I have a very strong Jewish identity.

Yes, it matters very much to me that I am Jewish. I used to think that there were many differences between Jews and non-Jews, but now that I'm older and know more non-Jewish people, I think that there are very few Jews who remain within the faith and do not intermarry. I would say that the main difference between Jews and non-Jews is the humour and outlook on life. Jews have a very distinctive *shtick* that non-Jews seem not to understand unless they've had prolonged exposure! I still find that the people who understand me the best are fellow Jews because they understand what it means to be Jewish.

Being Jewish gives me a sense of belonging, knowing that my faith has survived trials and tribulations for thousands of years. Being Jewish makes me feel that my parents were successful in bringing me up to be a positively contributing member of both Jewish society and secular society.

I hope that with the ease of information exchange that more people learn about Jews. Last week, a coworker asked about my necklace, which I told him bore my Hebrew name. He told me that I don't look Hebrew (I told him that I was Jewish, not Hebrew). In any case, there are still people who are very uneducated about Judaism and hopefully they can learn more on the Internet. I just pray that it is *correct*! But, I don't think that anyone's Jewishness will be affected by the increase in technology. Some will learn more about their roots and feel closer to them, while others will meet a non-Jewish lover on a *chat* line. It will all balance out.

Ann Waterman
EDITOR, PUBLICATIONS CONSULTANT
Seekonk, Massachusetts

Does it make a difference to me that I am Jewish? That is like asking whether it makes a difference to me that I am female, or middle-aged, or handicapped. It is who I am, and it affects the way I see the world and everything I do. I think that what makes a difference is that I like being Jewish. I like people to know that I am, and that I see my Judaism as one of the best and most positive things about me. There are visible items of Judaica in my office as well as in my home, and lengthy conversations with me usually manage to touch on Judaism in at least some capacity (my daughter's NEFTY involvement, a recent holiday gathering, an article I've written for the *Jewish Herald*, etc.).

The Jewish value that stands out most in my mind is care for the sick. Although this principle is part of many cultures, Jews have a unique and special way with this *mitzvah*. When my husband was in the hospital, he was visited by many Jews (strangers) from all over the spectrum of Judaism. We also developed a very strong bond with the people in the next room. I say "people" rather than "patients" because the whole family was there, from early morning till well into the night. The patient ("Bubby," as they called her) had had a stroke and could not speak. Her family sat by her bedside and spoke to her constantly, both in Yiddish and in English—they were trying to teach her to speak all over again as if she were a child, and they had no way of knowing if she was responding or even if she was aware of them. But every night after they went home, I could hear her softly crying. It was one of the greatest privileges of my life to be able to tell them this. They cried for joy.

Another aspect that impresses me is how the rapid development in technology is bringing Jews from around the world closer together. Thanks to the Internet, I've conversed with Jews all over the United States and around the world, sharing our interests and often finding solutions to problems I face. I've also downloaded Passover recipes, found answers to Jewish questions, and even located Jewish clip art and fonts for my work. It's been wonderful and can only get better.

241

Julian Yudelson
ASSOCIATE PROFESSOR OF MARKETING,
ROCHESTER INSTITUTE OF TECHNOLOGY
Rochester, New York

How can I begin to count the ways? It is easier for me to imagine what I'd be like if I were blind, or handicapped, than to imagine what it would be like not to be Jewish. Judaism defines so many aspects of my life. Although I am not Orthodox, I have never known a Friday night that was not Shabbos. My children have all had a day school education, and that has defined where I could work. I met my wife at a Jewish teen event. Last week in Jerusalem, I saw my three-year-old granddaughter bend over to kiss each *mezuzah* in a gift shop.

As a system for shaping human behavior, Judaism is more right than any other approach. It may be misunderstood, or misapplied, but the basic system is right. I believe that to be true even when I vary from the traditional norms.

Jewish values are hard to define, since most of the non-Jews I know have good values, and some of the Jews I know have rotten values. One value that I hold dear that is intrinsically Jewish is *kol Yisrael chaveirim*—all Israel are one family, friends, cousins, responsible to and for each other. I also believe that Judaism (though not all Jews) has a qualitatively different approach to relating to others and our world. *Tikkun olam* is a Jewish reality. We may differ on how to go about it, but as Jews we should be able to agree on the goal: a better world for everyone.

It is hard to think of important situations where my Jewishness did not guide my actions. As a teenager, I gave money to a total stranger who was emigrating to Canada, just because I saw him as a fellow Jew. To go way back, when I marched for open housing in Milwaukee, Wisconsin, in the 1960s, I did it because I knew that it was wrong to oppress the stranger. I advocated the Vietnam war because I believed that there was more *tzedek* (justice) on our side than there was on the side of the Viet Cong. I have tried to raise my children as committed Jews (and seem to have succeeded). They are much more observant than I am and I am proud that they have excelled in this area, where I fell short.

AFTERWORD

⌀

On Jewish Weddings, Tradition, and Continuity

by Elvira Nadin

"As the weddings get bigger and bigger, the sandwiches get smaller" was how Harry Golden summed up the blandness of Jewish weddings in the 1950s. This was a time when children and grandchildren of Jewish immigrants wanted to do things the American way. My own experience with Jewish weddings some decades later makes for a telling comparison with how Jews of today define and continue their Judaism into a new millennium. The Jewish wedding is symbolic of many important aspects of Judaism: family, tradition, faith, joy, continuity. If Freud were alive, he would probably agree that at each Jewish wedding, all the participants experience how much Judaism—by which he understood religion—and how much Jewishness—by which he understood tradition and identity—participate in the makeup of the new families arising from a particular wedding.

Golden's description of the Old World-style Jewish weddings he had attended as a boy on the Lower East Side of New York before World War I aroused colorful romantic visions in me. I *had* to attend such a wedding. The religious ceremony that my husband and I had in Romania, a land where both political and historical anti-Semitism combine, was not the joyful public celebration that Golden recalled, although it was memorable as a testimony to Jewish survival under a heartless regime. As my husband was a Romanian citizen at the time of our wedding, he and I had to be married in Romania, according to Ceausescu's edict. A state ceremony was compulsory and had to precede any religious wedding. I insisted on a religious ceremony, reasoning that Judaism had been around long before this communist dictatorship and would be around long after it disappeared. After we obtained permission for the religious service from the chief rabbi of Romania—almost as difficult to get as permission from the Romanian government—our religious wedding took place in the cafeteria of the Jewish home for the aged. Old men whom my husband and I had never seen before, nor after, were roused from their meals by the officiating rabbi and told that a wedding was to take place. The ten men asked no questions as they left their tables and participated with enthusiasm. Four men held up the corners of the *chupah*; but they could not hold it high enough to prevent my husband's head from forming a peak in the chupah whenever he stood up straight. Although the presiding rabbi was Orthodox, moreover a Chasid, he put a used light bulb, instead of a relatively expensive wine glass—or plate, according to Romanian-Jewish custom—on the ground for my husband to crush underfoot. The sound of cheap glass popping resounds louder in my memory than the hearty "mazel tov!" of the old Jews made happy by an event they never thought they'd be part of again.

Some years later, we arrived in the United States (I returning to the country of my birth, my husband immigrating) with our three small children. Shabbat became the focal point of our week; we started to attend the local synagogue and to integrate into the Jewish community. Living in a Jewish neighborhood and having friends of marriageable age gave me the hope that my wish to be a guest at a real Jewish wedding would be fulfilled—not that ours, having taken place in the land in which Tristan Tzara was born and raised, was unreal, or surreal. And one day, the invitation to the marriage of the daughter of friends arrived. I telephoned right away to say that we—two adults and three children—would be happy to attend. A pause on the other end. "I don't know how to say this, but we have to keep costs down, so . . . we can accept only the children of family members." So this was not to be the wedding that Golden described, a celebration for all generations, with children running all over the place. It was a case of economics overriding tradition.

The family members could be described as conscious Jews, but not religious, who celebrated the holy days and were devoted to continuity. The parents of the bride had made sacrifices to pay for putting their children through years of Jewish day school, even though the local public school was excellent. The bride and groom were both professionals who wanted a Jewish wedding and were prepared for it. The rabbi, doubtless realizing that the guests were less conversant with Judaism than the bride and groom, carefully explained every word and act of the religious ceremony. One would think that the Jewish couples present had never had their own religious wedding!

A year later, we received another wedding invitation. The groom, a medical student—as was the bride—used to converse with my husband about Judaism and philosophy. Raised in the age of the yuppies, he had become "religious" over the years and promised us a "real chasidic wedding." The children will love this, I thought, and confidently wrote down "5" in the space provided for number of guests on the elegant RSVP card included with the invitation. A few days later, the groom's mother called and told me that with all the friends and relatives attending, it would be impossible to include our children in the reception. But they were welcome to attend the wedding ceremony. Well, this wedding would not be so chasidic as promised. As I learned later, it never could be.

The Sabbath prior to the wedding, the *aufruf* was held. As the groom made his way to the *bimah*, we congregants pelted him with hard candies, which the children present afterwards collected. The night before the wedding, both bride and groom had started their fast and still had empty stomachs as the guests arrived Sunday morning. We munched on the pre-wedding appetizers and greeted the bride and mothers of both parties. The bride's mother, a widow who had raised eight children by herself, was all smiles. The groom's mother was not so radiant. Was this the right girl for her son? (A question that every Jewish mother asks herself.) How many of the guests recalled that this girl looked quite striking in the bikini she wore at the Jewish Center outdoor swimming pool, where there were no hours set aside for women only? The bride, coming from a family of admirable women, seemed amused, if not joyful. My husband went with other males to the groom's *tish* in the designated room. An hour later, the groom appeared before his bride. After inspecting her to make sure he was getting his Rachel and not Leah—this bride did have four sisters, after all—he handed her the marriage contract and covered her in the act called *bedeken*. (If nothing else, one can learn a lot of corrupt German at a Jewish wedding!) The guests were requested to take seats—men on one side of the aisle, women on the other—in a hotel room usually reserved for conferences, where the light of day or night never penetrates. Since I had not yet attended a truly traditional wedding, I was ignorant of the fact that the chupah was meant to be under the cover of heaven, not of a ceiling.

Our young rabbi was already under the *chupah*. The bride entered, face covered, accompanied by her female relatives. The groom was brought in, father on one side, a future brother-in-law on the other, both holding him up by his arms. He looked scared, and it seemed he would make a break and run if the men were to let go. Under the *chupah*, the bride circled her betrothed seven times, representing the sevenfold blessing. The rabbi, the most chasidic person at the wedding, also explained every step of the ritual. The seven blessings were performed. I could tell by the sound of crystal breaking that this groom crushed a real wine glass under foot. The ceremony over, the bride and groom departed for their chamber, for the *yichud*, the union of man and wife. Today, this time alone entails breaking their fast. Once upon a time, the marriage was consummated right after the ceremony; the "proofs of virginity" mentioned in the Torah were then handed over to the bride's parents for safekeeping, should they need them if their daughter's honor was ever questioned. What luck that the sages decided to do away with this custom! No one should ever say that Orthodox rabbis, even in the case of a "real chasidic" wedding, impose impossible burdens on women.

My husband took our kids home and returned for the reception. In the large banquet hall, where men and women were free to mingle, I had already found the place designated for us, a table with two lovely couples from our synagogue. Had children been accepted, our table would have had to provide seating—and food—for three couples and ten children.

Here, too, Harry Golden would have been disappointed, and not just in the food. Sure, there was klezmer music—on acoustic instruments. Sure, there were dances—for women alone, for men alone, for couples together. The slow circle dance for women reminded me of the *sardana* I had witnessed in Barcelona, and which Jews took with them upon their expulsion from Spain. Livelier *horas* recalled my four years in Romania. The climax was the traditional dance in which the bride and groom are lifted in their chairs by many, if not all strong, men and hold on to each other by grasping the ends of a handkerchief as they are carried around the room. The bride still looked amused.

Something was missing. Was it genuineness? Was it spontaneity? If anyone disturbed this choreography through an unplanned, but heartfelt, outpouring of emotion, my husband and I did not stick around long enough to witness it. Was I justified in considering this wedding a sham when our fourteen-year-old son revealed that the religious groom and the bride—who after the honeymoon kept her beautiful long hair out of sight and would soon start wearing a wig—had been living together months before the wedding? (My innocent boy had been hired by the groom's mother to help her son move his belongings to his fiancée's apartment!) Years later, in another revival of tradition, a couple in Ukraine also had a chasidic wedding many years after they had been officially declared man and wife by a government functionary of a town converted to atheism during the Soviet regime. But unlike our yuppies, they lived apart for the six months preceding their renewed *yichud,* connecting themselves to a tradition they had discovered late.

My husband's new job took us to New York. Through a former student from his days as a college professor, he became involved in advising the design of Hebrew typefaces for use on computers and the Internet. The force behind this endeavor was the highly learned rabbi of a very pious group. One of the fringe benefits of this association was an invitation to the wedding of the rabbi's daughter. My husband assured me that this time I would not be disappointed. He himself had been to the chasidic wedding of his former student, an event he would never forget. We should make every effort to attend. I had, however, lost my hope of ever experiencing the type of wedding Golden had described, so I harbored no great expectations—and I wrote down "2" on the acknowledgment card.

The taxi driven by our Israeli neighbor took us to the Williamsburg section of Brooklyn, where a number of extremely Orthodox denominations live at levels ranging from the poverty of welfare recipients to the wealth of merchants at the Diamond Exchange in midtown Manhattan. As my husband and I entered the lobby of the Jewish community center, we noticed several old men and women—the *schnorrers* still familiar to Jews across America—sitting and asking for *tzedakah.* Reaching far back to his early childhood, my husband recalled similar scenes from precommunist Romania. But all traces of poverty vanished as we entered the reception hall where the bride was in attendance with her current and future female relations—sisters, mothers, grandmothers, and even a great-grandmother. Everyone was happy. There was no doubt that this *kallah* was worthy of comparison to the Shabbat bride praised in the song *Lecha dodi.* Many people were taking snapshots, and a professional was recording the event on videotape. I congratulated the bride, her mother, and grandmother, all strangers to me, but all emanating a beautiful vitality whose source was not just the immediate celebration. I was invited to partake of the prewedding appetizers.

Hello, Harry Golden! I thought that if I turned around, I would see him sampling every item from the lavish array of dishes. I was wondering how anyone would be able to partake of the postnuptial feast. Hot appetizers included spicy fried chicken livers and onions with rice, fried chicken wings, chicken in sauce, stewed sweetbreads, stuffed cabbage, the delicacies of eastern European *shtetls*. The cold table groaned under the weight of various salamis, cold meats, gefilte fish, smoked salmon and mackerel, and pickled herring. And I should not omit the sweet table, with fruit and cakes, punch and soda. The history of Jewish wanderings was displayed through the variety of foods set out.

A buzz went through the crowd: The wedding was about to take place. It was November, and the first snowflakes heralded an early winter. But this was no excuse to cast aside tradition and hold the wedding indoors in a hall where the *chupah* could not be placed under heaven. Outside the hall, old men in *streimls* held the posts of the *chupah*. The bride came, face covered, shoulders kept warm by a mink stole. Now I glimpsed the *chatan,* a *yeshivah bochur*—of impeccable antecedents I was told—devoted to Torah and the way of life that these Jews had lived for centuries. But he was so pale, and so weak-looking, a stark contrast to the robust and joyful bride. Immediate relatives joined the festivities out in the cold. I remained indoors, peering through the thick high windows, hoping to catch a hint of explanation. Harry Golden had not prepared me for this!

Clearly, this wedding was not like others I had attended, and I really wanted to know what was different that was going on. But outside or indoors, I would hear no explanation because none was given! If you did not already know, you had to watch, pay attention, and learn. Or you could ask—which I did—and be taught. The children—and there were many—stopped running around to stare in amazement for as long as their attention span held. Then they resumed running around. No one expected a silence that was obviously beyond the children's capabilities. They would attend many weddings and absorb the traditions as time went by. By the way, one of the first questions the bride's mother asked me was, "Where are your children?"

Vows exchanged, the bride and groom retired. We guests were to take seats, women on one side of the *mechitzah*, men on the other. You could tell the sections apart because the men's tables held gin and whiskey, while the women's tables held various liqueurs. "Take seats" is the right description, because none had been assigned. And if there was no room for a friend you just spotted, you brought over a chair, called the waitress to bring dishes, and squeezed the friend in. No one complained. I happened to sit with an older businesswoman, not at all religious, on my left and a group of young Satmar wives on my right and across from me. Kerchiefs covered their shaven heads and they conversed in Hungarian. An older woman came by, and they rose from their seats and would not sit again until she was comfortable. I recognized this Oriental respect for the elderly that I had witnessed under other circumstances in the nonreligious Hungarian home of my childhood. As the celebrated novelist Imre Kertesz put it, Hungarian Jews are more Hungarian than the Magyars! "These are the real Jews," said the nonreligious businesswoman. "No convert can feel this." I had many reasons to disagree with her, one being a friend of mine seated nearby, a former Christian converted to a zealous Lubavitcher. Keeping my opinion on who is a Jew to myself, I only responded that they were as real as the rest of us Jews.

The bride reappeared and took her place at the table reserved for her and her female relatives. A beautiful headdress now covered her hair, which from this moment on was an attraction reserved for her husband. Dinner was served: chicken soup with matzo balls followed by a second course of fish. Before the main course was served, my husband reminded me that our taxi would soon arrive. How I regretted that my experience with Jewish weddings had made me desire an early getaway. I would miss the dancing—strictly women with women and men with men, until the climax, when the *mechitzah* would be removed and the *gurtel* dance would take place. The bride, holding onto one end of a sash, would dance in turn with selected male relatives, who held onto the other end. The father-in-law came first, followed by father, uncles, brothers, until only the groom was left. But I had a chance to pick up at another wedding, in the same family, from where I left off at this wedding, and to learn a lesson that applies to Jews, Judaism, and continuity.

At the marriage of the same rabbi's son, I sat next to my Lubavitch convert friend and asked her how the rabbi's daughter, at whose wedding we had last seen each other, was doing. I expected to hear that her first child was due pretty soon, if not already born. My friend's answer shocked me: The daughter was divorced. It seems that, due to generations of marriages within a closed community, the groom had inherited a genetic disease, which—to put it as briefly and as charitably as possible—made him unable to fulfill all his husbandly duties. Obviously, not all marriages within the very religious communities have this result. But of the three weddings I had attended, the one having the greatest apparent claim to authenticity and continuity turned out to be the end of the line.

"The wedding does not make a marriage," is the conclusion I drew from this experience. Neither does apparent reference to Jewish tradition, however weak and contradictory it can seem, immediately classify the Jews of this tendency as either hypocrites or one step from assimilation. The other couples in this story, whose reference to tradition seemed tenuous or contrived, have strong, healthy, Jewish marriages and are raising their children with a living awareness of Judaism, or at least of Jewishness. The children will be educated, as the parents were, in Jewish schools. No, their Judaism will not be the same as that which the very pious have held to for centuries, a Judaism—better said, "Judaisms"—that many of us call "traditional," forgetting that these too were the result of changing conditions, environments, and requirements. Remember all those German words used in connection to Jewish weddings? They (along with Hebrew, Russian, Polish, Turkish, and other borrowed words) make up the Yiddish language that, like *gefilte fish*, *hamantaschen*, and the loaf called *challah*, date back to the accommodations that Jews made with the Germans (and other nations) in whose lands they settled—just as Jews had made earlier accommodations with the Greeks before and after Antiochus Epiphanes. The Judaism of these young families, like the Judaism and Jewishness of many of the individuals who responded to the thousands of letters that my husband and I sent out, will reflect a view and understanding of life, inculcated in a loving spirit, devoted to the conviction that Judaism and Jewishness make a difference worth preserving and carrying on. And one of these differences has to do with being open, with adapting what is useful to meet changing requirements of Jewish continuity. Closing off the outside in order to maintain a strict notion of what is authentically Jewish was a strategy of survival in a world of many autarchic and antagonistic worlds. Today, it is a sure formula for stagnation and self-destruction. Openness should not be misconstrued as surrender, but rather understood as an assertion of strength in difference.

The parents of the next generations of Jews might meet over the Internet, and thousands of guests around the world will share in the festivities, if not taste the food. In the Introduction, globality and self-defining nuclei were mentioned as being the paradigm of our age. Clearly, Jews have reflected this tendency throughout the Diaspora. As far apart as they are physically, Jews have held up as long as they conscientiously keep defining themselves as Jews and constituting themselves as such through how they live and act. As long as Jews actively define what is Jewish and do not leave it up to the Görings of the world to decide who is a Jew, Jewishness will not disappear or be absorbed into a homogeneous ethical humanism or its many variations. To be Jewish is not to exist in reaction to something else—another religion, other philosophies, other forms of humanism, and the various forms of inhumanity—but to affirm values and a way of living not reducible to other elements.

Glossary

—∽—

aliyah—"going up"; immigration to Israel

Ashkenazi—(plural, Ashkenazim) Jews of eastern European origin

aufruf—"calling up" of the bridegroom to the Torah on the Sabbath before his wedding

bimah—pulpit; the raised platform from which the Torah is read

chametz—leavened food, forbidden during Passover

Chanukah—eight-day Festival of Lights commemorating the Maccabean victory

Chasid, Chasidim—member(s) of an ultra-Orthodox Jewish sect

chasidic—referring to, or in the style of, a Chasid

chatan—bridegroom

chaver—(plural, *chaveirim*) friend

cheshbon ha-nefesh—"accounting of the soul," traditionally undertaken before Rosh Hashanah

chevra—society, social group

Chevra Kadisha Burial Society, a group of volunteers that prepares the deceased for burial

chupah—wedding canopy

chutzpah—nerve, hubris

daven—pray

freilach—joyful

goy—non-Jew

haftarah—weekly reading from a book of the Prophets

Haggadah—book containing the story of Exodus, read at the Passover Seder

halachah—Jewish law

Kaddish—prayer traditionally recited by a mourner

kallah—bride

kashrut—Jewish dietary laws

kedushah—holiness

Kiddush—blessing made over wine

kishka—gut

matza—(plural, *matzot*) unleavened bread

mechitzah—physical barrier used in the synagogue to separate men and women

mensch—(good) human being

mezuzah—(plural, *mezuzot*) parchment scroll containing the first paragraph of the *Shema*, attached to the doorpost of a Jewish home

Midrash—collection of the rabbinic tales based on Bible stories

mikveh—ritual bath

minhag—custom (in contrast to law)

minyan—(plural, *minyanim*) quorum of ten required to hold public prayer; the prayer service

mishpachah—family

mitzvah—(plural, *mitzvot*) commandment; good deed

nebechel—poor thing, pitiable person

niggun—melody

payis—sidecurls worn by ultra-Orthodox men

Pesach—Passover

pesachdik—suitable for Passover

Pirkei Avot—*Ethics of the Fathers*

rebbetzin—wife of a rabbi

schnorrer—beggar

Seder—(plural, Sedarim) traditional Passover feast

Sephardi—(plural, Sephardim) Jews of Spanish and Portuguese, and later Middle Eastern, origin

Shema—important prayer recited twice daily affirming faith in one God

Shoah—Holocaust

shetl—Jewish village or small-town community in eastern Europe

shul—synagogue

siddur—prayer book

tallit—prayer shawl

Talmud—Oral Law, consisting of the Mishnah and Gemara

talmudic—pertaining to the Talmud

tikkun olam—"repair of the world"; improving society

tochas—backside; buttocks

Tu Bishvat—festival of the New Year for trees

tzaddick—righteous person

tzedakah—charity, righteousness, justice

tzedek—justice

Yahrzeit—anniversary of a person's death

yarmulke—skullcap; also known as *kipa*

yeshivah—Jewish institution of learning

yeshivah bochur—young man enrolled at a *yeshivah*

Index of Respondents

━━◆━━